Critical
Issues
in
History

The Age of Revolution, 1770-1870

Critical
Issues
in History

UNDER THE EDITORIAL DIRECTION OF *RICHARD E. SULLIVAN*

SIX-VOLUME EDITION

TWO-VOLUME EDITION

Critical Issues in History

The Age of Revolution

1770-1870

EDITED WITH INTRODUCTIONS BY

DAVID L. DOWD

University of Kentucky

D. C. HEATH *and Company, Boston*

ILLUSTRATION CREDITS

Cover and page 519: Head of mine shaft, Houillère de Bézenet,
Ste. Barbe; Amédée Bûrat, *Les Houillèries,* 2 vols., Paris, 1868-70.

Library of Congress Catalog Card Number: 67-13486
Copyright © 1967 by D. C. Heath and Company
No part of the material covered by this copyright
may be reproduced in any form without written permission
of the publisher.
Printed in the United States of America.

Printed December 1966

Boston
Englewood
Indianapolis
Dallas
San Francisco
Atlanta

PREFACE

This volume, one of a six-volume set, is intended to engage students in *problem-resolving situations* as a technique for enriching their study of European history. The editors who collaborated in preparing these six volumes are convinced that this approach has great value in stimulating interest, encouraging critical thinking, and enhancing historical-mindedness, especially when it is used to supplement the more conventional techniques employed in teaching the general introductory course in European history.

The volume opens with an interpretive essay aimed at placing the five "problems" which follow in the perspective of the period. While all of the problems follow the same structure, the topics they treat are highly diverse: in one, a single man's role in history is debated, while the next examines an ideological issue; in one problem causes are sought, while the next weighs effects.

Each of the five problems is introduced by a short statement defining the issue and directing the student to the crucial questions involved. For the most part selections have been taken from the works of modern historians, with occasional use of the observations of contemporary witnesses. In choosing the selections, the editor has tried to avoid generating conflict for conflict's sake. Rather, he has sought to show how honest divergencies emerge among historians as a result of the complexities of history, varying initial assumptions, different approaches to evidence, and all the other factors that enter into interpretation of the past. The student's efforts to understand how differing interpretations arise and to resolve these differences should increase his ability to manipulate historical data and concepts and deepen his understanding of the historian's craft.

CONTENTS

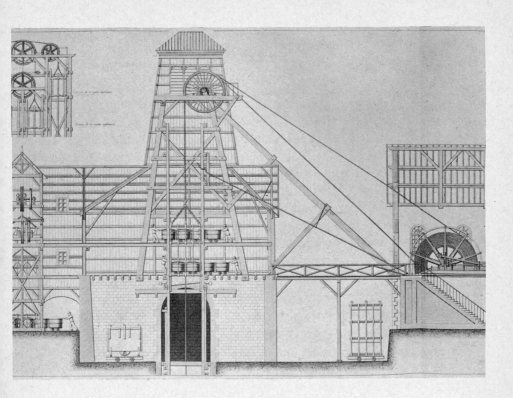

INTRODUCTION

To describe the period from 1770 to 1870 as an age of revolutions offers obvious advantages if we define "revolution" as a violent and sudden overthrow of an established political order. One recalls that 1770 was marked by the Boston Massacre, the first armed conflict of the American Revolution, and that the revolt of the Paris Commune in 1871 immediately followed the fall of the Second Empire of Napoleon III in the French Revolution of September 4, 1870, as well as the defeat of France by Germany in the Franco-Prussian War. The century in question also underwent social disturbances, economic revolutions, and massive demographic changes which made it, at least as much as our own, a truly revolutionary age. Other changes of a more gradual nature such as the great transformations in scientific thought and application, the "Industrial Revolution" and the "revolution of rising expectations" also developed during this hundred-year period.

No matter what our precise definition of "revolution" may be, the term does fit the age in question whether we apply the term to political upheavals such as the democratic and equalitarian revolutions of "1789," of the 1820's, of the 1830's and of "1848", or to the social upheavals and profound economic changes which go under the name of "Industrial Revolution", or to the so-called "scientific revolution." The historical problems selected for this section of the book are focused on "revolutionary" aspects of the period: the roots of political revolts, the characteristics and results of those revolutions, the fluid political tendency known as "liberalism," the powerful force of "nationalism," and the basic social, economic, and technological changes associated with the phrase "Industrial Revolution."

Nevertheless, one must remember that the period was also characterized by movements of counterrevolution, of conservatism, and of internationalism; and that the older, traditional patterns of society and of economic production were continued on a broad scale over most of the European World. Since the number of problems included here must be limited, certain other significant themes such as rapid and far-reaching scientific developments and the impact of science upon human life, society, and economic, political, and military institutions; developments in the arts, music and literature, including "neo-Classicism," "Romanticism" and "Realism;" basic conflicts between Church and State and various interrelations between religious and secular institutions and ideas; and the development of new movements such as Socialism and Communism have had to be passed over.

The century between 1770 and 1870 also witnessed a spectacular increase in Europe's population. Since early in the eighteenth century, population figures had been increasing by leaps and bounds. New jobs and a greater supply of food and clothing were required for Europe's expanding population. Population pressure challenged the traditional economy and the ingenuity of monarchs and statesmen in expanding their frontiers or colonizing their underdeveloped areas.

Although the problems selected tend to concentrate on Europe, it must be kept in mind that the colonial empires and overseas trade of the European states, their exploitation, and the rivalries that they engendered were a vital part of the history of this period. In its overseas possessions Europe imposed its own values, its own interests, and its own institutions. Authoritarian autocracy, military and police rule, bureaucratic centralization, religious intolerance, all produced some measure of discontent among European colonists and natives in the Americas, in Africa, and in Asia. During the period under discussion revolutions broke out not only in North America, but in Latin America as well. Europeans were fascinated by that American Revolution which by precept and example made such significant contributions to reforms of a political and social nature. In the end the revolutionaries of the thirteen colonies won their independence because France, Spain, and Holland supported them against their hated rival, England. Eventually other colonists could count upon other hostile coalitions to aid them in their bids for independence. On the other

The Age of Revolutions

hand, Canada achieved dominion status within the British Empire through evolutionary means in 1867.

Ever-increasing trade with Africa, the Americas, Asia, and other areas beyond Europe greatly enriched Europeans between 1770 and 1870. The world-wide trade associated with their emerging oceanic empires had already created a global economy by the 1770's. During the subsequent century vast new wealth was accompanied by and contributed to by increasing technological and scientific knowledge. This knowledge engendered more wealth, and the two together merged in a significant new idea, the conception of progress.

Those years which preceded the French revolution of 1789 are often referred to as the "Age of Enlightenment." Educated men and women believed that they lived in an enlightened era and that the bad times of barbarism were past. At first the idea of progress was popular only among the educated elite. In 1770 this belief was held not only by the "philosophes," but also by the "enlightened despots," progressive-minded monarchs, and by their ministers and officials. By 1871 even the mass of Europeans had come to think of their age as one of "progress" but reforms were expected to come from constitutional monarchs and from their parliaments rather than from the fraudulently "enlightened" despots and their ministers of the previous century.

Profound modifications also occurred in the economic realm. Many aspects of agriculture, commerce, and industry were "revolutionized" between 1770 and 1870. These economic changes, sometimes described as "industrial capitalism," provided Europe with new machines, new processes, and a new type of entrepreneur, the industrial capitalist who pushed for freedom of enterprise and enormously expanded the production of goods. The so-called "Industrial Revolution" spread new techniques and new machines from England to the continent and then to all parts of the Western world.

Social and political reforms, favored at first by enlightened despots, later were carried out by revolutionaries in the Americas, in Switzerland, in the Netherlands, in France, in Italy, and in the Germanies, and proposed in Spain and Portugal and briefly in Poland and Hungary. This "world revolution in the West" profoundly modified Europe and its colonies by the achievement of an "Age of Democratic Revolution" which did not end in 1800, but rather which continued into the nineteenth century. By 1871, most Europeans enjoyed certain constitutional and liberal institutions, or at any rate, they possessed the machinery of representative government and of parliaments. Out of the revolutionary upheavals of this period also emerged our contemporary world of mass culture and nationalism. By 1871 the world which had been largely transformed economically was also revolutionized politically in another way by the emergence of large consolidated nation states. The great powers had appeared. They were Great Britain, France, Germany, Austria-Hungary, and Russia. There were some doubts as to whether Italy would really become a great power but almost all realized that the United States would one day play a major role in the world, but not yet.

1

THE ROOTS OF REVOLUTION

One of the most controversial and widely discussed problems for historians and other scholars is that of the causes of Revolutions. In 1931, the American historian Louis Gottschalk published an essay entitled, "The French Revolution; Conspiracy or Circumstance?," in which he classified and analyzed the work of various historians according to the attitude which they adopted toward the problem of revolutionary causation: those who believe that the coming of revolution is to be attributed to the force of circumstances as compared with those who believe that it is a result of a conspiracy and therefore the work of men.

Probably the Abbé François Lefranc (1739–1792), who wrote a pamphlet entitled, *The Veil Withdrawn*, in 1791, was one of the earliest to blame the outbreak of revolution in France and Europe upon a conspiracy, and he appears to have been the first to attribute the revolution to the Freemasons. This theme was taken up and elaborated in a curious work entitled *A History of Jacobinism*, published in 1798 in Hamburg, Germany by the émigré Abbé Augustin de Barruel (1741–1820). The "Conspiracy Thesis" still has supporters today though few, if any, among professional historians. The essay of Professor Henri Peyre on the influence of eighteenth century ideas on the French Revolution gives a much more reasonable and convincing analysis of the role which was played by ideas and intellectuals in the coming of this and other revolutions.

Among the advocates of the "circumstance theory" one of the first was Antoine Barnave (1761–1793), a contemporary of the French Revolution and one of its greatest orators, who argued that the Revolution in France was the summit of a European revolution and also that it was the result of changes in the social and economic structures, notably the rise of the wealthy, industrial bourgeoisie which desired to participate in the government of France. This for Barnave was the basic cause of the Revolution and also explained why the upheaval was more violent and more profound in Western Europe where the bourgeoisie were richer, more numerous, and more powerful than elsewhere. Much later Karl Marx argued in a somewhat similar way, but one need not be a Marxist in order to stress the significance of social and economic factors in the causal pattern of Revolutions. On the other hand the aristocracy not only fiercely defended its privileges and positions but also in what historians have come to call a "feudal reaction" demanded an even greater share of political power. The selection from the French historian Jacques Godechot discusses the role of social and economic forces in the coming of the Revolution.

The essay by the British historian George Rudé on the outbreak of the French Revolution also stresses social conflicts but shifts the major interest from the "bourgeoisie" to "the crowd" and to "popular movements."

The final selection is a suggestion by Lawrence Stone, a Princeton University historian of sixteenth and seventeenth century English revolutions, that the historian should consider some newer theories of Revolution which have been advanced by social scientists of the present day, particularly political scientists and sociologists. It demonstrates that the last word has not been said on the subject.

While the first three selections are oriented toward the late eighteenth-century revolutions of 1770–1799, the last indicates various ways in which there are common patterns of causation to be found not only among the revolutionary movements of the eighteenth century but parallels with those of the nineteenth century and, possibly, those of the twentieth century.

HENRI PEYRE

THE INFLUENCE OF IDEAS ON REVOLUTION

Henri Peyre (1901 –   ), a native of Paris, France, is Sterling Professor of French and chairman of the French Department at Yale University and one of the most widely recognized figures in French literary history in the United States. He passed the Agrégation (1924) and took his doctorate at the University of Paris (1936). He has taught at Yale since 1928, but he has also been on the faculty of Bryn Mawr and the University of Cairo, and has served as visiting professor at the Universities of Lyons, Buenos Aires, and Chicago, and at Columbia and Cornell.

Despite the fact that he is known primarily for his work on the history of French literature since the seventeenth century, he has a broad and profound knowledge in the fields of comparative literature, literary criticism, and intellectual history.

If there is really one almost undisputed conclusion on the origins of the Revolution reached by historical studies coming from radically opposite factions, it is that pure historical materialism does not explain the Revolution. Certainly riots due to hunger were numerous in the eighteenth century and Mornet[1] draws up the list of them; there was discontent and agitation among the masses. But such had also been the case under Louis XIV, such was the case under Louis-Philippe and deep discontent existed in

[1] Daniel Mornet (1878–1954), Les Origines intellectuelles de la Révolution française (Paris: A. Colin, 1933). Mornet's study of the gradual spread of the new ideas is a "model of intellectual probity and discretion" which analyzes the degree of penetration of the philosophic spirit and the specific concepts and influence of the most widely read writers of the eighteenth century. He demonstrates that the ideas of the "philosophes" could not have produced the Revolution without (1) widespread misery among the people and (2) an aroused public opinion which demanded reform. [Editor's note.]

From Henri Peyre, "The Influence of Eighteenth Century Ideas on the French Revolution," Journal of the History of Ideas, Vol. X, (1949), pp. 72–87. Translated by Arthur L. Kurth. Reprinted by permission of the author and the Journal of the History of Ideas.

France in 1920 and 1927 and 1934 without ending in revolution. No great event in history has been due to causes chiefly economic in nature and certainly not the French Revolution. France was not happy in 1788, but she was happier than the other countries of Europe and enjoyed veritable economic prosperity. Her population had increased from 19 to 27 millions since the beginning of the century and was the most numerous in Europe. French roads and bridges were a source of admiration to foreigners. Her industries such as ship-fitting at Bordeaux, the silk-industry at Lyons and the textile-industry at Rouen, Sedan and Amiens were active while Dietrich's blast-furnaces and the Creusot were beginning to develop modern techniques in metallurgy. The peasants were little by little coming to be owners of the land. Foreign trade reached the sum of 1,153 million francs in 1787, a figure not to be attained again until 1825. The traffic in colonial spices and San Domingo sugar was a source of wealth. Banks were being founded and France owned half the specie existing in Europe. So misery in France was no more than relative. But truly wretched peoples such as the Egyptian fellah, the pariah of India or even the Balkan or Polish peasant or Bolivian miners for example rarely bring about revolutions. In order to revolt against one's lot, one must be aware of his wretched condition, which presupposes a certain intellectual and cultural level; one must have a clear conception of certain reforms that one would like to adopt; in short, one must be convinced (and it was on this point that the books of the eighteenth century produced their effect) that things are not going well, that they might be better and that they will be better if the measures proposed by the reformist thinkers are put into practice.

Eighteenth-century philosophy taught the Frenchman to find his condition wretched, or in any case, unjust and illogical and made him disinclined to the patient resignation to his troubles that had long characterized his ancestors. It had never called for a revolution nor desired a change of regime; it had never been republican and Camille Desmouslins[2] was not wrong in stating: "In all France there were not ten of us who were republicans before 1789." Furthermore he himself was not one of those ten. But only an over-simplified conception of influence would indulge in the notion that political upheaval

completely embodies in reality the theoretical design drawn up by some thinker. Even the Russian revolution imbued as it was with Marxian dialectic did not make a coherent application of Marxism or quickly found it inapplicable when tried. The reforms of limited scope advocated by L'Esprit des Lois, L'Homme aux quarante écus, L' Encyclopédie and the more moderate writings of Rousseau struck none the less deeply at the foundations of the ancien regime, for they accustomed the Frenchman of the Third Estate to declaring privileges unjust, to finding the crying differences between the provinces illogical and finding famines outrageous. The propaganda of the "Philosophes" perhaps more than any other factor accounted for the fulfillment of the preliminary condition of the French revolution, namely, discontent with the existing state of things.

In short, without enlarging upon what is already rather well known we may say that eighteenth-century writers prepared the way for the Revolution, without wishing for it, because:

a) They weakened the traditional religion, winning over to their side a great number of clerics, and taught disrespect for an institution which had been the ally of the monarchy for hundreds of years. At the same time they had increased the impatience of the non-privileged groups by uprooting from many minds the faith in a future life which had formerly made bearable the sojourn in this vale of tears that constituted life for many people of low estate. They wished to enjoy real advantages here on earth and without delay. The concept of well-being and then that of comfort slowly penetrated among them.

b) They taught a secular code of ethics, divorced from religious belief and independent of dogma, and made the ideal of conduct consist of observation of this system of ethics, which was presented as varying in accordance with climate and environment. Furthermore they gave first importance in this ethical code to the love of humanity, altruism and service due society or our fellowmen. The ideas of humanity, already present in the teaching of Christ, in Seneca and Montaigne but often dormant, suddenly exert fresh influence over people's minds.

c) They developed the critical spirit and the spirit of analysis and taught many men not to believe, or to suspend judgment rather than accept routine traditions. In D'Argenson, Chamfort, Morelly, Diderot, Voltaire of course, D'Holbach, Condillac and many

---

[2] A radical revolutionary leader who was an important figure in the early stages of the French Revolution; ultimately he moved toward a more conservative position and was guillotined in 1794. [Editor's note.]

others, and even in Laclos and Sade,[3] we will find the effort to think courageously without regard for convention or tradition, that will henceforth characterize the French intellectual attitude. From this time on, inequality with respect to taxation, the tithe paid to the Church, and banishment or persecution for subversive opinions will shock profoundly the sense of logic and critical spirit of the readers of the "Philosophes."

d) Lastly, these very thinkers who have often been depicted as builders of Utopias are the creators of history or the historical sense, or almost so. Montesquieu studiously examined the origins of law and constitutions and saw men "conditioned" by soil and climate in contrast with the absolute rationalists who were foreign jurists and not Frenchmen. Boulainvilliers[4] and many others of lesser fame studied France's past. Voltaire's masterpiece is probably his work on general history. The result of this curiosity about history was two-fold: it encouraged faith in progress and convinced numbers of Frenchmen that it was their task to fulfill humanity's law, to endeavor to increase the sum of liberty, relative equality, "enlightenment" and happiness in the world; it also proved to many men of the law who examined old documents and the titles of nobility and property, that the privileges of nobility were based on a flimsy foundation. The respect that

these bourgeois or sons of the people might have felt for the aristocrats was accordingly diminished, at the very moment when the bourgeois saw the nobles not only accept with admiration but take under their protection destructive writings produced by the pens of commoners: sons of tailors (Marmontel), vine-growers (Restif),[5] cutlers (Diderot) and watch-makers (Rôusseau). And the history of the origins of royal sovereignty itself seemed to them scarcely more edifying than that of the feudal privileges.

As for the means of dissemination of those ideas or new beliefs that the philosophes were spreading between the years 1715 and 1770 or 1789, it will suffice to enumerate them rapidly, for numerous studies have examined them: they were the salons, although very few of the future revolutionaries frequented society gatherings; the clubs, that more and more called for tolerance, preached deism, demanded the abolition of slavery (Société des Amis des Noirs) and dreamed of imitating the American Revolution (Club Américain); books or tracts which made their appearance as works of small format, easily carried or hidden, lively and sharp in style and prone to surprise and arouse the reader; periodicals; the theatre especially after the coming of the "drame bourgeois" and the "comédie larmoyante," and then with Beaumarchais; and the education given in the secondary schools. Mornet's book sums up the essential material on the subject that can be found in documents. The other means of spreading new ideas, such as conversation, which is doubtless the most effective means man has always used to borrow and pass on new views, elude documentary research.

It is among the actors in the great revolutionary drama that investigations of broader scope might show us which of the ideas of the eighteenth century exerted influence and how and why they did so. Sieyès, among others, has been the subject of an exhaustive intellectual biography which has established with precision what the young abbé coming to Paris from Fréjus to devise constitutions owed to Descartes, Locke, and Voltaire in particular (for the negative side of his ideas), to Rousseau (for his impassioned logic) and to Mably. (Paul Bastid, Sieyès et sa pensée, 1939). Another recent book, by Gérard

[3] Diderot, Voltaire, and Condorcet need no identification. Rene Louis de Voyer de Paulmy, Marquis d'Argenson (1694–1757) was a lawyer, a government official, scholar, and writer in the era of Louis XV; he was greatly admired by Voltaire. Sebastien Chamfort (1741–1794) was a popular man of letters and raconteur who was highly critical of all the conventions of late eighteenth century society and whose writings helped to shape revolutionary opinion. Morelly was an eighteenth century political writer about whom almost nothing is known; however, the socialistic ideas which he set forth in a large number of writings had considerable influence on later socialistic and communistic thought. Baron d'Holbach (1723–1789) was a German-born philosopher who lived in Paris and attracted a number of literary and philosophical figures to his circle; he contributed a considerable number of scientific articles to the Encyclopédie; in his philosophical writings he propounded a materialistic concept of the universe and a morality based on the quest for happiness, ideas which provoked a counterattack from Voltaire and many others. Etienne Bonnot de Condillac (1715–1780) was an associate of Diderot, Rousseau and Duclos and an exponent of the doctrine of sensationalism. Pierre Laclos (1741–1803) was a French soldier and writer of the Revolutionary era; his most famous book was the novel, Liaisons dangereuses. The Marquis de Sade (1740–1814) was a French novelist whose descriptions of debauchery, cruelty, and perversion shocked his age; his own personal conduct nearly equalled his fictional accounts and finally resulted in his commitment to an insane asylum; the word "sadism" was derived from his name. [Editor's note.]

[4] Henri Boulainvilliers (1658–1722) was a French political writer whose works defended the feudal regime as the ideal form of government; his ideas were based on an extensive study of French history. [Editor's note.]

[5] Jean Francois Marmontel (1723–1799) was a French dramatist, historian, and journalist; among his writings were several articles in the Encyclopédie. Nicolas Edme Restif (1734–1806) was an influential novelist, especially effective in portraying the seamy side of eighteenth-century French society. [Editor's note.]

Walter, is a study of Babeuf (1937). It would be instructive to know how the minds of many of the revolutionaries were developed and by what books and meditations they were influenced; such men range from Mirabeau and Danton to Marat, from Rabaut de Saint-Etienne[6] to Hérault de Sechelles[7] and from Desmoulins or Brissot[8] to generals of the Convention who may have read Raynal and Rousseau with passionate interest, as Bonaparte did later. Only when many monographs have been written devoting at least as much if not more attention to the history of ideas and the psychology of the protagonists in the Revolution than to the facts of their lives of action, will we be able to make sure generalizations about the influence of Montesquieu or Rousseau on the France of '89 or '93.

Montesquieu and Rousseau are certainly the two great names worthy of consideration in some detail. The presiding judge of the High Court of Bordeaux obviously did not want the Revolution; had he lived to see it, he would not have approved of its reorganization of the judiciary, nor its audacity in reform, nor the Declaration of the Rights of Man, nor even the interpretation of certain principles he himself had enunciated. Still he is one of the spiritual fathers of the first two revolutionary assemblies. Like so many other men who have made history, he influenced the fateful years of 1789-92 by what he did say almost involuntarily, by the thoughts other men read in his sentences and by the tone even more than by the content of his writings. His great work breathes a veritable hatred of despotism founded on fear; it shows no moral respect for monarchy, and so helped to alienate the most reasonable minds from it. The great principle of the separation of powers presumes the right to seize from the king the united powers that he believed he held as a whole by divine right. Finally, Montesquieu, however elevated his position as a citizen or as a magistrate may have been, uttered words which will assume a mystic authority in later times on the subject of the people's

inherent good qualities and its ability to select its leaders: "The common people are admirable in choosing those to whom they must delegate some part of their authority," or "When the common people once have sound principles, they adhere to them longer than those we are wont to call respectable people. Rarely does corruption have its beginning among the people."

Finally, in his admirable XIth book, Montesquieu had defined liberty in terms that were to remain etched in people's memories: this liberty required stable laws, which alone could establish and protect it. These laws were also to correct economic inequality. Certainly its historical examples adduced in great profusion, highly technical juridical considerations, certain generalizations that had been too cleverly made symmetrical and its lack of order made this voluminous treatise hard to read. But Montesquieu's influence was not one of those that can be gauged by the number of readers: it expressed itself in action thanks to a few thoughtful minds who found in it a sufficiently coherent overall plan capable of replacing the old order which obviously was crumbling. Montesquieu's influence inspired a more important group of revolutionaries who were familar with only a few chapters of his work, but these chapters were filled with the love of freedom and the great feeling for humanity that condemned slavery and the iniquitous exploitation of some men by others.

Montesquieu's influence on the French Revolution began to decline at the time when Rousseau's was coming to the fore. Many studies have been devoted to the subject of Rousseau and the French Revolution; and the subject deserves still further study, for perhaps no more notable case of the effect of thought on life exists in the whole history of ideas and of dynamic ideas in particular. But this broad subject has too often been narrowed down by the most well-meaning historians. So many dogmatic and partisan statements had portrayed Rousseau as the great malefactor who was guilty of the excesses committed by the Terrorists and as the father of collectivism that, as a reaction, the best-disposed scholars set about proving by facts and texts that the author of the Contrat Social was guiltless of so many misdeeds. As a result they have belittled his influence. But there is some narrowness and naïveté in these scholarly arguments.

According to some, everything that Rousseau wrote

[6] Jean Paul Rabaut Saint-Étienne (1743–1793) was a revolutionary leader of the "Girondins" who was guillotined in 1793. [Editor's note.]

[7] Marie Jean Hérault de Séchelles (1759–1794) was a key figure in the radical faction of the Revolution, ultimately serving as a member of the Committee of Public Safety; eventually he was accused of treason by Robespierre and executed in 1794. [Editor's note.]

[8] Jacques Pierre Brissot (1754–1793) was a journalist who played an important role in shaping opinion in the early stages of the Revolution; his circle of associates and followers eventually emerged as the so called "Girondins"; he was guillotined in 1793 along with the other "Girondins." [Editor's note.]

already existed before his coming in the works of a number of writers and thinkers both at home and abroad and Jean-Jacques brought forth very little that was new. That is quite possible, and scholars have been able to make fruitful inquiries into the sources of the *Discours sur l'Inégalité* and the *Contrat*. But the fact remains that whatever Rousseau borrowed from others he made his own; he rethought it and above all felt it with a new intensity and set it off to advantage by his own passion and his own talent. What he owes to Plato or Locke suddenly "shook" the men of 1792 only because Rousseau had charged it with a new electric current.

Furthermore Rousseau is rife with contradictions and the most ingenious men of learning (Lanson, Höffding, Schinz and E. H. Wright) have not yet succeeded in convincing us of the unity of his thought. For Corsica and Poland he proposes finely adapted and moderate constitutions that do not seem to have sprung from the same brain as the *Contrat Social*. He writes a very conservative article on *l'Economie politique* for the fifth volume of the *Encyclopédie* while in his second *Discours* he had propounded anarchical theses burning with revolutionary ardor. "To expect one to be always consistent is beyond human possibility, I fear!" he himself had admitted in the second preface of the *Nouvelle Héloïse*. We will not go so far as to pay homage to Rousseau for his contradictions and may choose to reserve our unalloyed admiration for other systems of thought more dispassionate and logical than his. But an author's influence does not have much to do with the rigor and coherence of his philosophical system. In fact, it would not be hard to show that the thinkers who have contributed the most toward changing the face of the world exerted influence because of their contradictions, since very different periods and highly diverse individuals drew from them various messages of equal validity. Let us add with no ironic intention that because of this the ingenuity of the learned will never tire of seeking the impossible golden key to these disconcerting enigmas and that the hunger for systems, among those lacking the necessary imagination to construct new ones, will always exert itself to bring about a happy synthesis of the successive assertions of a Plato, a Montaigne, a Locke, Rousseau, Comte or Nietzsche.

After all, as the historians tell us quite correctly, the *Contrat Social* is only a part of Rousseau's political thought and not the most important part in the eyes of his contemporaries; the author himself attributed only a rather limited importance to this logical Utopian book. Rousseau never seriously contemplated a revolution in France; he did not think that a republic was viable, or perhaps even desirable for France. One might even make the assertion supported by texts that Jean-Jacques, that *bête noire* of the anti-revolutionaries from Burke to Maurras, Lasserre and Seillière[9] was a timid conservative. It is quite true (M. Mornet has proved this once again) that the influence of the *Contrat Social* was very weak between the years 1762 and 1789; the book caused so little disturbance that Rousseau was not even molested; and it is probable that Rousseau would have been frightened by certain inferences that were later drawn from his ideas. What he wrote in 1765 in no way justifies an assertion on our part that he would still have written the same thing in 1793 and so it is quite as conceivable that Rousseau might have violently changed his point of view and espoused the cause of the revolutionaries, had he lived long enough to receive their acclaim. And above all, without having consciously wanted the Revolution, Rousseau did a great deal, if not to cause it, at least to give it direction when it had broken out. The success of Rousseau's works and the reception accorded them in his life-time have been investigated in sufficient detail. From now on groups of research men might well give their attention to the enormous influence Rousseau exerted on the men of the Convention and on those of the Empire or the Restoration or on the Romantics. Granted that Rousseau was neither a republican nor a revolutionary, he was in revolt and that is no less important. A. Aulard[10] who was not inclined to over-estimate the influence of the intellectuals on the French Revolution nevertheless accurately described the paradoxical result of any fairly broad study of this subject: "All these men in

[9] Edmund Burke (1729–1797) was an influential English political figure and author who eloquently supported tradition and the established order against the threat of revolution stirring throughout the western world in the late eighteenth century. Pierre Lasserre (1867–1930) was a French writer known especially for his nationalist and conservative opinions and his severe criticism of more liberal literary figures in late nineteenth and early twentieth century French society. Ernest Seillière (1866–1955) was a sociologist who likewise supported conservative causes; he had an especially keen interest in imperialism and patriotism. Charles Maurras (1868–1952) was a journalist and literary critic of a conservative, anti-democratic bent; he ultimately supported the Vichy regime after the fall of France in 1940 and was sentenced to life imprisonment after the liberation in 1945. [Editor's note.]

[10] A well known conservative republican historian of the French Revolution who stressed political factors. [Editor's note.]

revolt want to keep the monarchy and all of them blindly deal it mortal blows. The French, monarchists to a man, take on republicanism without their knowledge."

Not one of the men of the Revolution adopted Rousseau's philosophical system outright in order to put it into practice; that is only too plain. Not one of them understood Rousseau's thought in its subtleties, its contradictions and its alterations as the scholar of the present-day can understand it with the aid of much posthumous documentation: this is scarcely less obvious. Whatever chagrin it may cause minds devoted to strict methods, the unparalleled effect produced on the imagination of posterity by Montaigne, Rousseau or Nietzsche can be credited to quotations drawn from their contexts and probably perverted from their original sense. This influence is not so much an influence of ideas as it is an influence of *idées-forces*, . . . and exerts its power more by setting men's sensibilities aflame than by convincing their minds.

"Man is born free, and everywhere he is in chains." This peremptory formula from the first chapter of the *Contrat Social*, in conjunction with a few others which declared the sovereignty of the people inalienable and affirmed the right to revolt in the event of the usurpation of powers by the government, contributed immeasurably toward crystallizing in the general mind from 1789 on the resolve to make the king subject to the only true rights which were inherent in the people. On October 5th 1789 Robespierre and Barrère contended that the sovereign could not oppose the constituent power which was superior to him. The passion for equality which wildly inspires the Revolutionaries and the modern world after them owes no less to Rousseau's fundamental idea that law should rectify natural inequality (which he was not foolish enough to overlook) by means of civic equality . . . the *Contrat Social* stated in striking terms: "For the very reason that the force of things always tends to destroy equality, the force of legislation must always tend to maintain it." The . . . same work castigated the vices to which kings are prone, for if they are not narrow or evil on attaining the throne — "the throne will make them so." That does not make Rousseau a partisan of republicanism or a democrat; but had it not been for such aphorisms, Saint-Just never would have proclaimed in his fine *Discours concernant le jugement de Louis XVI* of November 13th 1792: "Royalty is an eternal

crime against which every man has the right to rise up and take arms . . . One can not reign in innocence."

The *Discours sur l'Inégalité* contained pages of impassioned rhetoric that were even more effective. The English writer C. E. Vaughan, who is a scrupulous commentator on the political writings of Rousseau, did not hesitate to state, after years of reflection of this subject: "Wherever, during the last century and a half, man has revolted against injustice and oppression, there we may be sure that the leaven of the second *Discours* has been working." . . . Doubtless Rousseau had never dreamed of the application of his declamations against property: but he had set forth the idea that inheritances ought to be whittled down by fiscal measures and that those who owned no lands ought to receive some, without necessarily advocating collectivism. He had also uttered against wealth words whose echoes will ring down the centuries: "It is the estate of the wealthy that steals from mine the bread of my children. . . . A bond-holder whom the State pays for doing nothing is scarcely different in my eyes from a highwayman who lives at the expense of the passers-by . . ., every idle citizen is a rogue."

The precautions with which Jean-Jacques had surrounded some of his bold affirmations quickly disappeared in the heat of action. The chapter called "Du Peuple," in the *Contrat Social*, was most cautious: but its author had nevertheless hinted in it that sometimes, in the life of peoples, "the State, set aflame by civil wars, is so to speak reborn from its ashes, and regains the vigor of youth in leaving the arms of death." People retained phrases from the *Emile* too, — the prophetic phrases in which the educator had proclaimed to the people of his time that they were approaching the era of revolutions when men would be able to destroy what men had built. These few phrases, gaining added violence in tone from the fact that they were detached from contexts that often contradicted them, seemed charged with new meaning when the great upheaval had broken out. Such was also the case of the mystic system of happiness taught by the Genevan "philosophe's" entire work. Man is born good; he is made to be happy; he may become so if he reforms himself and if his governments are reformed. We know how the echo of these doctrines will resound in the noble formulas of Saint-Just, who was perhaps the revolutionary most deeply steeped in Rousseau's thought.

The aspect of Rousseau that Albert Schinz called "the Roman Rousseau" exerted no less influence on that other myth which prevailed or raged among the men of the Revolution (and among the women, too, as in the case of Madame Rolland), the myth of the ancients and their passion for liberty and virtue. "The world has been empty since the day of the Romans," cried Saint-Just; and he stated to the Convention on February 24th 1793: "The Republic is not a Senate, it is virtue." The whole of Saint-Just's remarkable youthful work entitled: *Esprit de la Révolution et de la Constitution de la France* is imbued with Rousseauist themes and ends on this cry of regret: "France has only now conferred a statue upon J. J. Rousseau. Ah! Why is that great man dead?"

Robespierre, whom Michelet maliciously called a "weak and pale bastard of Rousseau" because of his cult of the Supreme Being, was indebted to Rousseau to no lesser degree than Saint-Just, although he does not show the mark of the born writer that stamps the formulas of the terrorist guillotined at the age of twenty-seven. It was by assiduous reading of Rousseau that he formed his style: and his style served him as a powerful weapon. It seems that the young student from Arras met Rousseau in 1778, the year of his death, and never forgot it. "I saw thee in thy last days, and this memory is a source of proud joy for me," he declares later in his *Mémoires,* placed under the aegis of Rousseau, and promised to "remain constantly faithful to the inspiration that I have drawn from thy writings." Dozens of sentences which reiterate formulas from the *Contrat Social* might be extracted from his speeches. It was Rousseau who had helped to turn Robespierre away from Catholicism, and of course he was the man from whom Robespierre borrowed his cult of the Supreme Being; his *Observations sur le projet d'Instruction publique* presented to the Convention in 1793 are based on the Rousseauist faith: "If nature created man good, it is back to nature that we must bring him." His speech made at the Jacobin Club on January 2nd 1792 against the war at that time desired by the Girondins rendered homage to Rousseau in impassioned terms: "No one has given us a more exact idea of the common people than Rousseau because no one loved them more." The secret of the enormous influence exerted by Rousseau lay less in the substance of his thought than in the burning tone of a man who had lived his ideas and had suffered (or thought he had) because he had sprung from the people and had known poverty. "According to the principles of your committee," declared Robespierre to the Constituent Assembly on August 11th 1791, "we ought to blush at having erected a statue to J. J. Rousseau, because he did not pay the property-tax." The history of ideas and their influence on persons and things is full of elements that defy all possibility of quantitative or statistical measurement. How can one estimate all that the men of the Revolution owed Rousseau in the way of fervor, mystic hope, logic that was impassioned and even fierce on occasion and — what is not less important, even for history, as Danton, Saint-Just and Robespierre were aware — the imperious and incisive style that made their formulas resound in twenty countries and across one hundred and fifty years? "One does not make revolutions by halves" or "the French people are voting for liberty for the world" — these aphorisms or decrees of Saint-Just, like certain phrases of Mirabeau, or a multitude of orators of lesser stature, and of Bonaparte himself, would not have been uttered, and would not have had the resonance that has kept them alive, if these men had not been imbued with the spirit and the style of the Citizens of Geneva.

The history of the cult of Rousseau during the French Revolution is easier to trace than that of his deep influence on the revolutionaries. The former has been studied in part, and the manifestations of this idolatry of Rousseau are often amusing. The setting-up of the bust of Jean-Jacques in the Constituent Assembly on June 12, 1790, the consecration of a street of Paris named after him in the same year, the repeated editions of the *Contrat Social* (4 editions in 1790, 3 in 1791, etc.), the constitutional articles put under his aegis, the decree ordering that Rousseau's ashes be brought to the Pantheon in 1794 and the pious emotion of the crowd, and lastly, the invocation to "his generous soul" by the Incorruptible One in his speech of May 7th 1794 on the religion of the Revolution and the pompous application of his declamations on the Supreme Being; all these things have been mentioned more than once and recently, too. But the way in which Rousseau's influence profoundly modified the men and women of the revolutionary and imperial era, and then the romantics great and small, and the continuators of the Revolution, in and out of France, in the nineteenth and twentieth centuries: these are the questions that intellectual history seems to have been reluctant to investigate.

Its timidity is regrettable and our knowledge of the past suffers twice over because of it: first, because history that devotes itself too exclusively to what we call material facts such as a military victory, the fall of a ministry or the opening-up of a railroad-track, seriously falsifies our perspective of what took place. The development of the Napoleonic legend, the quietly working influence of Rousseau or Voltaire, the growth of anti-clericalism and the elaboration of socialist myths are phenomena which are partly literary or sentimental in nature, but are second to no other order of phenomena in importance and in the effects they had on the course of human affairs. Our knowledge of the past suffers additionally because historians, by turning aside from the history of ideas and sentiments with their vigorous influence on the lives of men, abandon these research subjects to men less trained than themselves in exact methods of study; the latter are disposed to write with the sole intent of finding in the past arguments to support their political views or their partisan claims. Meanwhile youth is tempted to reject history as it is officially presented, as an endless series of wars, diplomatic ruses, crimes, examples of intense selfishness and the impotent efforts of men to bring more reason into the world. It refuses to lend credence to those who advise it that man has remained a religious and ideological animal even more than an "economic" creature. Youth's awakening, when it is suddenly placed face to face with the terrible power of ideas, myths and fanaticisms in the world, is sometimes a rude shock, as we have seen recently.

The Frenchmen in particular who have thought fit in the past few years to deny their eighteenth-century thinkers as traitors to the classic and monarchical tradition of France have only to open their eyes in order to ascertain that no French tradition is more alive than that of the Century of Enlightenment. Pascal and Descartes are doubtless greater; Montaigne has more charm and Saint Thomas more logical power: but it is Voltaire and Rousseau, and sometimes Montesquieu and Condorcet, that one finds almost always behind the living influence of France on the masses and the ideologies of South America, of the United States itself, of central and eastern Europe and that one will find tomorrow in Africa and Asia. The world of today expects from post-war France, and France herself expects from her political thinkers who had lost the habit of expressing themselves in universal terms during the last fifty years, a renewal and modernization of her liberal ideas of the eighteenth century, boldly adapted to the social and economic problems of today, but still inspired by the same faith in man and his possibilities.

Students from other countries remind the French of this fact, lest they forget it too readily. Their studies on the influence of Voltaire and Rousseau on the French Revolution and the revolutions that ensued elsewhere in the world are becoming more numerous and sometimes more objective than the French ones. A Slavic scholar Milan Markovitch in a large and exhaustive book on *Rousseau et Tolstoi* (1928) set forth in detail the Rousseauism of the Russian novelist, who in his adolescence carried the portrait of Jean-Jacques around his neck like a scapular and wrote the following message to the newly-founded Rousseau Club on March 7th 1905: "Rousseau has been my teacher since the age of fifteen. Rousseau and the Gospel have been the two great influences for good in my life." The German thinker Ernst Cassirer devoted a little book written in 1945 to commemoration of the admiration for Rousseau expressed by Goethe and Fichte as well as Kant who declared: "Rousseau set me right. . . . I learned to respect human nature." Thoreau and D. H. Lawrence are indebted to the Genevan for a good half of their thinking. George Eliot, on meeting the philosopher Emerson in Coventry in 1848, found herself being asked by him what her favorite book was; Rousseau's *Confessions,* she answered; at which the American transcendentalist cried: "It is mine too." Shortly afterwards, on February 9th 1849, she wrote Sara Hennel these extremely lucid sentences on the mechanism of intellectual influence:

I wish you thoroughly to understand that the writers who have most profoundly influenced me are not in the least oracles to me. . . . For instance, it would signify nothing to me if a very wise person were to stun me with proofs that Rousseau's views of life, religion, and government were miserably erroneous,—that he was guilty of some of the worst *bassesses* that have degraded civilized man. I might admit all this: and it would be not the less true that Rousseau's genius has sent that electric thrill through my intellectual and moral frame which has awakened me to new perceptions; . . . and this not by teaching me any new belief. . . . The fire of his genius has so fused together old thoughts and prejudices, that I have been ready to make new combinations.

In the face of such proofs of a fruitful and life-giving though possibly dangerous influence, an

The Age of Revolutions

important English historian who was moreover an admirer of Burke and usually more moderate in his statements, but was conscious of the importance of ideas in the events of this world, Lord Acton, was impelled to exclaim: "Rousseau produced more effect with his pen than Aristotle, or Cicero, or St. Augustine, or St. Thomas Aquinas, or any other man who ever lived."

JACQUES GODECHOT

STRUCTURAL CAUSES OF REVOLUTIONS

Born in French Lorraine, Jacques Godechot (1907 –   ) received his doctorate in history from the Sorbonne, and has been a professor of history at the University of Toulouse and Dean of the Faculty of Letters there since 1961. He is also president of the Société des Etudes Robespierrists, and officer and member of numerous other professional societies, governmental commissions, and international organizations. He has published significant works on *Les Commissaires aux armées sous la Directoire* (1938), *Histoire de l'Atlantique* (1947), *Les Institutions de la France sous la Révolution et l'Empire* (1952), *La Grande Nation* (1956, two volumes), *La Contre-Revolution* (1961), *Les Révolutions* (1963), *La Pensée Revolutionaire* (1964), *La Prise de la Bastile* (1965), *L'Epoque impériale en France et en Amérique* (1966), as well as *France and the Atlantic Revolution* (1965), from which our selection has been taken. He has also contributed chapters on the French Revolution to *L'Histoire de la Société française* (1953) and to *The New Cambridge Modern History*, Vol. IX, (1965). As the most distinguished living French historian of the Revolutionary and Napoleonic periods, he has been honored by many French and foreign scholarly societies, including the American Historical Association, which recently elected him an Honorary Life Member.

Causes common to a revolutionary movement extending over half of Europe and the European-colonized part of America necessarily lay very deep in the character of society. In the first place, these causes were certainly bound up with transformations in the social structure itself. This was asserted in 1793 by Barnave, a French revolutionary and former member of the Constituent Assembly, who died later that year on the guillotine. In an interesting book, *Introduction to the French Revolution,* which was published for the first time in 1843 and republished in 1960, Barnave showed that everywhere in Europe society had been originally feudal, with the immense majority of inhabitants living under the domination of the landed aristocracy. Possession of the land had been the only source of wealth and the basis of power. The great discoveries of the sixteenth century and the rise of transoceanic navigation led to development of a new social class, the commercial bourgeoisie, and to the growth of great cities, in particular the ports situated on either side of the ocean – London, Paris, Rouen, Antwerp, Amsterdam, Hamburg, New York, and Philadelphia.

The commercial bourgeoisie of these great cities spurred the expansion of industry, which became very rapid after the late eighteenth century thanks to the invention of the steam engine and other machines. The labor force expanded rapidly too. The revolution originated ultimately in the desire of the new classes, especially the bourgeoisie, to come to power. Nor, declared Barnave, was the revolution limited to a single country; it was a "European revolution with France at its apex."

Present-day historians, recognizing the truth of Barnave's ideas, have also been struck by their "Marxist" formulation. They regret, however, that Barnave spoke of a purely "European" revolution, for the revolutionary movement first showed its force across the Atlantic. It would be better to speak either of the "Revolution of the West" or of the "Atlantic Revolution."

If as a whole the pattern described by Barnave is correct, it is nevertheless rather vague. It can now be made more precise as a result of the numerous studies of the social structure of the Western countries made during recent years. Although these studies bring out very noticeable regional differences, they also demonstrate incontestable similarities.

Two types of social structure can be distinguished in Europe and America. In some regions, the peasants were usually owners of the land; in other regions they worked as serfs or slaves upon lands belonging to large landowners, who were generally noblemen. Europe west of the Elbe and North America above the Potomac belonged to the first type of structure. In these countries the tiller of the soil was either its absolute owner, in the Roman sense of the word, or a manorial tenant—actually the owner of the land subject to the payment of manorial dues which varied in importance according to the region. Or he might be a renting farmer, paying either a money rent or a share of the crop. Of course, there were landless peasants, whom the French called *brassiers* because they had their only arms (*bras*) with which to work; but they could move about freely and take up another trade if they wished. Property in land was generally small and scattered. Although the nobility and the Church still owned an important portion of the land—in some regions as much as 30 to 40 percent of the acreage—it must not be forgotten that a large fraction of the nobles' lands and the greatest part of the clergy's land were rented to peasantry. This was the fundamental agrarian structure of western Germany, the Low Countries, France, northern Italy, and northern Spain. In England small landed property was becoming less important, giving way to great enclosed estates which the landlord farmed with free wage-laborers. In central and southern Italy and in most of Spain large estates or

latifundia predominated, but the agricultural workers who cultivated them—very badly, it may be added—lived in big villages of urban character and were completely free. Furthermore, the agrarian system presented significant variations. In the west and south of Western Europe, the fields were generally irregular in form and were enclosed by hedges; this system further strengthened the peasant's individualism. In the north, on the contrary, the open-field system prevailed. The parcels of land were grouped into "fields" (*soles*) or "seasons"; everyone who cultivated the same seasonal field was compelled to plant the same crop. Once the harvest was brought in all the inhabitants of the village, including those who possessed no land, were entitled to bring their livestock to graze upon the stubble. This was the system of "stubble right" (*vaine pâture*), to which the *brassiers* were strongly attached. However, the big landowners, noble and bourgeois alike, increasingly sought the abolition of stubble rights so that they could make their fields more productive.

This structure of peasant society in Western Europe forms an extraordinary contrast to the system that prevailed east of the Elbe river. While west of the Elbe serfdom remained exceptional (in France in 1789 there were less than a million serfs—more precisely *mainmortables,* peasants who could not inherit property without paying a fee to their lord), serfdom was the rule beyond the Elbe. The peasant serfs were almost never owners, tenants, renters, or even sharecroppers. They were *adscripti glebae,* bound to the soil and sold with it. The peasants of Eastern Europe, in their immense majority without any education, passively accepted the rule of the lord, who enjoyed very extensive and almost absolute powers over them. The mentality of the Prussian Junker and the Polish or Hungarian magnate was therefore very different from that of the French squire, the British landlord, or even the Neapolitan baron. South of the Potomac in the British North American colonies, and in the French, Spanish, and Portuguese colonies of Central and South America the land was tilled by black slaves imported from Africa. Conditions resembled those on the estates of Eastern Europe, although the white proprietors would have been indignant to hear themselves compared to Polish or Russian noblemen. They considered slavery a "peculiar institution" bound up with the tropical or equatorial climate; they saw no reason whatever for it to disturb their feeling of belonging to the Western world, which they held to be the vanguard of civilization.

If we pass from the peasantry to an examination of the structure of the other social classes, the contrast between the regions of Eastern and Western Europe becomes even sharper. Everywhere in Western Europe there existed a rich and active bourgeoisie which inhabited numerous large cities. London, Paris, and Naples exceeded 500,000 inhabitants; Hamburg, Liverpool, Amsterdam, Nantes, and Bordeaux attained or passed 100,000 and it would take too much space to list the cities with more than 50,000 inhabitants. East of the Elbe it is possible to cite only Warsaw, Moscow, and St. Petersburg among cities with more than 100,000 population. In Western Europe the bourgeoisie formed a powerful class whose wealth was comparable to, and sometimes even surpassed, that of the nobility. They were in control of almost all trade and the largest part of industry. Furthermore, industry had begun a full-scale revolution in 1750. The invention of the steam engine and various other machines, especially in the textile industry, resulted in the appearance of the first large factories, most of which were in the hands of the bourgeoisie. East of the Elbe, however, the bourgeoisie was extremely small in numbers. Internal trade was almost entirely in the hands of Jews; foreign trade was conducted by the nobility or even by the state.

In Western Europe one of the principal causes of social disturbances consisted in the rise of the bourgeoisie. They possessed wealth and desired power. They did in fact participate in the exercise of power in England, the Netherlands, and several regions of Italy but wanted to gain power in France and to have a larger share of it in Italy, Ireland, and the British colonies of America.

We thus see that the rise and ambitions of the bourgeoisie formed one of the elements of social disorder in the West. But other factors of more acute character resulted from the expansion of the population.

Nowadays sociologists agree that quantitative changes of the population structure are among the essential causes of the revolutions of the contemporary world. No one disputes that the acquisition of independence by the countries of North Africa was essentially prompted by an increase in their population at a rate so rapid that some writers have characterized it as "demented." Why should it have been otherwise in the past? More and more numerous studies of the demographic evolution of the West in the eighteenth century show that a considerable increase also occurred then. Of course it was not a new phenomenon: the population of the globe has been growing ever since the origin of mankind. But today we are quite sure that this growth was not continuous but came in spurts. Europe probably did not have many more inhabitants at the end of the seventeenth century than it had at the end of the fifteenth. During the eighteenth century, on the contrary, the population of Europe doubled on the average, although the increase varied according to the region. It was very large in England but less in France. In Venice the population actually became smaller. The figures on population in Poland and Russia are uncertain, but the fact of growth is indisputable. More important perhaps than the increase in numbers as such was the modification of the demographic pattern. Between the fifteenth and the eighteenth centuries the failure of the European population to grow had been the consequence of a series of profound crises, epidemics (generally called "plagues"), and wars. Plagues and wars in particular resulted in catastrophic drops in the population. To be sure, the high birth rate permitted a rapid return to the previous figure, but then new crises followed which prevented any further rise. Infant mortality was considerable. More than half the newborn did not live beyond one year of age. Life expectancy was short; the average life extended little beyond twenty-four years. This whole pattern was transformed during the eighteenth century. Although infant mortality remained very high and decreased only very, very slowly, the adult mortality rate diminished considerably; thus life expectancy increased. In France the total population, which had never exceeded 18 million since the fourteenth century, passed this figure around 1730 and reached 26 million in 1789. The population of the whole of Europe passed from 100 million to about 200 million between 1700 and 1800.

This was a phenomenon of capital importance. The increase of the population created two fundamental problems. One was subsistence: would the augmentation of food production keep up with the growth in the population? The other was employment: would the surplus population be able to find work? These questions preoccupied the scientists and philosophes of the eighteenth century. They gave various and often contradictory replies. The Englishman Thomas Malthus, a pessimist, favored reducing the number of births.

In any case we are in the presence of the fact that

the European population doubled. What were the consequences of this increase? Did it cause the disorders and the revolution? So far as expansion of food production is concerned, the problem is very complex. It seems well established at the present time, thanks to recent studies, that the increase in the European population was due first of all to improvement of agricultural production. The discovery of America in the late fifteenth and sixteenth centuries made available to Europeans new plants which either were more nutritious or had a bigger yield than the crops which had long been cultivated in Europe. These included maize (American corn), which had a yield of 32 to 1, while the best varieties of wheat sowed in Europe yielded only three or four to one; the potato, which grew very well in poor soils; tobacco, whose leaf was in great demand and sold at a very high price; and vegetables such as the kidney bean and the pumpkin. These plants were introduced into Europe as early as the sixteenth century but were accepted slowly, and the consequences of their cultivation only became evident in the eighteenth century. There is no doubt that they improved the diet of the European peasant and thereby contributed to increasing his resistance to disease. Hence adult mortality fell. The progress of hygiene and medicine does not seem to have played a major part in reducing mortality. But as the European population increased, the surplus in agricultural products decreased. Other ways for increasing production had to be considered. The English agronomists and the French physiocrats began scientific study of the process of cultivation of the soil. They recommended development of pasturage by means of artificial meadows, abandonment of triennial or biennial rotation of crops (which left as much as half the ground fallow each year), development of industrial crops, selection of seed, and suppression of open pasture by means of the enclosure of farmlands. These suggestions were often adopted. In France, butcher shops increased in number and had spread even to the smallest villages by the end of the eighteenth century. Nonetheless it does seem a fact that agricultural production was unable to keep up with the increase in the population. After 1770, bad crops due to weather conditions (excessive rainfall or heat) resulted in famines such as Western Europe had not seen for fifty years.

Employment was a different problem. When population began to increase, men easily found jobs in agriculture, which was developing rapidly. In certain countries of Western Europe, like France, the Netherlands, Germany and especially England, the start of the Industrial Revolution and the building of big factories resulted in the creation of new jobs. But soon there were not enough jobs, and unemployment developed. The number of jobless vagrants in France on the eve of the revolution was considerable. Here is the significant complaint made by the villagers of La Caune, near Châlons, in their grievance list (cahier de doléances) in 1789: "The number of our children makes us despair. We do not have the means to feed or clothe them." An inquiry conducted by the "committee on mendicancy" of the Constituent Assembly in 1790 revealed that in about half of France (44 departments out of 86) the number of the "indigent" (that is, the unemployed) was more than 10 percent; in six departments, including Haute-Garonne, Le Nord, and Pas-de-Calais, it reached one-fifth of the population. In England and Germany the employment situation was less difficult: in the former country big industry was more developed; in the latter overseas emigration was more important. However, despite the great extent of vacant land, the arrival of an increasing number of immigrants in America confronted that country with problems like those which the increase in population placed before Europe.

The considerable increase in the population of the Western world resulting from introduction of new plants of American origin into Europe must be considered incontestably one of the major causes of the revolutions of the Atlantic world. Indeed, it was from the innumerable unemployed that were recruited not the leaders, but the troops, of the revolutionary armies.

The difficulties met after 1770 by a young population in the full flood of expansion are bound up with the economic cycle. The business cycle has not been studied in its entirety for the whole of the West but only in some individual countries—England, Spain, Holland, and especially France. Tables of prices and sometimes of wages have been established and curves drawn. The examination of these curves demonstrates that in a general manner prices rose slowly from about 1730 to 1770. From 1770 to 1790 we observe a plateau marked by very accentuated sawteeth in the curves. These peaks and hollows on the graphs are the indicators of repeated economic crises, which appear to be the origins of the demographic crises revealed by the birth and death curves. Where in most cases the birth rate clearly exceeded the death rate between 1730 and 1770, from 1770 until 1790 a surplus of deaths is often observable. The demographic curves thus reproduce the sawteeth of the price curve and confirm the existence of serious and profound crises. The shape of the price curve in Western Europe has been explained by variation of the imports of precious metals. The discovery of gold in Brazil in the Minas Gerães and its introduction into European monetary circulation brought an increase in prices after 1730. The slowing of gold shipments around 1770 is one of the causes of the slackening of the increase in prices and hence of the economic stagnation.

Although wages increased, they lagged far behind prices, so that wage-earners—farm laborers, artisans, and factory hands—found themselves in a less favorable situation. In France prices increased on the average from 48 to 65 percent between 1730 and 1789, but wages rose only from 11 to 26 percent. Comparing the rise of *nominal wages* with the increase in the cost of living, we observe a fall in *real wages*. This fall was the consequence on the one hand of the rapid increase in the population of working age and on the other hand of the weak development of big industry in France. In fact, Watt's steam engine, perfected in England between 1769 and 1776, was not put to use in France until 1785 at the metallurgical factory of Le Creusot. The smelting of iron ore by means of coke instead of charcoal was practiced in England and Germany as early as 1750, but not before 1785 in France. Where the British textile industry used 20,000 jennies in 1789, France possessed only 7,000. In the last decade of the eighteenth century, England had numerous factories employing more than a hundred workers, but France had only a few—several metallurgical plants in Le Nord, Alsace, Lorraine, and Le Creusot. Western Germany and Belgium were perhaps better equipped than France, but northern Italy was definitely behind France. At the end of the eighteenth century, England had at least a twenty years' headstart over the most developed countries on the continent.

The transformation of agriculture as recommended by the English agronomists and the French and Italian physiocrats did not create new jobs for the excess population. On the contrary, extension of pasturage, development of artificial meadows, enclosures, partition of common lands, and suppression of open grazing had the inevitable consequence of reducing the number of farm jobs. Livestock rais-

ing requires fewer hands than tilling the soil. When communal lands and open grazing were abolished, the poor *brassier* could no longer keep a cow or sheep and was reduced to the status of a rural proletarian. The modernization of agriculture therefore had the result of increasing the number of available workers. In England most of them were rapidly absorbed by industry, then in the process of rapid expansion. On the continent they were driven into unemployment and destitution and became elements of social disorder.

International trade also felt the effect of these changes. England became an even more intense competitor in the great international markets, clashing sharply with France especially. French merchants hoped to find compensation in increased trade with the United States, as seemed to be promised by the treaty of 1778, but they were disappointed. Instead of opening new outlets to French trade, the Anglo-French treaty of commerce of 1787 (the "Eden treaty") merely increased English exports to France and hence the economic struggle between the two countries.

In America the situation was somewhat different. The economic cycle does not seem to have developed there as it did in Europe, although the problems of employment and economic competition were similar. In the second half of the eighteenth century the local aristocracy tended to monopolize the land and to assemble vast estates, in particular in the Hudson valley. The surplus population resulting from the excess of births and the arrival of immigrants had difficulty in finding land in already cleared regions. The land-seeker had to go West as a pioneer. As for the merchants, the numerous fiscal measures adopted by the British government after 1763, especially the tax on tea, cut into their trade and drove them into opposition. In summary, after 1770, in America as in Europe, the economic cycle was unfavorable, increasing general insecurity and encouraging social agitation. . . .

The Atlantic Revolution also had political causes. The slow but continuous rise of prices during the course of the eighteenth century affected not only individuals but also the states. The financial resources of governments, coming essentially from taxes, rapidly became insufficient to cover their expenses. This was all the more true because expenses rose considerably as a result of the great wars that disturbed the first two-thirds of the eighteenth century. From 1700 to 1783 there took place the War of the Spanish Succession, which lasted twelve years, the War of the Polish Succession, which lasted four, the War of the Austrian Succession, which lasted seven, and the Seven Years' War: in all a total of thirty years of war out of sixty-three, or almost one year out of every two. The states had to introduce new taxes in order to meet their enormous military expenses. But nowhere was it possible to demand more of the peasants and the bourgeois, who until then had borne the principal share of government expenditures. It became imperative to abolish the fiscal privileges of the nobility and the clergy. Although this meant a frontal attack on privileged institutions, most sovereigns did not hesitate to adopt this policy. To justify their conduct, they employed the theories of those philosophes who sang the praises of absolute monarchy provided it was "enlightened." Thus "enlightened despotism" was born. It was characteristic particularly of the reigns of Frederick II in Prussia, Catherine II in Russia, Maria Theresa and Joseph II in the Holy Roman Empire (Germany), and sovereigns of lesser importance in Italy and Spain.

In a majority of states the aristocracy organized (in Montesquieu's phrase) in "intermediate corporations" resisted this policy of the enlightened despots, which tended to strengthen the power of the state and to diminish or even to abolish totally the aristocrats' privileges. Russia and the Ottoman Empire were the only countries in Europe that were not the arena of such struggles. This was a consequence of the social structure of these states: the weakness of the nobility and the bourgeoisie, which were badly organized, and the huge numbers of the peasantry, who were subject to unlimited burdens of taxation and labor services. In most other countries of Europe and the European colonies of America, the privileged corporations, in the name of the "historic rights" which Montesquieu defended, resisted the demands of the state. In Sweden it was the Riksdag, composed of the representatives of the four orders (nobility, clergy, bourgeoisie, peasantry), with the aristocracy predominant, which opposed the monarchy until the coup d'état of King Gustavus III in 1772. In Poland, Bohemia, and Hungary the diets, composed only or almost only of the nobles and the bishops, relentlessly resisted every effort to reinforce the central power, to make the executive more powerful, and to modernize the administration of the state. In Prussia there existed no national diet but only provincial assemblies (*Landtäge*), in which the nobility held the preponderant influence; they too attempted to struggle against the claims of the monarch. In Italy the aristocracy dominated most of the states. In old republics like Venice and Genoa they ruled as they pleased, but where the states were headed by princes, as in Lombardy and Tuscany, they opposed the princes' reforms. The situation was similar in most of the German principalities, in the Austrian Netherlands and in the United Provinces. In France the aristocracy was the master of the *parlements*, the courts of justice which claimed the right to present their views on all legislative enactments. They also dominated the provincial Estates which still existed in Languedoc, Brittany, and Burgundy. Even in Great Britain the aristocracy remained very powerful in Parliament. The assemblies of the English colonies of North America represented primarily the local aristocracy. The great administrative bodies of the French colonies in the Antilles were in the hands of the privileged classes, and in the Spanish colonies the *cabildos* were likewise composed of aristocrats.

In all these countries—that is, throughout the West—the aristocracy formed a front against the claims of the sovereigns. They strove not only to maintain their position but also to improve it, by obtaining confirmation of their privileges and monopolies, by having land registers brought up to date, and by more harshly than ever requiring from their vassals recognition of their privileges and payment of the feudal dues owed to them (for they too were the victims of the price rise and needed more money). This attitude of the nobility has been studied especially in France, where it has been called the "aristocratic reaction," the "reaction of the nobility," and the "feudal reaction." But the aristocratic reaction was not a specifically French phenomenon; it was a phenomenon of the West as a whole.

The sovereigns first attempted to break the aristocratic reaction by traditional means—that is, by decrees and commands and by invoking their theoretical omnipotence. But the interests at stake were such that the resistance of the privileged classes became more and more stubborn. The sovereigns then gave thought to the counsels of philosophes of the Voltairean tendency, who held all subjects to be equal before the monarch, and they sought the alliance of the Third Estate against the privileged orders. In France, Louis XV suppressed the parlements in 1771 upon the advice of his ministers Maupeou,

Terray, and D'Aiguillon,[1] and reformed the fiscal system by placing slightly greater burdens upon the privileged groups. In Sweden Gustavus III amended the constitution by his own authority in 1772; he reduced the powers of the aristocratic Riksdag and governed with the support of the bourgeoisie and the peasantry. In the Hapsburg states, Maria Theresa compelled the "constituted corporations" of Austria, Bohemia, the southern Netherlands, and Lombardy to accept heavier taxation and a new customs tariff in 1775. In 1765 the British government extended the Stamp Act to its possessions of North America without consulting the colonial assemblies. Faced by their resistance, the king withdrew the Stamp Act the next year, but he affirmed the superiority of the Crown over the colonial assemblies by the Declara-

[1] Nicolas Augustin de Maupeou (1714–1792) served in several offices, finally becoming chancellor in 1768. Joseph Marie Terray was ecclesiastical counsellor to the parlement of Paris and comptroller general of finances until replaced by Turgot in 1774. The Duc d'Aiguillon (1720–1788), a descendant of Richelieu, became minister of foreign affairs in 1773 and minister of war in 1774. Between 1770 and 1774 this trio constituted a triumvirate which virtually governed France. Their conduct of affairs evoked considerable discontent. [Editor's note.]

tory Act. In the same period Louis XV also proclaimed his authority over the French parlements, the citadels of the aristocracy, in the famous "flagellation" session.

If sovereigns sought the support of the people, the privileged orders did not hesitate to do so too. Outbidding the rulers, the aristocrats proclaimed themselves to be the only defenders of the people. In France the members of the parlements took the name of "Fathers of the People." For a dozen years the bourgeoisie sincerely believed that they had no better defenders than the parlements; not until 1788 did the duplicity of the parlements become apparent. In the English colonies of America, the assemblies sought support against the British sovereign among the merchants, small farmers, and artisans. In general the people were encouraged not only by the philosophes but also by the privileged orders to enter into struggle against the sovereign. In most countries of the West the "aristocratic reaction" inevitably led to a revolt of the nobility and soon thereafter to a revolt of the people.

GEORGE E. RUDÉ

SOCIAL CONFLICT AS A CAUSE OF REVOLUTION

George E. Rudé, born in 1910, the son of a Norwegian, was raised and educated in England at Trinity College, Cambridge. He took his Ph.D. at London University. Since 1960, he has been in Australia at the University of Adelaide, where he is Professor of History. His numerous publications include his dissertation, *The Crowd in the French Revolution* (1959), *Wilkes and Liberty* (1962), *Revolutionary Europe, 1783–1815* (1964), and *The Crowd in History* (1964). Together with three other students of Georges Lefebvre, Albert Soboul, Richard Cobb, and Kåre Tønnesson, he has helped to reveal for the first time the role of the popular classes in revolutionary movements in France and England in the eighteenth century. He has contributed a chapter to *The New Cambridge Modern History*, Vol. VIII (1965).

Although there is a tendency to re-open the debate on the causes of the French Revolution, most reputable historians of the event have by now accepted the thesis that the Revolution was the product of a conflict of social classes rather than the outcome of a conspiracy hatched by *philosophes*, lawyers, dis-

George E. Rudé, "The Outbreak of the French Revolution." World Copyright: The Past and Present Society, Corpus Christi College, Oxford. This article is reprinted with the permission of the Society and the author from *Past and Present, A journal of historical studies*, No. 8 (November, 1955).

gruntled officials or Freemasons.[1] Since the publication of Jaurès' *Histoire Socialiste* at the turn of the century, a serious effort has been made, as well, by a number of historians to treat the problems, aspirations and movements of the peasant and urban masses in their own right instead of as an echo or reflection of the speeches and actions of the revolutionary leaders in Paris.

Such studies have, of course, done more than merely throw a fresh light on the general causes and course of the Revolution; they have made it possible to measure with greater accuracy the point of revolutionary outbreak and the part played by the masses of town and countryside in relation to it. The revolutionary explosion, therefore, no longer appears as a more or less fortuitous climax to a series of purely political, though interrelated, crises — the rejection of Calonne's proposals by the Notables, the convocation of the States General, the dismissal of Necker, etc. — but as the sharp collision of a complex of social forces at a moment of acute revolutionary crisis.

Even when this is accepted, however, the picture may still become lop-sided if one or other of the social forces, whose coming together — either in alliance or in opposition — provoked the revolutionary crisis, is not seen in its proper perspective. The most familiar distortion of this kind is that which presents the revolutionary action of the peasant and urban masses as "waiting upon" that of the *bourgeoisie*, or even of the privileged orders themselves. Mathiez,[2] in particular, has made us familiar with the picture of the origins of the great Revolution as a gradual "unfolding" of minor revolutions — first the "*revolte nobiliaire*"; then the "*révolution bourgeoise*"; and, finally, the popular revolution. While such a presentation is convenient and has more than a grain of truth in it, it tends to reduce the intervention of the masses to one of secondary importance and fails to show that the popular movement, while intensified and accelerated by the revolutionary crisis, had its origins in the Old Régime and, in fact, preceded by many years the revolutionary activity of the *bourgeoisie*.

On the other hand, writers like Daniel Guérin have gone to the opposite extreme by exaggerating the independence and the degree of coherence and political maturity of the popular movement, and particularly emphasizing those aspects of it which appear to look forward to the working class movements of the 19th and 20th centuries.[3] In the view of such historians, of course, it is not the wage-earners or *sans-culottes*,[4] but the *bourgeoisie* itself which ceases to be a revolutionary force.

Yet another tendency has been to present the revolutionary crisis almost exclusively in terms of more or less short-term economic factors, particularly of rising or falling prices. No-one will deny the great contribution made to our knowledge of the origins of the Revolution by Ernest Labrousse: before his work appeared,[5] little was known of the movements of prices and wages in 18th century France, particularly in the crucial years preceding the revolutionary outbreak. Labrousse's insistence, however, on the primacy of "natural" (i.e. uncontrollable economic) over "anthropomorphic" causes has the effect of reducing the popular movement to the automatic product of purely economic factors.[6]

The present study introduces new material to illustrate the range and diversity of the movement in town and countryside — particularly in the Paris region — in the years leading up to the Revolution; it also attempts to place the revolt of the privileged orders and the Parlements (the "*révolte nobiliaire*") and the revolutionary action of the *bourgeoisie* in the crisis of 1788 – 9 in their correct historical setting; but, above all, it is concerned to trace the main stages and currents of the popular movement during the last years of the Old Régime up to the point where its "merger" with that of the *bourgeoisie* touched off the revolutionary explosion.

Let us begin with the year 1775. There had, of course, been numerous other movements provoked

[1] The main exponents of this "conspiracy" — thesis are Taine, Gochin and Gaxotte. More recently, a more modern version of it has been put forward by J. L. Talmon in his *Origins of Totalitarian Democracy* (1952).

[2] Albert Mathiez was an important historian of the French Revolution [Editor's note.]

[3] D. Guérin, *La Lutte de Classes sous la I^e République* (2 vols. 1946).

[4] The term *sans-culottes* is here used, as elsewhere in this article, to denote the mass of small producers and the non-propertied classes of town and countryside. Strictly speaking, it did not come into use until after June 1792; but then it tends also to acquire a wider, political significance.

[5] C.-E. Labrousse, *Esquisse du Mouvement des Prix et des Revenus en France au XVIII Siècle* (2 vols. 1933); *La Crise de l'Economie Française a la Fin de l'Ancien Régime et au Début de la Révolution* (vol. 1. 1944).

[6] *La Crise de l'Economie Française*, pp. 180 et seq.

by hunger and the high cost of bread in earlier periods of the century—as, for example, in 1725, 1739–40, 1752 and 1768;[7] but that of 1775 is not only the nearest to the point of revolutionary outbreak, but the most extensive, the best documented and that which bears the closest resemblance to the popular movements of the Revolution itself. Turgot had been appointed Comptroller-General in August 1774. He started with no particular record of unpopularity as far as the common people were concerned: at any rate, his predecessor and most vocal opponent, the Abbé Terray, was, soon after his appointment, burned in effigy in the Faubourg St. Antoine.[8] Yet, to the delight of his enemies at Court, he was soon to lose any semblance of popular favour by his over-haste in applying Physiocratic doctrine to the grain-trade: an *arrêt* of 13 September restored freedom of trade in grain and flour. This, combined with a bad harvest, led to a shortage and a rapid rise in the price of corn, flour and bread in the following spring and summer. The price of the 4-lb. loaf in Paris (normally 8–9 *sous,* though, in recent years, more often 10–11 *sous*) rose up to 11½ *sous* in early March and to 13½ *sous* at the end of April. Grain riots had already broken out in Dijon, Tours, Metz, Rheims and Montauban—and, in their wake, sprang up that particular series of riots, centred in Paris and its adjoining provinces, known to history as *"la guerre des farines."* The movement spread from market to market and took the form of a popular price-control of wheat, flour and bread—the price of bread being generally fixed at 2 *sous* per pound, that of flour at 20 *sous* a bushel and wheat at 12 *francs a setier* (2 quintals). Starting on 27 April at Beaumont-sur-Oise, twenty miles north of Paris, it reached Pontoise on the 29th, St. Germain on 1 May, Versailles on the 2nd and Paris itself on the 3rd. It then spread eastwards and southwards up the valleys of the Seine and Marne, lingered for several days in the markets and villages of Brie, reached Beaumont-sur-Gâtinais (50 miles south of Paris) on the 9th, and petered out somewhere near Melun on the 10th.

It is instructive to note the main features of this remarkable movement. It was essentially a spontaneous movement—in spite of some historians' claim to the contrary—provoked by hunger and the fear of shortage. It saw the massive invasion of markets and farms by urban poor, farm-labourers, village artisans, and even occasional farmers and well-to-do *bourgeois.* It was directed, in the main, against farmers or prosperous peasants *(laboureurs),* grain-merchants, millers and bakers; and aroused some sympathy among other classes—certain priests, for example, either encouraged, or did little to restrain their parishioners from taking part in the movement, and more than one market official helped it along by himself fixing a "just" price for grain or flour.

Why, then, did a movement of such magnitude and bearing striking similarities with certain movements of the Revolution yield no tangible result? In the first place, the food crisis itself, though protracted, was overcome by the end of the summer: prices began to fall in October. Secondly, Turgot managed to crush the movement by a combination of propaganda—via the Bishops—and the use of troops, who remained entirely loyal to the Government. More important still, the bulk of the peasantry was not involved: the question of tithes, feudal dues or game laws did not arise. Lastly, and perhaps most important of all, the *bourgeoisie* had not yet begun to challenge the existing order and, in any case, were bound to be hostile to a movement directed against members of their own class and against a Minister, whose accession to office they had hailed with enthusiasm and whose reforms—including that of free trade in grain—they actively supported: in several towns, in fact, the *milice bourgeoise* was mustered in order to crush the riots.[9] The main lesson of 1775 was, in short, that, in the conditions of 18th century France, no isolated movement of wage-earners, artisans and village poor could hope to yield revolutionary results. This truth was to be realized on more than one occasion both before and during the Revolution.

The twelve years that followed (1775 to 1787) were, despite a general sharpening of the longer-term economic crisis,[10] years of comparatively stable food prices and social peace. In Paris, at least, the

[7] *Journal et Mémoires du Marquis d'Argenson* (9 vols. 1859), i, 54; ii, 153, 159, 184, 213; iii, 61–2, 131–73; vii, 81–7, 218–333, 353–9. See also S. Lacroix, *Actes de la Commune de Paris* (2nd series. 8 vols. 1900–14), vi, 398.

[8] Métra, *Correspondance secrète, politique et littéraire . . . depuis la Mort de Louis XV* (18 vols. London, 1787–90), i, 87.

[9] For the movement of 1775, see my study, "La taxation populaire de mai 1775 à Paris et dans la région parisienne," shortly to appear in *Annales Historiques de la Revolution Française.*

[10] See Labrousse, *Esquisse . . .* ii, 597–608. Already in 1778, there were said to be 120,000 poor and needy in Paris out of a population of about 600,000. (M. C. Bloch, *L'Assistance et l'Etat en France à la Veille de la Révolution* (1908), p. 6).

price of bread remained remarkably steady: from the manuscript Journal of the Parisian bookseller Sébastien Hardy we learn that, whereas, in the period 1767–75, the price of the 4-lb. loaf rarely fell below 11 *sous* (and, for a few days in November 1768, actually reached 16 *sous*), in the later period, the normal price was 8 or 9 *sous*, and it only rose to 10½ or 11 *sous* for very brief spells in 1784.[11]

Popular movements during these years were scattered and sporadic, arising on a number of separate issues. In June 1778, bread riots took place in Toulouse and Grenoble; in both, rioters were fired on by troops.[12] In 1784 and 1786, there were protest movements in Paris against the *barriéres*, or ring of customs posts, recently erected by the Farmers-General to tax livestock, meat, wine, firewood and other commodities entering the capital;[13] and, also in 1786, Hardy noted protests against the cost of meat and firewood.[14] In Paris, too, there appears to have been a resurgence of anti-clerical feeling among the people: Hardy recorded a number of incidents between 1783 and 1789[15] that are reminiscent of the hostility to Jesuits in the 1720's and to the Archbishop of Paris over the *billets de confession* in 1752.[16]

More remarkable perhaps is the number of strikes, involving the journeymen in a number of trades and, in the case of the Lyons silk-workers, assuming almost insurrectionary proportions. Jules Flammermont may be right in attributing these, in part at least, to the special penal measures in restraint of combination introduced in August 1776 and to the anger of the workers at the reversal of the decision to abolish the guilds;[17] but it is worth observing that, in 18th century France, a crop of strikes usually coincides, as here, with a period of comparatively stable prices. In 1776, a general strike broke out among Parisian bookbinders who were demanding a 14-hour day.[18] In July 1785, there was a large-scale and successful strike of Paris building-workers against a wage-cut imposed by the employers; in March 1786, the carpenters were on strike again and, this time, Hardy reported "une espèce de fermentation" among the journeymen of several trades.[19] In January of the same year, the carriers and porters of the capital struck against the institution of a rival monopoly by Court favourites, and seven to eight hundred of them marched to Versailles to see the King.[20] In Lyons, the strikes of the silk-weavers led to widespread rioting and bloodshed.[21] Yet, with the exception of the movement in Lyons, which had its sequel in the domination by the *maîtres-ouvriers* of the meetings called to draw up the *cahiers de doléances* for the silk industry in 1789, it is doubtful if these labour disputes gave any appreciable impetus to the widespread and varied popular movement that was to arise in the period of revolutionary crisis.

The year 1787 saw the opening of the "*révolte nobiliaire*" which served as a curtain-raiser to the revolutionary crisis of 1788–9. In February, an empty exchequer and mounting deficit forced the Government to convene the Assembly of Notables. Calonne, as Comptroller-General, proposed a number of stop-gap measures to meet the crisis, including a stamp-duty and a tax on landed estates. The privileged orders refused to co-operate. Calonne was dismissed on 8 April and succeeded by Loménie de Brienne, Archbishop of Toulouse. Brienne's proposals being no more acceptable than Calonne's, the Notables in turn were dismissed on 25 May, and the "*révolte nobiliaire*" began. The opening shot was fired, as so often in the past, by the Paris Parlement which, while accepting Brienne's plan to relax controls on the sale and export of grain and protesting against the stamp-duty, refused absolutely to register the decree on the land-tax and demanded that the States General be convened to deal with the matter. When the decrees were, none the less, promulgated in a *lit de justice* in August, the provincial Parlements rallied to the support of Paris, and Brienne was forced to capitulate; the decrees on the land-tax and stamp-duty were withdrawn on 21 Sep-

[11]S. Hardy, *Mes Loisirs, ou Journal d'événements tels qu'ils parviennent à ma connaissance* (Bib. Nat. fonds français, nos. 6680–7), vols. 1–7, *passim*.

[12]Hardy, *op. cit.*, iv, 9; Métra, *op. cit.*,v., 295.

[13]Hardy, vi, 18, 35, 435.

[14]*Ibid*, vi, 332, 479.

[15]*Ibid*, v, 322–3, 394–5, 410; vi, 330, viii, 184.

[16]E. J. F. Barbier, *Journal historique et anecdotique du Règne de Louis XV* (4 vols. 1847), i, 263–4; *Journal et Mémoires du Marquis d'Argenson*, vii, 226–7.

[17]J. Flammermont, "Mémoire sur les grèves et les coalitions ouvrières à la fin de l'Ancien Régime," *Bull. du Com. des Trav. hist. et scient.* (Section des sciences econ. et soc.), 1894, pp. 194–205.

[18]Hardy, iii, 281.

[19]*Ibid.*, vi, 149–50, 315.

[20]*Ibid.*, vi, 266–71.

[21]Jaurès, *Histoire, Socialiste de la Révolution Française* (8 vols. Paris, 1922–4), i, 97–116; Hardy, vi, 413–4, 424–5.

tember and the Paris Parlement was reinstated a few days later.[22]

The return of the Paris Parlement from exile was the occasion of wild scenes of jubilation in the Place Dauphine, the rue du Harlay and other approaches to the Law Courts. Calonne was burned in effigy, bonfires were lit on the Pont Neuf, fireworks and squibs were let off at the Guards. From Hardy's description and from the arrests made on 28 September (the climax of the disturbances) it is clear that the shock-troops in these riots were formed by the clerks of the Palais—"une jeunesse effrénée" Hardy calls them—and the apprentices and journeymen of the luxury trades in the Place Dauphine; the "populace" of the surrounding quarters joined them but played only a subordinate part.[23] The bourgeoisie was as yet uninvolved.

In the months that followed it was the economic crisis, above all, that brought the "fourth estate" once more into the picture, either on their own account or (as in Paris) as the temporary ally of the dissident privileged orders. Brienne's return to the "free trade" measures of Turgot had led to a sharp rise in the price of grain; by July 1788, in the North at least, speculators were at work again and widespread complaints were voiced against forestalling and hoarding.[24] At Troyes, the milice bourgeoise was already mustered in April to overawe the textile workers;[25] and, in Paris, as we shall see, the high price of bread was to contribute to a popular outbreak in the late summer. Peasant revolt, however, lay dormant until the following spring, when long-simmering discontent with food-prices and seignorial exaction was to be touched off into violent outbreak by the political ferment emanating from the local electoral assemblies.

Meanwhile, the political crisis had sharpened. Brienne had fallen back on the expedient of raising a loan, which the Paris Parlement was willing to accept, provided the States General should be summoned. But negotiations broke down again in November; the Duke of Orléans and two conseillers

were exiled; and, in May 1788, the Parlement issued a declaration, condemning the whole system of arbitrary government, including the lettres de cachet. The Government riposted by ringing the Palais with troops, forced the Parlementaires to surrender their ringleaders to royal justice and promulgated six edicts, prepared by Lamoignon, the garde des sceaux, which restricted the jurisdiction of the Parlements and vested the royal courts and officials with greater powers. A new phase of violence followed: there were mass riots in Grenoble and Rennes in June;[26] in the Dauphiné, nobility and Third Estate joined forces against the Crown in July. In early August, troops were concentrated around the capital for fear of an "insurrection," not so much of the Palais clerks and apprentices as of the menu peuple of the markets and the Faubourgs St. Antoine and St. Marcel.[27]

These fears proved well-founded. The Government was compelled to bow before the storm and promised that the States General would be called in May 1789; on 24 August, Brienne was replaced by Necker and the Parlement was recalled soon after. The news was greeted with another outburst of celebrations in the Place Dauphine and the approaches to the Palais: bonfires were lit and the occupants of coaches crossing the Pont Neuf were compelled to bow low to the statue of Henri IV and to shout "A bas Lamoignon!" A new factor, however, was to extend these disturbances far beyond the scope and limits of those of the previous year. On 17 August, the price of the 4-lb. loaf, after remaining at 9 sous, rose to 9½ sous, on the 20th to 10 sous, on 2 September to 10½ sous, and on 7 September to 11 sous. Under this stimulus, the inhabitants of the Faubourgs joined in the riots on the third day (29 August) and changed their whole character: they spread to the markets and University quarter, continued—with short lulls—until the end of September and took a heavy toll in casualties and arrests; the latter were mainly composed of craftsmen and wage-earners of widely-scattered districts.[28] The Parisian sans-culottes had entered the arena as a decisive force, but not yet as the ally of the bourgeoisie; the real revolutionary crisis was yet to come.

[22] For a brief, but adequate, account of the "révolte nobiliare," see G. Lefebvre, La Révolution Française (Peuples et Civilisations No. XIII, 1951), pp. 107–12; also A. Goodwin, The French Révolution (Hutchinson's Univ. Lib., 1953), pp. 27–42.

[23] Hardy, vii, 178–255; Arch. Nat. Y 13014.

[24] G. Lefebvre, Les Paysans du Nord pendant la Révolution Française (1924), pp. 339–41.

[25] G. Lefebvre, La Grande Peur de 1789 (1932), pp. 55–6.

[26] For Rennes, see B. de Moleville, Histoire de la Revolution de France (14 vols. 1801–3) ii, 100–20.

[27] Hardy, viii, 35.

[28] For a detailed account of the above, see Hardy, op. cit., viii, 58–109; for the arrests, see Bib. Nat. MSS Collection Joly de Fleury, doss. 1113; and Arch. Nat. Y 9491, 9989, 11206, 11517, 18756, 18795.

This developed in the winter of 1788–9 and was to bring about a radical realignment of classes. The harvest was generally bad, and, in the Paris region, crops had been flattened by a freak hailstorm in July.[29] There followed a winter of phenomenal severity which threw thousands out of work and brought further thousands of villagers flocking to the capital;[30] in December, Hardy wrote of 80,000 unemployed.[31] The price of the 4-lb. loaf in the Paris markets rose to 12 *sous* on 8 November, to 13 *sous* on the 28th, to 14 *sous* on 11 December and, finally, to 14½ *sous* on 1 February; it was to remain at this level until after the fall of the Bastille.[32] In April, in the grain-starved markets of the Paris region, the price of wheat rose to the fantastic sum of 40–44 *francs* the *setier*.[33] Meanwhile, the crisis in industry—itself the offshoot of the agrarian crisis,[34] though doubtless aggravated by the results of the Commercial Treaty with England in 1786[35]—had thrown thousands out of work in every textile centre: according to the reports of the industrial inspectors for September 1788 to January 1789, there were 46,000 unemployed in Amiens, 10,000 in Rouen, 8,000 in Falaise, 30,000 in Carcassonne, 25,000 in Lyons; while at Troyes and Sedan half the looms were idle.[36]

It was against this economic background that the *bourgeoisie* made its entry on the revolutionary stage. The cause of conflict had its roots deep in the Old Régime: while colonial trade, land-values and luxury spending had enormously increased in the course of the century, capital investment and expansion of manufacture were everywhere impeded by the restrictions imposed by privileged corporations, feudal landowners and Government on the elementary capitalist freedoms—the freedom to hire labour, the freedom to produce and the freedom to buy and sell. Yet, while the ensuing conflict owed its eventual sharpness and finality to these deeper social antagonisms, the clash between the *bourgeoisie* and the privileged orders arose, in the first instance, over representation and voting in the States General. Already in September, the Paris Parlement had shattered its reputation as the spokesman for "popular liberties" by demanding that the States General be constituted as in 1614—i.e. that each order should have equal representation and vote separately. An even more forthright insistence on the maintenance of privilege was voiced in the Manifesto of the Princes of the Blood in December. Necker, however, persuaded the Council to allow the Third Estate double representation; but the question of voting "par tête" (as demanded by the *bourgeoisie*) or "par ordre" (as insisted by the nobility and clergy) remained open and led to bloody clashes between nobles and commoners at Rennes. By January, the new alignment of forces was becoming clear and Mallet du Pan noted that it was no longer a question of a constitutional conflict between the King and the *privilégiés* but a "war between the Third Estate and the two other orders."[37] In February, the conflict was raised to a higher pitch by the publication of the Abbé Sieyès' pamphlet *Qu'est-ce que le Tiers Etat?*, in which the *bourgeoisie*, for the first time, laid claim to control the destinies of the nation irrespective of the wishes or privileges of the other orders.

It is not surprising that, with these developments, the winter of 1788–9 should see the beginnings of a popular movement of an altogether vaster scope and intensity than those of the preceding years. This movement had other, even more significant, features: it became a continuous movement that did not cease until after the point of revolutionary outbreak; it grew from a movement concerned, in the first place, with purely economic ends into one with more or less clearly defined political aims; it developed a common bond of interest between the wage-earners, craftsmen, wine-growers,[38] and small tradesmen of town and countryside against monopolists, hoarders and grain-speculators; this movement, in turn, began to "merge" with that of the small peasant proprietors against feudal game laws, tithes and dues; and, finally (though not always in point of time), the movement of townsmen and vil-

[29] Arch. Nat. H 1453.

[30] See A. Tuetey, L'*Assistance Publique a Paris pendant la Révolution* (4 vols. 1895–7), vol. I, p. cxlii.

[31] Hardy, viii, 168.

[32] *Ibid*, viii, 154–5, 408, 426.

[33] Arch. Nat. H. 1453.

[34] Labrousse, *La Crise de L'Economie Française*, pp. xxxviii–xl.

[35] The older view—that the Vergennes Treaty was a primary cause of the depression—is argued by Charles Schmidt in "La crise industrielle de 1788 en France," *Revue Historique*, lcvii (1908), 78–94; this is contested by L. Cahen, "Une nouvelle interprétation du traité franco-anglais de 1786–7," *Rev. Hist.*, clxxxv. (1939), 257–85; and by Labrousse (*loc. cit.*)

[36] Schmidt, *loc. cit.*

[37] Quoted by Lefebvre, *La Révolution Française*, p. 113.

[38] For the importance of the wine-growers as a factor in the revolutionary crisis, see Labrousse, *op. cit.*, pp. 207–630.

lagers "merged" with the political action of the *bourgeoisie* against feudal privilege and the whole apparatus of government of the Old Régime.

The revolt against shortage and rising prices started in the last days of December 1788 and is recorded in the reports of the Intendants (or their *sub-délégués*) of several provinces. It variously took the form of pillaging of grain-boats and granaries; of enforcing price-control of bread, flour and wheat; of rioting in bakers' shops and markets, and at town halls; of assaulting customs officials, dealers and farmers; and the widespread destruction of property. In December and January, such reports come in from Brittany and Touraine; in March and April, from Burgundy, the Ile de France, Languedoc, Nivernais, Orléanais, Picardy, Poitu, Provence and Touraine; in May and June, from the Limousin and Lyonnais; in July, from Champagne and Normandy.[39] Hardy records bread-riots at Rheims in March and at Nancy and Toulouse in April.[40]

In the Faubourgs and markets of Paris, the high cost of meat and bread provoked a mounting wave of anger[41] which broke out into destructive violence in the Réveillon Riots in the Faubourg St. Antoine at the end of April.[42] Ten "smugglers" were arrested at the *barrières* in early May; this movement reached its climax on 12–14 July, when 40 of the 50-odd customs posts ringing the capital were burned down.[43]

In the country north of Paris, the fight against famine developed into a movement against the game laws and the hunting rights of the nobility. On the estates of the Prince de Conti at Cergy, Pontoise, l'Ile Adam and Beaumont, peasants and land-workers, having reaped no harvest owing to the ravages of hail, set out to trap and destroy the rabbits that infested their fields. The movement spread in the spring to Conflans Ste. Honorine and adjoining villages, and led to clashes with the *maréchaussée*.[44] At Oisy, in the Artois, the peasants of a dozen villages banded together to exterminate the Count of Oisy's game and refused in future to pay him the traditional *siyeté*, or *terrage*.[45] More violent clashes occurred near Corbeil and at Chatou; south and west of the capital, whole parishes, suspected of large-scale poaching on royal and aristocratic preserves, were disarmed in June.[46] In Lorraine and the Hainaut, landless peasants and small *laboureurs* joined forces in opposition to enclosure edicts and land clearance schemes.[47] Meanwhile, peasant revolt against royal taxes and seignorial exactions had broken out in Provence in March, at Gap in April, and in the Cambresis and Picardy in May.[48] This movement led, in turn, into that far vaster movement of July and August which, spreading over regions as widely scattered as Alsace, Normandy, the Hainaut, Mâconnais and Franche-Comté, left in its trail the widespread destruction of *chateaux* and manorial rolls.[49] Yet peasant hostility to enclosure and encroachment on rights of pasture led also to attacks on capitalist farmers; and, in more than one case again, the *milice bourgeoise* joined forces with the *maréchaussée* to repress peasant disorder.[50]

Yet, in spite of such contradictions, as the crisis deepened, *bourgeois* and *sans-culottes* were drawn into closer partnership in opposition to the privileged orders and the feudal régime. The urban and peasant masses were never to be fully won for the *bourgeois* conception of "freedom"—this was to remain a cause of division throughout the Revolution—but it was in their common interest to remove the fetters on production and the high cost of food occasioned by internal customs duties and fiscal charges; to clip the wings of (if not to dispossess entirely) the tithe-owner and the extractor of feudal

[39] Arch. Nat. H 1453.

[40] Hardy, viii, 262, 278.

[41] For this *"fermentation"* in Paris and the posting of troops at bakers' shops and in markets to contain it, see Hardy, viii, 158–184, 310, 344, *et seq.*

[42] Although the immediate cause of the riots were remarks attributed to two manufacturers concerning wages, it is evident that the real issue was that of the shortage and high cost of bread. (See my article, "The Motives of popular Insurrection in Paris during the French Revolution," *The Bull. of the Inst. of Hist. Research*, xxvi (1953), 53–74.).

[43] Arch. Nat. Y 18795, pp. 446–7; Z^{1a} 886.

[44] Arch. Nat. H 1453.

[45] Lefebvre, *Les Paysans du Nord*, p. 356.

[46] Arch. Nat. O^1 1036. Villages in the neighbourhood of the Royal forests of Fountainebleau, St. Germain, etc. had been protesting against damage done to their crops by rabbits, deer, etc. almost continuously for the past 15 years. There is, however, no sign of armed revolt in these districts until April 1789 (*ibid.*).

[47] M. Bloch, "La lutte pour l'individualisme agraire dans la France du xviiie siècle," *Annales d'Histoire économique et sociale*, ii (1930), 532–43. I am indebted to Mr. Alun Davies for this reference, as for several other valuable suggestions concerning the peasant movement of the period.

[48] Lefebvre, *La Révolution Française*, p. 130.

[49] Lefebvre, *La Grande Peur*, pp. 146 et. seq.

[50] Lefebvre, *La Révolution Française*, p. 138.

rente and *champart*; to reduce taxes and the ruinous costs of government; to compel the privileged orders to make a fair contribution to the national exchequer; to curb the monopolists and Farmers-General; to destroy such relics of ancient tyrannies as the Bastille, the *lettre de cachet* and the vexatious inquisitions of the Parlements. It is precisely such demands that we find voiced most frequently in the *cahiers de doléances* which began to be drawn up in the early months of 1789—usually drafted, it is true, by the professional *bourgeoisie*, but often endorsed by meetings of peasants, small tradesmen and workshop masters, and even though more rarely (as at Rheims, Marseilles, Troyes and Lyons) by guilds of journeymen or *maîtres-ouvriers*.[51]

And the States General roused such ardent hopes —"la grande espérance," Georges Lefebvre has called it[52]—because it was widely believed that, cleared of the obstruction and domination of the privileged orders, it could realize a radical programme of this kind. From these hopes stem the enthusiastic adoption of the slogan, *"Vive le Tiers Etat!"* (which is certainly thought to include the "fourth Estate" as well),[53] and the passionate belief, once the Court Party began to threaten to dash these hopes to the ground, in the existence of an aristocratic plot." It was in direct response to this stimulus that the Parisian journeymen, labourers, workshop masters and shop-keepers—already roused to action by the ruinous cost of bread, meat and wine—rallied to the call of the revolutionary leadership installed at the Palais Royal and—less certainly—to that set up by the Electors of the Paris Third Estate at the Hôtel de Ville; it was also this conviction that the Court Party was preparing to disperse the States General and to subdue Paris with the aid of foreign troops, far more than the gold of the Duke of Orleans, that won over the main body of the Paris garrison, the Gardes Françaises—so recently engaged in shooting down the Réveillon rioters—to the side of the Revolution. When Necker, the popular Finance Minister, was dismissed by the King on 12 July, the people of the Faubourgs and the markets joined with the *bourgeois* revolutionaries and the disaffected troops in carrying through the Paris insurrection—the first great armed uprising of the Revolution. The gunsmiths, arsenals and religious houses were raided for arms, the hated *barrières* were destroyed, a *milice bourgeoise* (including journeymen, but excluding "vagrants" and unemployed workers) was organized, a revolutionary government was installed at the Hôtel de Ville, and, finally, the Bastille was taken by storm. The popular movement had fully "merged" with that of the revolutionary *bourgeoisie;* the example was quickly followed in other parts of France.

Labrousse tells us that the Bastille fell on the very day when the price of grain throughout France reached its cyclical peak.[54] This is no doubt significant, but it would be a mistake to attempt to explain the revolutionary crisis wholly in such terms. To do so would be to discount entirely the revolutionary action of the *bourgeoisie* and the permeation of the Parisian *menu peuple* with the political ideas and slogans of the Third Estate. It is evident that the basic motive prompting popular action was the high cost of food and the fear of famine. This continued to be so and is the most constant element in the repeated upsurge of the popular movement during the years of the Revolution—in August-November 1789, in the years 1792–3 and, above all, in 1795.[55] Yet there was a similar fear of famine in 1768; and, in 1775, as we have seen, the fears thus aroused led to a massive movement of popular protest; yet in neither case did a revolutionary outbreak result. This was because the economic and political crisis as a whole—and not one single aspect of it, however important—had not fully matured and because the conflict of social classes which it occasioned was as yet only one-sided and partial; above all, it was because one of these classes, the *bourgeoisie*, although dissatisfied with the inequalities, the corruption, the extravagance and the restrictions of the Old Régime, had not yet begun seriously to challenge the absolute monarchy or the privileged orders, or the social system on which they depended. It was

[51] For the latter, in particular, see G. Laurent, *Cahiers de Doléances pour les Etats Genéraux de 1789* (6 vols. Rheims, 1906–30), iv, 94–5; G. Fournier, *Cahiers de Doléances de la Sénéchaussée de Marseille* (Marseille, 1908), pp. 70, 228–34; J.-J. Vernier, *Cahiers de Doléances du Bailliage de Troyes et de Bar-sur-Seine pour les Etats Généraux de 1789* (3 vols. 1909), i, 179–80; C.-L. Chassin, *Le Génie de la Révolution* (2 vols. 1863), i, 428–33.

[52] *Op. cit.*, pp. 130–1.

[53] The earliest popular use that I have found in police records of the term *"tiers état"* in this militant sense is on 21 April 1789 (Arch. Nat. Y 18762). The slogan *"Vive le Tiers Etat!"* was heard in the Réveillon Riots a week later (Arch. Nat. KK 641, fo. 17).

[54] Quoted by Lefebvre, "Le mouvement des prix et les origines de la Révolution francaise," *Ann. Hist. Rév. Franc.*, xiv (1937), p. 324.

[55] For an elaboration of this point, see my aforementioned article in *The Bulletin of the I.H.R.;* also "Prices, Wages and popular Movements in Paris during the French Revolution," *Econ. Hist. Rev.*, vol. vi, No. 3, April 1954, pp. 246–67.

only when the *bourgeoisie* entered the revolutionary struggle, as it did in the winter of 1788–9, that the popular masses were able to acquire a political direction and a set of political aims and concepts — such concepts as Third Estate, Nation, "*complot aristocratique*" and the Rights of Man — without which they would have expended their energies on actions limited to economic ends. This is not to underrate the importance of their contribution; without their intervention, the *bourgeois* revolutionaries of July 1789 — many of whom were stricken by panic at the crucial moment of insurrection — would have been doomed and the recently constituted National Assembly dispersed by royal troops. Yet, for all their vacillations and fears — fears of the Court Party and of the masses themselves — in the social conditions of the day, the insurrection could not have been successfully carried out without the direction and political guidance of the deputies, journalists, pamphleteers and Electors of the Third Estate.

It was, in fact, to be one of the great lessons of the French Revolution that the popular movement, however militant and widespread, could only succeed and survive as an effective revolutionary force as long as it was allied to an important section of the *bourgeoisie*; conversely, that the *bourgeoisie* could only carry out its historical task of destroying feudal property relations as long as they, or a substantial part of them, maintained their links with the broad masses of town and countryside. Nothing is to be gained by omitting one side or other of this picture, as some historians have done. In July, 1789, as we have seen, at the moment of revolutionary crisis, the immediate interests of the masses coincided with those of the main body of the *bourgeoisie* and even of a minority of the privileged class itself. In the following autumn, as so often in the course of the Revolution, the preoccupation of the Parisian *menu peuple* with the problems of high prices and shortage threatened to disrupt the alliance by directing their main fury against the monopolists and the newly constituted city authorities; and it was only by the harnessing of this movement to the political tasks set by the Constitutional Monarchists that the Royal Family was brought to Paris and the National Assembly was once more saved. Similar situations arose — though with changing forms of alliance, as the *bourgeois*-democratic revolution advanced — in the years 1791–4; but in the summer of 1794, when the Revolutionary Government was compelled by its own contradictions to sacrifice the interests of the *sans-culottes*, the alliance was broken and Robespierre fell an easy victim to the intrigues of his enemies. In the spring and early summer of 1795, attempts were made to reconstitute it at the time of the massive popular insurrections of *Germinal* and *Prairial*; but, at the crucial moment, the radical wing of the *bourgeoisie* deserted, either from weakness or from fear of the masses, and the popular movement was finally crushed. It was only to rise again — and under very different conditions — in 1830.

LAWRENCE STONE

SOCIAL AND ECONOMIC THEORIES OF REVOLUTION

Lawrence Stone (1919–), though educated at the Sorbonne and at Oxford University, has been Dodge Professor of History at Princeton University since 1963. He was a Fellow of Wadham College, Oxford, from 1947 to 1963, a member of the Institute for Advanced Studies, Princeton, 1960–61, and he has published significant studies on English social history of the sixteenth and seventeenth centuries, notably in his most recent work, *The Crisis of the Aristocracy, 1558–1641* (1965), and numerous articles and books dealing with other aspects of English history since the Middle Ages. He is interested in comparative studies in history and sociology and in interdisciplinary studies such as the one selected for presentation here.

In attacking the problem of revolution, as most others of major significance in history, we historians should think twice before we spurn the help offered by our colleagues in the social sciences, who have, as it happens, been particularly active in the last few years in theorizing about the typology, causes, and evolutionary patterns of this particular phenomenon. The purpose of this article is not to advance any new hypothesis, but to provide a summary view and critical examination of the work that has been going on.

The first necessity in any inquiry is a careful definition of terms: what is, and what is not, a revolution? According to one view, it is change, effected by the use of violence, in government, and/or regime, and/or society. By *society* is meant the consciousness and the mechanics of communal solidarity, which may be tribal, peasant, kinship, national, and so on; by *regime* is meant the constitutional structure—democracy, oligarchy, monarchy; and by *government* is meant specific political and administrative institutions. Violence, it should be noted, is not the same as force; it is force used with unnecessary intensity, unpredictably, and usually destructively. This definition of revolution is a very broad one, and two historians of the French Revolution, Crane Brinton and Louis Gottschalk, would prefer to restrict the use of the word to the major political and social upheavals with which they are familiar, the "Great Revolutions" as George S. Pettee calls them.

Even the wider definition allows the historian to distinguish between the seizure of power that leads to a major restructuring of government or society and the replacement of the former elite by a new one, and the coup d'état involving no more than a change of ruling personnel by violence or threat of violence. This latter is the norm in Latin America, where it occurred thirty-one times in the ten years 1945–1955. Merle Kling has arrived at a suggestive explanation of this Latin American phenomenon of chronic political instability, limited but frequent use of violence, and almost complete lack of social or institutional change. He argues that ownership of the principal economic resources, both agricultural and mineral, is concentrated in the hands of a tiny, very stable, elite of enormously wealthy monoculture landlords and mining capitalists. This elite is all-powerful and cannot be attacked by opposition groups within the country; externally, however, it is dependent on foreign interests for its markets and its capital. In this colonial situation of a foreign-supported closed plutocracy, the main avenue of rapid upward social mobility for nonmembers of the elite leads, via the army, to the capture of the government machine, which is the only accessible source of wealth and power. This political instability is permitted by the elite on the condition that its own interests are undisturbed. Instability, limited violence, and the absence of social or institutional change are therefore all the product of the contradiction between the realities of a colonial economy run by a plutocracy and the facade of political sovereignty—between the real, stable power of the economic elite and the nominal, unstable control of politicians and generals.

The looser definition of revolution thus suits both historians of major social change and historians of the palace coup. It does, however, raise certain difficulties. Firstly, there is a wide range of changes of government by violence which are neither a mere substitution of personalities in positions of power nor a prelude to the restructuring of society; secondly, conservative counterrevolutions become almost impossible to fit into the model; and lastly, it remains hard to distinguish between colonial wars, civil wars, and social revolution.

To avoid these difficulties, an alternative formulation has recently been put forward by a group of social scientists working mainly at Princeton. They have dropped the word "revolution" altogether and put "internal war" in its place. This is defined as any attempt to alter state policy, rulers, or institutions by the use of violence, in societies where violent competition is not the norm and where well-defined institutional patterns exist. This concept seems to be a logical consequence of the preoccupation of sociologists in recent years with a model of society in a stable, self-regulating state of perpetual equipoise. In this utopian world of universal harmony, all forms of violent conflict are anomalies, to be treated alike as pathological disorders of a similar species. This is a model which, although it has its uses for analytical purposes, bears little relation to the reality familiar to the historian. It looks to a society without change, with universal consensus on values, with complete social harmony, and isolated from external threats; no approximation to such a society has ever been

Lawrence Stone, "Theories of Revolution," in *World Politics*, Vol. XVIII, No. 2 (January, 1966), pp. 159–176. Reprinted with the permission of *World Politics*.

seen. An alternative model, which postulates that all societies are in a condition of multiple and perpetual tension held in check by social norms, ideological beliefs, and state sanctions, accords better with historical fact, as some sociologists are now beginning to realize.

The first objection to the all-embracing formula of internal war is that, by covering all forms of physical conflict from strikes and terrorism to civil war, it isolates the use of violence from the normal processes of societal adjustment. Though some of the users of the term express their awareness that the use of violence for political ends is a fairly common occurrence, the definition they have established in fact excludes all times and places where it *is* common. It thus cuts out most societies the world has ever known, including Western Europe in the Middle Ages and Latin America today. Secondly, it isolates one particular means, physical violence, from the political ends that it is designed to serve. Clausewitz's[1] famous definition of external war is equally applicable to internal war, civil war, or revolution: "War is not only a political act, but a real political instrument; a continuation of political transactions, an accomplishment of them by different means. That which remains peculiar to war relates only to the peculiar nature of its means."

It is perfectly true that any means by which society exercises pressure or control, whether it is administrative organization, constitutional law, economic interest, or physical force, can be a fruitful field of study in its own right, so long as its students remain aware that they are looking at only one part of a larger whole. It is also true that there is something peculiar about violence, if only because of man's highly ambivalent attitude towards the killing of his own species. Somehow, he regards physical force as different in kind from, say, economic exploitation or psychological manipulation as a means of exercising power over others. But this distinction is not one of much concern to the historian of revolution, in which violence is a normal and natural occurrence. The concept of internal war is too broad in its comprehension of all types of violence from civil wars to strikes, too narrow in its restriction to normally nonviolent societies, too limited in its concern with one of many means, too arbitrary in its separation of this means from the ends in view, and too little concerned with the complex roots of social unrest to be of much practical value to him.

The most fruitful typology of revolution is that of Chalmers Johnson, set out in a pamphlet that deserves to be widely read. He sees six types, identified by the targets selected for attack, whether the government personnel, the political regime, or the community as a social unit; by the nature of the carriers of revolution, whether a mass or an elite; and particularly by the goals and the ideologies, whether reformist, eschatological, nostalgic, nation-forming, elitist, or nationalist. The first type, the *Jacquerie*, is a spontaneous mass peasant rising, usually carried out in the name of the traditional authorities, Church and King, and with the limited aims of purging the local or national elites. Examples are the Peasant Revolt of 1381, Ket's Rebellion of 1549, and the Pugachev rebellion in Russia in 1773–1775. The second type, the *Millenarian Rebellion*, is similar to the first but with the added feature of a utopian dream, inspired by a living messiah. This type can be found at all times, in all parts of the world, from the Florentine revolution led by Savonarola in 1494, to the Anabaptist Rebellion in Münster led by John Mathijs and John Beukels in 1533–1535, to the Sioux Ghost-Dance Rebellion inspired by the Paiute prophet Wovoka in 1890. It has attracted a good deal of attention from historians in recent years, partly because the career of Hitler offered overwhelming proof of the enormous historical significance of a charismatic leader, and partly because of a growing interest in the ideas of Max Weber. The third type is the *Anarchistic Rebellion*, the nostalgic reaction to progressive change, involving a romantic idealization of the old order: the Pilgrimage of Grace[2] and the Vendée[3] are examples.

The fourth is that very rare phenomenon, the *Jacobin Communist Revolution*. This has been defined as "a sweeping fundamental change in political organization, social structure, economic property control and the predominant myth of a social order, thus indicating a major break in the continuity of development." This type of revolution can occur only in a highly centralized state with good communications and a large capital city, and its target is government, regime, and society—the lot. The result

<hr/>

[1] Karl von Clausewitz (1780–1831) was a Prussian general whose concepts on military strategy played an important role in modern thought about warfare. [Editor's note.]

[2] A popular religious uprising in North England in 1536–1537. [Editor's note].

[3] The Vendée was an antirevolutionary uprising in an area of western France known as the Vendée which began in 1793. [Editor's note.]

is likely to be the creation of a new national consciousness under centralized, military authority, and the erection of a more rational, and hence more efficient, social and bureaucratic order on the ruins of the old ramshackle structure of privilege, nepotism, and corruption.

The fifth type is the *Conspiratorial Coup d'État,* the planned work of a tiny elite fired by an oligarchic, sectarian ideology. This qualifies as a revolutionary type only if it in fact anticipates mass movement and inaugurates social change—for example the Nasser revolution in Egypt or the Castro revolution in Cuba; it is thus clearly distinguished from the palace revolt, assassination, dynastic succession-conflict, strike, banditry, and other forms of violence, which are all subsumed under the "internal war" rubric.

Finally, there is the *Militarized Mass Insurrection,* a new phenomenon of the twentieth century in that it is a deliberately planned mass revolutionary war, guided by a dedicated elite. The outcome of guerrilla warfare is determined by political attitudes, not military strategy or matériel, for the rebels are wholly dependent on broad popular support. In all cases on record, the ideology that attracts the mass following has been a combination of xenophobic nationalism and Marxism, with by far the greater stress on the former. This type of struggle has occurred in Yugoslavia, China, Algeria, and Vietnam.

Although, like any schematization of the historical process, this sixfold typology is concerned with ideal types, although in practice individual revolutions may sometimes display characteristics of several different types, the fact remains that this is much the most satisfactory classification we have so far; it is one that working historians can recognize and use with profit. The one obvious criticism is semantic, an objection to the use of the phrase "Jacobin Communist Revolution." Some of Johnson's examples are Communist, such as the Russian or Chinese Revolutions; others are Jacobin but not Communist, such as the French Revolution or the Turkish Revolution of 1908–1922. It would be better to revert to Pettee's category of "Great Revolutions," and treat Communist revolutions as a subcategory, one type, but not the only type, of modernizing revolutionary process.

Given this classification and definition of revolution, what are its root causes? Here everyone is agreed in making a sharp distinction between long-run,

underlying causes—the preconditions, which create a potentially explosive situation and can be analyzed on a comparative basis—and immediate, incidental factors—the precipitants, which trigger the outbreak and which may be nonrecurrent, personal, and fortuitous. This effectively disposes of the objections of these historians whose antipathy to conceptual schematization takes the naive form of asserting the uniqueness of each historical event. .

One of the first in the field of model-building was Crane Brinton who, as long ago as 1938, put forward a series of uniformities common to the four great Western revolutions: English, French, American, and Russian. These included an economically advancing society, growing class and status antagonisms, an alienated intelligentsia, a psychologically insecure and politically inept ruling class, and a governmental financial crisis.

The subjectivity, ambiguity, and partial self-contradiction of this and other analyses of the causes of specific revolutions—for example the French Revolution—have been cruelly shown up by Harry Eckstein. He has pointed out that commonly adduced hypotheses run the spectrum of particular conditions, moving from the intellectual (inadequate political socialization, conflicting social myths, a corrosive social philosophy, alienation of the intellectuals) to the economic (increasing poverty, rapid growth, imbalance between production and distribution, long-term growth plus short-term recession) to the social (resentment due to restricted elite circulation, confusion due to excessive elite recruitment, anomie due to excessive social mobility, conflict due to the rise of new social classes) to the political (bad government, divided government, weak government, oppressive government). Finally there are explanations on the level of general process, such as rapid social change, erratic social change, or a lack of harmony between the state structure and society, the rulers and the ruled. None of these explanations are invalid in themselves, but they are often difficult or impossible to reconcile one with the other, and are so diverse in their range and variety as to be virtually impossible to fit into an ordered analytical framework. What, then, is to be done?

Fundamental to all analyses, whether by historians like Brinton and Gottschalk or by political scientists like Johnson and Eckstein, is the recognition of a lack of harmony between the social system on the one hand and the political system on the other. This situation Johnson calls *dysfunction,* a word derived from the structural-functional equilibrium model of the sociologists. This dysfunction may have many causes, some of which are merely cyclical, such as may develop because of personal weaknesses in hereditary kingships or single-party regimes. In these cases, the revolution will not take on serious proportions, and will limit itself to attacks on the governing institutions, leaving regime and society intact. In most cases, however, including all those of real importance, the dysfunction is the result of some new and developing process, as a result of which certain social subsystems find themselves in a condition of relative deprivation. Rapid economic growth, imperial conquest, new metaphysical beliefs, and important technological changes are the four commonest factors involved, in that order. If the process of change is sufficiently slow and sufficiently moderate, the dysfunction may not rise to dangerous levels. Alternatively, the elite may adjust to the new situation with sufficient rapidity and skill to ride out the storm and retain popular confidence. But if the change is both rapid and profound, it may cause the sense of deprivation, alienation, anomie to spread into many sectors of society at once, causing what Johnson calls multiple dysfunction, which may be all but incurable within the existing political system.

In either case the second vital element in creating a revolutionary situation is the condition and attitude of the entrenched elite, a factor on which Eckstein rightly lays great stress. The elite may lose its manipulative skill, or its military superiority, or its self-confidence, or its cohesion; it may become estranged from the nonelite, or overwhelmed by a financial crisis; it may be incompetent, or weak, or brutal. Any combination of two or more of these features will be dangerous. What is ultimately fatal, however, is the compounding of its errors by intransigence. If it fails to anticipate the need for reform, if it blocks all peaceful, constitutional means of social adjustment, then it unites the various deprived elements in single-minded opposition to it, and drives them down the narrow road to violence. It is this process of polarization into two coherent groups or alliances of what are naturally and normally a series of fractional and shifting tensions and conflicts within a society that both Peter Amman and Wilbert Moore see as the essential preliminary to the outbreak of a Jacobin Revolution. To conclude, therefore, revolution becomes *possible* when a condition of multiple dysfunction meets an intransigent elite: just such a conjunction occurred in the decades immediately before the English, the French, and the Russian Revolutions.

Revolution only becomes *probable* (Johnson might say "certain"), however, if certain special factors intervene: the "precipitants" or "accelerators." Of these, the three most common are the emergence of an inspired leader or prophet; the formation of a secret, military, revolutionary organization; and the crushing defeat of the armed forces in foreign war. This last is of critical importance since it not only shatters the prestige of the ruling elite, but also undermines the morale and discipline of the soldiers and thus opens the way to the violent overthrow of the existing government.

The first defect of Johnson's model is that it concentrates too much on objective structural conditions, and attempts to relate conditions directly to action. In fact, however, as Eckstein points out, there is no such direct relationship; historians can point to similar activity arising from different conditions, and different activity arising from similar conditions. Standing between objective reality and action are subjective human attitudes. A behaviorist approach such as Brinton's, which lays equal stress on such things as anomie, alienation of the intellectuals, frustrated popular aspirations, elite estrangement, and loss of elite self-confidence, is more likely to produce a satisfactory historical explanation than is one that sticks to the objective social reality. Secondly, Johnson leaves too little play for the operation of the unique and the personal. He seems to regard his accelerators as automatic triggers, ignoring the area of unpredictable personal choice that is always left to the ruling elite and to the revolutionary leaders, even in a situation of multiple dysfunction exacerbated by an accelerator. Revolution is never inevitable—or rather the only evidence of its inevitability is that it actually happens. Consequently the only way to prove this point is to indulge in just the kind of hypothetical argument that historians prudently try to avoid. But it is still just possible that modernization may take place in Morocco and India without revolution. The modernization and industrialization of Germany and Britain took place without revolution in the nineteenth century (though it can be argued that in the latter case the process was slow by twentieth-century standards, and that, as is now becoming all too apparent, the modernization was far from complete). Some think that a potentially revolutionary situation in the United States in the 1930's was avoided by political action.

Lastly it is difficult to fit into the Johnson model the fact that political actions taken to remedy dysfunction often themselves precipitate change. This produces the paradoxical hypothesis that measures designed to restore equilibrium in fact upset equilibrium. Because he begins with his structural-functional equilibrium model, Johnson is a victim of the fallacy of intended consequences. As often as not in history it is the *unintended* consequences that really matter: to mention but one example, it was Louis XVI's belated and half-hearted attempts at reform that provoked the aristocratic reaction, which in turn opened the way to the bourgeois, the peasant, and the sans-culotte revolutions. Finally the dysfunction concept is not altogether easy to handle in a concrete historical case. If societies are regarded as being in a constant state of multiple tension, then some degree of dysfunction is always present. Some group is always in a state of relative deprivation due to the inevitable process of social change.

Recognition of this fact leads Eckstein to point out the importance of forces working *against* revolution. Historians, particularly those formed in the Western liberal tradition, are reluctant to admit that ruthless, efficient repression—as opposed to bumbling, half-hearted repression—involving the physical destruction of leading revolutionaries and effective control of the media of communication, can crush incipient revolutionary movements. Repression is particularly effective when governments know what to look for, when they have before their eyes the unfortunate example of other governments overthrown by revolutionaries elsewhere. Reaction, in fact, is just as infectious as revolution. Moreover diversion of energy and attention to successful—as opposed to unsuccessful—foreign war can ward off serious internal trouble. Quietist—as opposed to activist—religious movements may serve as the opiate of the people, as Halévy suggested about Methodism in England. Bread and circuses may distract popular attention. Timely—as opposed to untimely—political concessions may win over moderate opinion and isolate the extremists.

Basing himself on this suggestive analysis, Eckstein produces a paradigm for universal application. He sees four positive variables—elite inefficiency, disorienting social process, subversion, and available rebel facilities—and four negative variables—diversionary mechanisms, available incumbent facilities, adjustive mechanisms, and effective repression. Each type of internal war, and each step of each type, can, he suggests, be explained in terms of these eight variables. While this may be true, it is fair to point out that some of the variables are themselves the product of more deep-seated factors, others mere questions of executive action that may be determined by the accidents of personality. Disruptive social process is a profound cause; elite inefficiency a behavior pattern; effective repression a function of will; facilities the by-product of geography. One objection to the Eckstein paradigm is therefore that it embraces different levels of explanation and fails to maintain the fundamental distinction between preconditions and precipitants. Secondly, it concentrates on the factors working for or against the successful manipulation of violence rather than on the underlying factors working to produce a revolutionary potential. This is because the paradigm is intended to apply to all forms of internal war rather than to revolution proper, and because all that the various forms of internal war have in common is the use of violence. It is impossible to tell how serious these criticisms are until the paradigm has been applied to a particular historical revolution. Only then will its value become apparent.

If we take the behaviorist approach, then a primary cause of revolutions is the emergence of an obsessive revolutionary mentality. But how closely does this relate to the objective material circumstances themselves? In every revolutionary situation one finds a group of men—fanatics, extremists, zealots—so convinced of their own righteousness and of the urgent need to create a new Jerusalem on earth (whether formally religious or secular in inspiration is irrelevant) that they are prepared to smash through the normal restraints of habit, custom, and convention. Such men were the seventeenth-century English Puritans, the eighteenth-century French Jacobins, the twentieth-century Russian Bolsheviks. But what makes such men is far from certain. What generates such ruthlessness in curbing evil, such passion for discipline and order? Rapid social mobility, both horizontal and vertical, and particularly urbanization, certainly produces a sense of rootlessness and anxiety. In highly stratified societies, even some of the newly-risen elements may find themselves under stress. While some of the *arrivistes* are happily absorbed in their new strata, others remain uneasy and resentful. If they are snubbed and rebuffed by the older members of the status group to which they aspire by reason of their new wealth and position, they are likely to become acutely conscious of their social inferiority, and may be driven either to adopt a pose *plus royaliste que le Roi* or to dream of destroying the whole social order. In the latter case they may try to allay their sense of insecurity by imposing their norms and values by force upon society at large. This is especially the case if there is available a moralistic ideology like Puritanism or Marxism to which they can attach themselves, and which provides them with unshakable confidence in their own rectitude.

But why does the individual react in this particular way rather than another? Some would argue that the character of the revolutionary is formed by sudden ideological conversion in adolescence or early adult life (to Puritanism, Jacobinism, or Bolshevism) as a refuge from this anxiety state. What is not acceptable is the fashionable conservative cliché that the revolutionary and the reformer are merely the chance product of unfortunate psychological difficulties in childhood. It is possible that this is the mechanism by which such feelings are generated, though there is increasing evidence of the continued plasticity of human character until at any rate post-adolescence. The main objection to this theory is that it fails to explain why these particular attitudes become common only in certain classes and age groups at certain times and in certain places. This failure strongly suggests that the cause of this state of mind lies not in the personal maladjustment of the individuals or their parents, but in the social conditions that created that maladjustment. Talcott Parsons treats disaffection or "alienation" as a generalized phenomenon that may manifest itself in crime, alcoholism, drug addiction, daytime fantasies, religious enthusiasm, or serious political agitation. To use Robert Merton's formulation, Ritualism and Retreatism are two possible psychological escape-routes; Innovation and Rebellion two others.

Even if we accept this behaviorist approach (which I do), the fact remains that many of the underlying causes both of the alienation of the revolutionaries and of the weakness of the incumbent elite are economic in origin; and it is in this area that some interesting work has centered. In particular a fresh look has been taken at the contradictory models of Marx and de Tocqueville, the one claiming that popular revolution is a product of increasing misery,

the other that it is a product of increasing prosperity.

Two economists, Sir Arthur Lewis and Mancur Olson, have pointed out that because of their basic social stability, both preindustrial and highly industrialized societies are relatively free from revolutionary disturbance. In the former societies, people accept with little question the accepted rights and obligations of family, class, and caste. Misery, oppression, and social injustice are passively endured as inevitable features of life on earth. It is in societies experiencing rapid economic growth that the trouble usually occurs. Lewis, who is thinking mostly about the newly emerging countries, primarily of Africa, regards the sense of frustration that leads to revolution as a consequence of the dislocation of the old status patterns by the emergence of four new classes—the proletariat, the capitalist employers, the urban commercial and professional middle class, and the professional politicians—and of the disturbance of the old income patterns by the sporadic and patchy impact of economic growth, which creates new wealth and new poverty in close and conspicuous juxtaposition. Both phenomena he regards as merely transitional, since in a country fully developed economically there are strong tendencies toward the elimination of inequalities of opportunity, income, and status.

This model matches fairly well the only detailed analysis of a historical revolution in which a conscious effort has been made to apply modern sociological methods. In his recent study of the Vendée, Charles Tilly argues that a counterrevolutionary situation was the consequence of special tensions created by the immediate juxtaposition of, on one hand, parish clergy closely identified with the local communities, great absentee landlords, and old-fashioned subsistence farming, and, on the other, a large-scale textile industry on the putting-out system and increasing bourgeois competition. Though the book is flawed by a tendency to take a ponderous sociological hammer to crack a simple little historical nut, it is nonetheless a suggestive example of the application of new hypotheses and techniques to historical material.

Olson has independently developed a more elaborate version of the Lewis theory. He argues that revolutionaries are déclassé and freed from the social bonds of family, profession, village or manor; and that these individuals are the product of rapid economic growth, which creates both *nouveaux riches* and *nouveaux pauvres*. The former, usually middle-class and urban artisans, are better off economically, but are disoriented, rootless, and restless; the latter may be workers whose wages have failed to keep pace with inflation, workers in technologically outdated and therefore declining industries, or the unemployed in a society in which the old cushions of the extended family and the village have gone, and in which the new cushion of social security has not yet been created. The initial growth phase may well cause a decline in the standard of living of the majority because of the need for relatively enormous forced savings for reinvestment. The result is a revolution caused by the widening gap between expectations—social and political for the new rich, economic for the new poor—and the realities of everyday life.

A sociologist, James C. Davis, agrees with Olson that the fundamental impetus toward a revolutionary situation is generated by rapid economic growth but he associates such growth with a generally rising rather than a generally falling standard of living, and argues that the moment of potential revolution is reached only when the long-term phase of growth is followed by a short-term phase of economic stagnation or decline. The result of this "J-curve," as he calls it, is that steadily soaring expectations, newly created by the period of growth, shoot further and further ahead of actual satisfaction of needs. Successful revolution is the work neither of the destitute nor of the well-satisfied, but of those whose actual situation is improving less rapidly than they expect.

These economic models have much in common, and their differences can be explained by the fact that Lewis and Olson are primarily concerned with the long-term economic forces creating instability, and Davis with the short-term economic factors that may precipitate a crisis. Moreover their analyses apply to different kinds of economic growth, of which three have recently been identified by W. W. Rostow and Barry Supple: there is the expansion of production in a preindustrial society, which may not cause any important technological, ideological, social, or political change; there is the phase of rapid growth, involving major changes of every kind; and there is the sustained trend toward technological maturity. Historians have been quick to see that these models, particularly that of Rostow, can be applied only to a limited number of historical cases. The trouble is not so much that in any specific case the phases—particularly the last two—tend to merge into one another, but that changes in the various sectors occur at irregular and unexpected places on the time-scale in different societies. Insofar as there is any validity in the division of the stages of growth into these three basic types, the revolutionary model of Olson and Lewis is confined to the second; that of Davis is applicable to all three.

The Davis model fits the history of Western Europe quite well, for it looks as if in conditions of extreme institutional and ideological rigidity the first type of economic growth may produce frustrations of a very serious kind. Revolutions broke out all over Europe in the 1640's, twenty years after a secular growth phase had come to an end. C. E. Labrousse has demonstrated the existence of a similar economic recession in France from 1778, and from 1914 the Russian economy was dislocated by the war effort after many years of rapid growth. Whatever its limitations in any particular situation, the J-curve of actual satisfaction of needs is an analytical tool that historians can usefully bear in mind as they probe the violent social upheavals of the past.

As de Tocqueville pointed out, this formula of advance followed by retreat is equally applicable to other sectors. Trouble arises if a phase of liberal governmental concessions is followed by a phase of political repression; a phase of fairly open recruitment channels into the elite followed by a phase of aristocratic reaction and a closing of ranks; a phase of weakening status barriers by a phase of reassertion of privilege. The J-curve is applicable to other than purely economic satisfactions, and the apex of the curve is the point at which underlying causes, the preconditions, merge with immediate factors, the precipitants. The recipe for evolution is thus the creation of new expectations by economic improvement and some social and political reforms, followed by economic recession, governmental reaction, and aristocratic resurgence, which widen the gap between expectations and reality.

All these attempts to relate dysfunction to relative changes in economic prosperity and aspirations are hampered by two things, of which the first is the extreme difficulty in ascertaining the facts. It is never easy to discover precisely what is happening to the distribution of wealth in a given society. Even now, even in highly developed Western societies with massive bureaucratic controls and quantities of statistical data, there is no agreement about the facts.

Some years ago it was confidently believed that in both Britain and the United States incomes were being levelled, and that extremes of both wealth and poverty were being steadily eliminated. Today, no one quite knows what is happening in either country. And if this is true now, still more is it true of societies in the past about which the information is fragmentary and unreliable.

Secondly, even if they can be clearly demonstrated, economic trends are only one part of the problem. Historians are increasingly realizing that the psychological responses to changes in wealth and power are not only not precisely related to, but are politically more significant than, the material changes themselves. As Marx himself realized at one stage, dissatisfaction with the status quo is not determined by absolute realities but by relative expectations. "Our desires and pleasures spring from society; we measure them, therefore, by society, and not by the objects which serve for their satisfaction. Because they are of a social nature, they are of a relative nature." Frustration may possibly result from a rise and subsequent relapse in real income. But it is perhaps more likely to be caused by a rise in aspirations that outstrips the rise in real income; or by a rise in the *relative* economic position in society of the group in question, followed by a period in which its real income continues to grow, but less fast than that of other groups around it. Alternatively it may represent a rise and then decline of status, largely unrelated to real income; or if status and real income are related, it may be inversely. For example, social scientists seeking to explain the rise of the radical right in the United States in the early 1950's and again in the early 1960's attribute it to a combination of great economic prosperity and an aggravated sense of insecurity of status. Whether or not this is a general formula for right-wing rather than left-wing revolutionary movements is not yet clear.

Moreover the problem is further complicated by an extension of the reference-group theory. Human satisfaction is related not to existing conditions but to the condition of a social group against which the individual measures his situation. In an age of mass communications and the wide distribution of cheap radio receivers even among the impoverished illiterate of the world, knowledge of high consumption standards elsewhere spreads rapidly, and as a result the reference group may be in another, more highly developed, country or even continent. Under these circumstances, revolutionary conditions may be created before industrialization has got properly under way.

The last area in which some new theoretical work has been done is in the formulation of hypotheses about the social stages of a "Great Revolution." One of the best attacks on this problem was made by Crane Brinton, who was thinking primarily about the French Revolution, but who extended his comparisons to the three other major Western revolutionary movements. He saw the first phase as dominated by moderate bourgeois elements; their supersession by the radicals; a reign of terror; a Thermidorian reaction; and the establishment of strong central authority under military rule to consolidate the limited gains of the revolution. In terms of mass psychology he compared revolution with a fever that rises in intensity, affecting nearly all parts of the body politic, and then dies away.

A much cruder and more elementary model has been advanced by an historian of the revolutions of 1848, Peter Amman. He sees the modern state as an institution holding a monopoly of physical force, administration, and justice over a wide area, a monopoly dependent more on habits of obedience than on powers of coercion. Revolution may therefore be defined as a breakdown of the monopoly due to a failure of these habits of obedience. It begins with the emergence of two or more foci of power, and ends with the elimination of all but one. Amman includes the possibility of "suspended revolution," with the existence of two or more foci not yet in violent conflict.

This model admittedly avoids some of the difficulties raised by more elaborate classifications of revolution: how to distinguish a coup d'etat from a revolution; how to define the degrees of social change; how to accommodate the conservative counterrevolution, and so on. It certainly offers some explanation of the progress of revolution from stage to stage as the various power blocs that emerge on the overthrow of the incumbent regime are progressively eliminated; and it explains why the greater the public participation in the revolution, the wider the break with the habits of obedience, and therefore the slower the restoration of order and centralized authority. But it throws the baby out with the bathwater. It is impossible to fit any decentralized traditional society, or any modern federal society, into the model. Moreover, even where it might be applicable, it offers no framework for analyzing the roots of revolution, no pointers for identifying the foci of power, no means of distinguishing between the various revolutionary types, and its notion of "suspended revolution" is little more than verbal evasion.

Though it is set out in a somewhat confused, over-elaborate, and unnecessarily abstract form, the most convincing description of the social stages of revolution is that outlined by Rex D. Hopper. He sees four stages. The first is characterized by indiscriminate, uncoordinated mass unrest and dissatisfaction, the result of dim recognition that traditional values no longer satisfy current aspirations. The next stage sees this vague unease beginning to coalesce into organized opposition with defined goals, an important characteristic being a shift of allegiance by the intellectuals from the incumbents to the dissidents, the advancement of an "evil men" theory, and its abandonment in favor of an "evil institutions" theory. At this stage there emerge two types of leaders: the prophet, who sketches the shape of the new utopia upon which men's hopes can focus, and the reformer, working methodically toward specific goals. The third, the formal stage, sees the beginning of the revolution proper. Motives and objectives are clarified, organization is built up, a statesman leader emerges. Then conflicts between the left and the right of the revolutionary movement become acute, and the radicals take over from the moderates. The fourth and last stage sees the legalization of the revolution. It is a product of psychological exhaustion as the reforming drive burns itself out, moral enthusiasm wanes, and economic distress increases. The administrators take over, strong central government is established, and society is reconstructed on lines that embody substantial elements of the old system. The result falls far short of the utopian aspirations of the early leaders, but it succeeds in meshing aspirations with values by partly modifying both and so allows the reconstruction of a firm social order.

Some of the writings of contemporary social scientists are ingenious feats of verbal juggling in an esoteric language, performed around the totem pole of an abstract model, surrounded as far as the eye can see by the arid wastes of terminological definitions and mathematical formulae. Small wonder the historian finds it hard to digest the gritty diet of this neo-scholasticism, as it has been aptly called. The more historically-minded of the social scientists, however, have a great deal to offer. The history of history, as well as of science, shows that advances depend partly on the accumulation of factual information, but rather more on the formulation of hypotheses that reveal the hidden relationships and common properties of apparently distinct phenomena. Social scientists can supply a corrective to the antiquarian fact-grubbing to which historians are so prone; they can direct attention to problems of general relevance, and away from the sterile triviality of so much historical research. They can ask new questions and suggest new ways of looking at old ones. They can supply new categories, and as a result may suggest new ideas.

2

THE CHARACTER OF THE REVOLUTIONS: CLASS STRUGGLES OR IDEOLOGICAL CONFLICTS?

One of the most significant recent controversies among professional historians concerns whether or not the revolutions of the eighteenth (and nineteenth) century were French or Western, that is to say, whether they were national or supranational in their character. Since there is already a very convenient volume edited by Peter Amann entitled The Eighteenth-Century Revolution: French or Western?, in the "Problems in European Civilization" series which deals with this absorbing question, we can refer interested students to this publication and to Jacques Godechot's book on France and the Atlantic Revolution of the Eighteenth Century from which a selection was included in the previous problem on the Causes of Revolution.

Instead, we shall use the space at our disposal to examine the role of classes versus that of ideas as the basis of controversial characterizations of the eighteenth- and nineteenth-century revolutions from 1770 to 1870.

To begin our inquiry we have selected Professor Robert R. Palmer's statement of how he came to write his monumental study, *The Age of the Democratic Revolution*. In this selection, the author includes not only his own analysis of what has come to be called the "Palmer Thesis," but also provides a clear insight into the processes by which historians go about the task of selecting their subjects and making generalizations. In this case, the generalization concerns the character of revolution. The selection also forms a connecting link with the Stone essay on the "Theories of Revolution" which dealt with the concepts and methods of the social scientists in their various interpretations of "revolution." Palmer, in this selection, is writing at the invitation of the Committee on Historical Analysis of the Social Science Research Council whose chairman, Louis Gottschalk, is appropriately enough one of this country's most distinguished specialists on the study of revolutions. Readers will note with interest that the Committee's interpretation of historical explanation addresses itself to the problem as to "whether the historian is competent from his own data and by his own methods to derive from history generalizations that are neither so limited as to be trivial nor so comprehensive as to be meaningless." Within this frame of reference Professor Palmer contributes his insights into the validity and meaning of the concept of "revolution" with special reference to his own study of the eighteenth-century revolutions, as well as making passing references to those of the nineteenth and the twentieth centuries.

Although Palmer is clearly aware of the various social groups in the eighteenth-century revolutions and mentions the concept of classes as one of the unifying themes of these revolutions, we have chosen an essay by Albert Soboul, a brilliant younger French Marxist historian of the revolution, who has lucidly stated the argument for the class struggle theme—an aristocratic resurgence followed by a bourgeois revolution. He clearly points out the significance of the assistance given to the "bourgeoisie" by the peasants and by the urban *sans-culottes* (whose historian he is). Note that according to Soboul the *sans-culottes* were not a class, but a group of political activists.

In contrast to these characterizations of the eighteenth-century revolutions by Palmer and by Soboul, we next introduce the theme of what Alfred Cobban has called "the Myth of the French Revolution." That is to say, Cobban attacks the interpretation of *La Grande Révolution* as a clash between "feudalism" and "bourgeois capitalism." In a book published in 1964 entitled *The Social Interpretation of the French Revolution*, Professor Cobban argues, as do the historians he is attacking, that the social pattern of eighteenth-century France was much more complicated than has usually been recognized. He stresses social cleavages among the peasantry and between town and countryside, phenomena long familiar to readers of Georges Lefebvre. He then proceeds to assume the controversial position that it was "landowners, *rentiers,* and officials" who seized control of the revolution and "consolidated the claims of property against the propertyless and of the richer, on all levels, against the poor." He concludes that the French Revolution was "not for, but against capitalism." Thus Professor Cobban, who has been highly critical of the work of Robert Palmer, castigates that of Albert Soboul as well. The selection from Cobban includes his chapter entitled "Plus ça change" from his beautifully written *History of Modern France,* in which he neither denies the importance of class nor of ideas, but in which he definitely restates the problem in his own terms.

Rather fittingly, I think, we conclude this section on the character of the revolutions of the eighteenth and nineteenth centuries with an essay by the greatest French Revolutionist of them all—the late Georges Lefebvre, who was highly respected by Palmer, Soboul, Cobban, and in fact, by professional historians of all persuasions. "The French Revolution in the Context of World History" sums up what all historians will agree to be among the most important characteristics of the French and other eighteenth-century revolutions, and evokes also the revolutions of 1830 and of 1848. The student should note carefully the way in which Lefebvre treats both the problems of the ideas of liberty and of equality and of the influence of class interests and of economic and social forces.

ROBERT R. PALMER

GENERALIZATIONS ABOUT REVOLUTION:
A CASE STUDY

The American historian Robert R. Palmer, who is Dean of the Faculty at Princeton University, has earned a distinguished place among leading scholars interested in the character of the eighteenth-century revolutions with his *Catholics and Unbelievers in Eighteenth-Century France* (1939), *Twelve Who Ruled: The Committee of Public Safety during the Terror* (1941), and a monumental study of great literary and scholarly merit, *The Age of the Democratic Revolution: A Political History of Europe and America, 1760–1800,* whose first volume, entitled "The Challenge," was published in 1959, and the second, "The Struggle," in 1964. Palmer also contributed a chapter entitled "Social and Psychological Foundations of the Revolutionary Era," to *The New Cambridge Modern History,* Volume VIII, (1965) and another on "The Influence of the American Revolution on Europe" to the new *Propyläen Weltgeschichte,* Volume VIII, (1960). The selection that follows was published in 1963 in *Generalization in the Writing of History,* edited by Louis Gottschalk.

The SSRC [Social Science Research Council] Committee on Historical Analysis, as I understand it, wishes to have some remarks made on the use of concepts in history, perhaps of the sort that may be made by one who has given little systematic attention to the problem but has been aware of it in the process of working on a particular piece of historical writing. For this purpose it may be that the work I am engaged in may serve as a case study. It is entitled *The Age of the Democratic Revolution,* with a subtitle, *A Political History of Europe and America, 1760–1800,* and is planned in two volumes, of which the first, on the years 1760–91, was published by the Princeton University Press in 1959. The following is drawn from experience in preparing this book and is offered with the apologies necessary in talking so much about myself but in the hope that it will at least provisionally serve a useful purpose.

I doubt that history is a social science but do believe that it should make use of concepts drawn from social science or any other useful source. In most histories, however, these general ideas will appear unobtrusively, to give meaning and relevancy to the particular. The *particular* is here taken to mean either single small items or the subject as a whole, such as the whole era 1760–1800 considered as one particular phenomenon or bit of human experience. I am here deliberately avoiding the often used term *unique.*

The original conception for a historical book, I suspect, does and should come from two altogether different kinds of sources—(1) the knowledge that workable bodies of information exist and (2) some general idea. In the present case it was known, or discovered, that a great deal existed in print, both of source collections and of historical treatments, pertaining to a dozen or more countries, which, however, no single person had ever tried to bring together. The general idea, held in advance, was that there had been a "revolutionary era" in all these countries, not adequately perceived as a "culture-wide" phenomenon in the various nationally oriented histories of the American and French Revolutions and other movements of the time. (I should perhaps make clear that terms like *culture-wide* do not appear in the book; whether or not such terms have any utility in social science, history in my opinion should be written in the ordinary language.)

There were therefore certain general ideas that antedate the composition of the book now being considered and that recur throughout it. Their role seems to have been at least threefold: (1) to provide a thesis or argument, of which the contents of the book are offered as empirical justification or evidence. (2) to give a basis for structure, or arrangement and interdependence of parts, and (3) to suggest relevancy and significance, which seems in the end to mean a relationship between these eighteenth-century events and persons now living.

The first of these antecedent ideas is that of Western Civilization as a unit. The term *Atlantic Civilization* is used at the outset but thereafter very sparingly, since it may arouse opposition or raise problems not essential for the purpose of the book. In 1955 Professor Jacques Godechot of Toulouse and I examined "Le problème de l'Atlantique du 18e au 20e siècle" at the Tenth International Congress of Historical Sciences, meeting at Rome; and some of our conclusions are taken over, but not argued, in the present book, notably the idea that the concept of an Atlantic Civlization had probably more validity in the period 1775–1825 than at any other time. The point is to maintain the existence of a certain culture area, "Western Civilization," as a zone having certain ideas and problems in common and a degree of mutuality of communications and influence. The book treats in some detail Anglo-America, Great Britain, Ireland, France, Belgium, Holland, Switzerland, Sweden, Poland, and the Hapsburg Empire including Belgium and Milan. Prussia and Russia figure less prominently. There is not explicit discussion of whether Russia belongs to "Western Civilization," but the account of the growth of aristocratic institutions under Catherine II points out European analogies. In the second volume events will be followed in the same countries, and more will be said on Germany and Italy as a whole, and on Canada, Latin America, and perhaps the Cape Colony. The attempt to use Western Civilization as the meaningful unit of inquiry is thought to have these advantages: (1) to be probably near to the truth, (2) to illuminate national histories by comparison and contrast, and (3) to have present-day relevancy in view of contemporary interest in the nature, character, and identity of Western Civilization itself.

A second general idea that antedates the book and recurs in it is that of revolution. Nowhere do I offer

Reprinted from "Generalizations about Revolutions: A Case Study", by Robert R. Palmer in *Generalizations in the Writing of History,* ed. Louis Gottschalk, pp. 66–76, by permission of the University of Chicago Press. Copyright © 1963 by the University of Chicago.

or commit myself to an explicit definition of this term. Its use is in part justified empirically; the American, French, Genevese, Belgian, and Polish "revolutions" form a large part of the content. Revolution is said also to be essentially a conflict or disagreement on fundamental interests and principles not reconcilable without struggle. Both or all sides in the conflict are regarded as equally real — that is, conservatism is not represented as the mere target of innovators. It is held that certain objectives, or views of society and of justice, which in some countries reached the point of outright revolution were present in other countries in a subrevolutionary way, yet recognizably in the same family of ideas, notably in the British and Irish movements for parliamentary reform and in the reforms of Joseph II of the Hapsburg empire.

Use of the concept *revolution* induced the author to face the question of the relationship between the revolutions of the eighteenth century and those of the twentieth. This question was essentially whether the eighteenth-century revolution, and the French Revolution in particular, were to be thought of as (1) a point in the genesis and growth of a continuing or "perpetual" revolution, "leading" to Marxism, communism, "totalitarian democracy," etc., or (2) a passing phase of crisis, conflict, excitement, and violence "leading" to what we understand by Western democracy. This problem is discussed briefly at the opening of the book, without claim to systematic rigor. The second alternative is favored. It is admitted, however, that there is a degree of truth in the first, the idea that the eighteenth-century revolution prefigured and in a way "caused" the twentieth-century revolution; this view is identified both with Marxist and with conservative treatments of the era of the French Revolution. It is insisted that late-eighteenth-century events were a true "revolution," that the term and concept of *revolution* has changed since then, that there are resemblances and differences between the eighteenth-century and twentieth-century revolutions, that one's attitude toward twentieth-century revolution (i.e., communism) should not affect one's attitude toward eighteenth-century revolution, etc.

A third recurring idea is that the eighteenth-century revolution was, or may be thought of as, democratic. Expecting this to be somewhat more contested, I justify it at some length at the outset, though the whole book is designed to persuade to this belief. The justification is, again, in part purely empiri-cal: it is shown that people at the time used the word *democratic* for the new movement, in a meaningful and reasonable way, whether to favor it or to oppose it. It is shown that this was precisely the period when the nouns *democrat* and *aristocrat* were coined in the various European languages. It emerges, in the first chapter and throughout the book, that the democratic movement was primarily anti-aristocratic. The term *democratic*, I think, is by no means forced upon the reader. He may call the movement whatever he likes. He is, however, asked to believe that there was a movement, in many countries and however named, against the monopolizing of public authority by certain in-groups; against the principle that some men are called upon to rule, others to be ruled; against inheritance of position, hereditary orders and estates, legal hierarchy, family self-perpetuation, property in office, co-opting governing bodies, etc. All the ideas thus contested are referred to as *aristocracy*. With *democracy* are associated the ideas that all authority is delegated, that public officers are responsible and removable, that persons should qualify for office without regard to family, rank, or church affiliation, that no person may govern by his own right or by right of status, leadership, or "history" — with an occasional hint that communist elitism or revolutionary vanguardism are if anything "aristocratic" (i.e., modern manifestations of what the eighteenth-century revolution was against). These hints remain implicit, and many readers may miss them; there is no attempt to engage in current debate. They suggest, however, how eighteenth-century matters may be made relevant to twentieth-century matters at a level of generalization that comprises both.

"Aristocracy" is discussed in the second and third chapters of the book as characteristic about 1760 of the society established in all countries, including the Anglo-American colonies. It is described in institutional terms, partly to give concreteness, partly because it was against certain definite institutions that the revolutionary and quasi-revolutionary movements were directed. Family self-perpetuation, intermarriage, inheritance of position, and privileged or special access to government and to its emoluments or profits are found to have been common phenomena over a wide range of institutions — the governors' councils in the British American colonies, the two houses of the parliaments of Great Britain and Ireland, the parlements and provincial estates of France, the town councils and estates of Belgium, Holland, Switzerland, Italy, and Germany, the diets of Hungary, Bohemia, Poland, and Sweden. For all these the term "constituted bodies" was invented. This term became one of the principal generalizations in the whole structure of the book.

The movement of ideas is discussed in the context of defense of and opposition to these "constituted bodies." Ideas of Montesquieu, Delolme, Rousseau, Burke, John Adams, Turgot, Sieyès, and various others are treated in this way. It is argued that ideas like the "sovereignty of the people" arose not as intellectual abstractions but as practical replies to claims of sovereignty, or at least of non-removability and non-responsibility, made by the constituted bodies. Ideas of "equality" are likewise represented as arising from the actual existing forms of inequality and in answer to the theoretical justifications of inequality and of special rights that were currently made. It is also maintained that if radical thought became unhistorical, abstract, and rationalistic, it was for the very good reason that historical argument was pre-empted and emphasized by exclusive, closed, hereditary, or co-optative constituted bodies. By this interpretation the history of ideas is, in short, woven closely into the history of real events and real conditions. The ground is thus removed from under the ancient historiographical dispute over whether the French Revolution arose from "ideas" or "circumstances"; or, in the terms of this dispute, the thesis of "circumstances" is favored, by showing that "ideas" had a constructive relevancy to real problems. I am aware that my whole book, though I hope not in an obvious or naïve way, is pro-revolutionary (and say as much, through a literary device, on the first page).

The concept of an "aristocratic resurgence" in the eighteenth century, long familiar to students of French history, is applied to Europe and America as a whole. Evidence is offered, that is, to show that the world was not only "aristocratic" but in some important ways becoming more so. The famous generalizations of Tocqueville—that history shows a long process toward equality of social conditions and that the Revolution only brought on violently what would have happened more slowly in any case—are viewed with a certain reservation. It is argued that exclusivism, aristocratic class-consciousness and emphasis on inheritance were increasing and that it was from these facts that bourgeois class-consciousness, frustrations, and social maladjustments were derived. Acute class-consciousness, along with ineffectual fiscal policies

and awkward administrative and personnel recruitment systems, is represented as one of the social evils resulting from these tensions. Social mobility and legal equality are represented as desirable not only ethically or to prevent personal frustration but to make a complex society operate more effectively. The terms integration, assimilation, segregation are used occasionally and discreetly but purposely in the belief that these abstractions will suggest relevancy to our own time.

Around the concept of the constituted bodies and their "official" philosophers (Montesquieu, Blackstone, Burke, etc.) the whole book is structured. It is shown that these bodies, and the privileges that they claimed, were challenged from contrary directions—both by kings or other higher authorities and by the "people" (that is, persons generally outside the governing classes, nobilities, patriciates, hereditary magistracies, etc.). Much political life consisted in the self-assertion of such bodies against a king or other superior: Whig elements in the British parliament against George III, the American colonial assemblies and the Irish parliament against the parliament of Great Britain, Dutch regents against the Prince of Orange, Belgian estates against the emperor, Swedish and Hungarian diets against their kings, general council against small council at Geneva, French parlements and provincial estates against Louis XV and Louis XVI. The demands of these bodies brought certain ideas into the arena of practical politics and debate, notably the ideas of sovereignty, the constitution, true liberty, real representation, etc. The movement became democratic, according to the thesis of the book, when in various ways in various countries certain dissatisfied persons, not content merely to liberate the constituted bodies from a superior authority, wished to reconstitute or open up these bodies themselves, make them more truly "representative" or elective, and subordinate them to the "people."

It is a secondary general idea throughout the book that what we know as conservatism first appeared not as a critique of the French Revolution of 1789 or 1793 but as a defense of parliaments, estates, diets, etc., against both royal and democratic encroachments on their established position. It is shown how Burke's philosophy was formed in opposition to parliamentary reform, notably in 1784. Contrariwise, the mounting radicalism of the democratic movement, even before 1789, is explained by the rigidity of the constituted bodies and the failure of moderate or gradual attempts at change.

Another subordinate general idea is that in no case did purely middle-class or "bourgeois" reform or revolution have any success, that successful revolution occurred only where the agricultural population generally collaborated with middle-class leaders, that this occurred only in America and France, and that the failure of democratizing efforts elsewhere— in England, Ireland, the Dutch Netherlands, Belgium, Switzerland, and in a sense Hungary and Poland—was due to the apathy or weakness of the agrarian mass or to the absence of a common ground on which urban and rural persons could work together.

The dependence of successful revolution or counterrevolution on military measures becomes also a general idea in the book. The foreign military intervention against revolution in Holland, at Geneva, and in Poland is described, and its significance is pointed out for the attempt at foreign military intervention in France in 1792 and, very briefly, for the so-called Holy Alliance of 1815. The success both of revolution and of a challenged conservatism (counter-revolution) is closely related to war: the independence of the United States in the form taken in 1783 is attributed to French intervention, the success of conservatism in Holland, Geneva, Poland, and Hungary (before 1792) is attributed in large part to armed intervention; and the ground is laid for a broad consideration, contemplated for the second volume, of the issues in the European war that began in 1792. It is argued that the needs of armed conflict in America in 1776—and it will be argued in the second volume that similar needs in France in 1792—had the effect of radicalizing and democratizing the movements in those countries beyond the intentions of original leaders. The relation of French military success to revolution in the 1790's throughout western Europe is thus also anticipated.

The American Revolution is made to occupy a central place in the book. Privileges of the American colonies within the British Empire, in such matters as tax immunity and local self-rule, are compared to analogous privileges in Europe, as in Brittany, Hungary, and Belgium. The American protest against the sovereignty or "absolute" power of Parliament is put in context with rising British radicalism that made the same protest. Whether the adoption of the federal constitution of 1787 resembled the "aristocratic

resurgence" of Europe of the 1780's is considered; this is related to the Beard thesis, but it is pointed out that Condorcet and others in 1788 and 1789 already regarded the new United States constitution as "aristocratic."

The degree to which the American Revolution was a true "revolution" is examined. It is held to have been revolutionary because of the repudiation of parliamentary sovereignty, the displacement and ejection of the old colonial aristocracy, the violence between patriot and loyalist, the extent of emigration and confiscation, and the successful implementation of the idea of (as it is called) "the people as constituent power." That there is and should be a power to constitute or reconstitute organs of state and that this power lies in the "people" and eventuates in a single written document or constitution drafted by an assembly for that purpose is represented as the essential or distinctive American revolutionary idea. Issue is taken with American neo-conservatives; John Adams is sharply differentiated from Burke and set up as a leading spokesman of the democratic revolution of the time.

A long chapter details the impact of the American Revolution on Europe. It is shown that this impact was very great, that it varied from country to country, that in part it was felt at a deep psychological level, heightening the expectancy of change, the sense of a new era, and the alienation and spiritual emigration from the European old regime, and that in part it was important in a practical and immediate way by helping to form a definite public opinion on political matters, with discussion on the formation of organs of government, written constitutions, and constituent assemblies. This, of course, leads into the French Constituent Assembly of 1789 and into the various such assemblies and conventions to be traced in several European countries in the forthcoming second volume.

The distinctive features of the French Revolution are set forth with some care, for although the purpose of the book is to describe a revolutionary era as a whole, there is no thought of minimizing national or other differences in a false search for uniformities. Various economic, demographic, psychological, and other explanations of the "causes" of the French Revolution are held to be of secondary value, as not accounting for the specific forms that the French Revolution took, notably its emphasis on certain political, constitutional, legal, and civic concepts.

The picture of a French Revolution that began as a "moderate" and became an "extreme" movement is likewise rejected as misleading. The true problem of the French Revolution is held to be why it was so radical or sweeping at the very beginning. In a way this is a concession to certain conservative and antirevolutionary schools of historiography, but enough has been said at this point in the book on the failure of a moderate opening-up of privileged bodies, both in France and elsewhere in Europe, to make the radicalism of 1789 seem an understandable consequence of pre-existing conservatism. This radicalism of the French Revolution in 1789 again raises the question of its resemblance to or difference from the American Revolution. The two revolutions are found to be very much alike in their principles and objectives. The difference is held to lie in the intensity and strength of opposition to these principles.

The book closes with the promulgation of the new French constitution in September, 1791. The notion, frequently heard from historians, that everything in the French Revolution had already been "accomplished" by 1791 is regarded as absurd. It is held that nothing had been accomplished except on paper, that the future of the new constitution was still very much in the balance, that intervention and restoration of the old order was a possibility in France, as shown by what happened in Belgium, Holland, Geneva, and Poland, the difference being that France was big enough to defend itself against intervention. The conservatism of Britain at this time is emphasized by the failure of parliamentary reform, even when sponsored by Pitt, and by the failure of Dissenters in 1789 to obtain equality of political rights. It is held that as of 1791, everywhere in the Western world except in America, the moderate attempts at democratization had come to nothing and that the new principles had an uncertain future in France. The first volume is therefore subtitled *The Challenge*. The second will be subtitled *The Struggle* and will deal with the Western world during the Wars of the French Revolution.

It will be seen that such concepts as I have mentioned are those arising in close conjunction with the empirical material itself. Larger concepts on causality, influence, or human nature remain purely implicit. Economic, social, and intellectual history is used to amplify what is essentially political and constitutional history; the book may therefore seem old-fashioned to some, and the subtitle, *A Political History . . .* , is included to disarm criticism from this quarter. I am sure that the material relates closely to many concepts arising in social psychology, the sociology of the family, social stratification, the theory of power and authority, of decision-making, law, moral philosophy, justice, and much else. These questions are rarely if ever explicitly canvassed. The historian's use and awareness of questions like these, I should think, appear in the quality of his judgments and the connections he makes in dealing with his empirical material—that is, his story.

ALBERT SOBOUL

CLASS STRUGGLES AND REVOLUTION

Albert Soboul is one of Georges Lefebvre's most brilliant and productive students. His massive doctoral dissertation, which he defended at the Sorbonne and published in 1958, dealt with *Les Sans-culottes Parisiens en 1'An II*, in almost 1,200 closely printed pages. He has also written a large number of monographs and articles and at least three histories of the French Revolution, including one published in 1964, in two volumes. Soboul has studied the Revolution "from below" through the popular movements of French peasants and *sans-culottes* in the light of Marxist conceptions. His contribution is significant for non-Marxists because of the exhaustive amount of research in original manuscript sources which he has carried out and synthesized. His work, along with that of George Rudé, Richard Cobb, and Kåre Tønnesson, all fellow students of Lefebvre, has added a new dimension to our knowledge of the Revolution, and permits us to see it from a point of view that has led to important revisions of earlier characterizations of the Revolution. Soboul is Professor of Modern History at the University of Clermont-Ferrand in France.

The French Revolution and the English revolutions of the 17th century were the culmination of a long economic and social evolution that made the bourgeoisie the mistress of the world.

This truth, which may pass for a commonplace today, had been proclaimed by the most conscious theoreticians of the bourgeoisie ever since the 19th century. Guizot proved that the characteristic feature of French, as of English, society, consisted essentially in the fact that between the people and the aristocracy there was a strong bourgeois class which had slowly defined the ideology and then created the leaders of a new society, of which 1789 was the consecration. Tocqueville spoke with "a sort of religious terror" "of this irresistible revolution which has been on the march for so many centuries over every obstacle, and that we still see today advancing in the midst of the ruins it has made." Taine sketched the slow climb of the bourgeoisie in the social scale, at the end of which it could no longer endure inequality. But for all their assurance that the birth and progress of the bourgeoisie had for their ultimate cause the appearance and development of personal wealth, first of commercial and then industrial enterprises, these historians hardly undertook a precise study of the economic origins of the Revolution or of the social classes that had made it.

Jaurès was the first, in his *Histoire socialiste*, to restore to the history of the Revolution its economic and social base, in a vast fresco swept away by eloquence. It still remains a valid monument. . . . Sagnac, and later Mathiez, went further and brought out the aristocratic reaction which culminated in 1787–88 in what Mathiez designates as "the revolt of the nobility": an expression for their fanatical opposition to any attempt at reform, and for their obstinate refusal to share their pre-eminence with the upper bourgeoisie. Thus was explained the violent nature of the French Revolution, in which the rise of the bourgeoisie was the result, not of gradual evolution, but of a sudden qualitative change.

But the Revolution was not the work of the bourgeoisie alone, even though it alone profited by it. Mathiez, following Jaurès, insists on the rapid disintegration of the Third Estate and the antagonisms which soon showed up between the various sections of the bourgeoisie and the popular classes; he takes into account the complexity of revolutionary history and the succession of its stages. Since France too at the end of the 18th century was still essentially rural, Georges Lefebvre turned from the Parisian scene and the big cities, which had almost exclusively occupied the attention of historians up to his time, and plunged into the study of the peasantry. Before him, peasant action had been thought of as a repercussion of urban movements, as something essentially directed, in accord with the bourgeoisie, against feudalism and the royal power. Georges Lefebvre, on the basis of precise social analyses, showed that within the framework of the bourgeois Revolution there developed a peasant trend with its own autonomous origin, procedures, crises and tendencies. . . .

The following pages . . . aim merely at sketching, beyond the basic antagonism of the society of the ancien regime, the complex complementary social antagonisms, which in the last analysis explain the evolution of the class struggles. Not only did the Revolution bring the bourgeoisie to power; in addition, without speaking of the aristocracy, it hastened the evolution, sometimes the destruction, of several categories of the old Third Estate. It permitted the flowering of the bourgeois society which had been in embryo so long.

I

The social structure at the end of the 18th century was still strongly marked by the pre-eminence of the aristocracy, a survival of the days when land, being the only form of wealth, gave its owners every right over those who worked it. Nevertheless, a long evolution had increased the power of personal property,

From Albert Soboul, "Classes and Class Struggles during the French Revolution," *Science and Society*, XVII (Summer, 1963), pp. 238–257 (footnotes deleted). Reprinted with the permission of *Science and Society*.

and of the bourgeoisie that held it. Thus faced each other two systems of production and two classes. But history had introduced differentiations into each of them.

The power of the aristocracy was based on landed property and the exercise of the seigneurial powers attached to the land. The economic evolution which brought personal wealth to the forefront, the rise in prices and the corresponding fall in feudal dues, all had produced within the solid ranks of the aristocracy an extreme inequality of fortune and a great diversity in conditions of existence. Above all, and this was the most important element of differentiation, a considerable portion of the landed aristocracy no longer disdained the revenues derived from capitalist enterprise, whether agricultural or industrial. In this way they came closer to the bourgeoisie.

It is obvious today that the French bourgeoisie led the Revolution. The bourgeoisie did not constitute a homogeneous element within the society of the 18th century. Sections of it were integrated into the social and economic structure of the ancien regime, and were to disappear with it. Others were the source of the new forms of capitalist production; their development was blocked by the traditional structure of society.

In the first category were commoners who shared in the privileges of the land-holding aristocracy or were part of the apparatus of the state; holders of office which they had bought; *fermiers généraux* [tax-farmers] and stockholders in the privileged financial companies, "a hybrid social force at the junction of the ancien regime and the new capitalism," according to Jaurès. But part of the capital of the *fermiers généraux* was invested in industrial enterprises. The second category consisted of the commercial and industrial bourgeoisie which was suffocating in the archaic framework of the economy.

The initiators of the new forms of production and exchange, the shipowners, merchants and manufacturers, were increasingly impatient with the impediments a still semi-feudal society placed in the way of their capitalist enterprises. Their importance at the end of the 18th century should not be exaggerated. Capitalism was still essentially commercial. But in the second half of the century great industrial enterprises in the modern sense appear in metallurgy, textiles and chemicals.

The spectacle of this economic activity gave the bourgeoisie an awareness of their class. Sieyès, in his famous pamphlet, defines the Third Estate by the *private* work and the *public* functions it performs. It is all the nation; the nobility can not be part of it, for it consumes "the better part of the product, without having had any share in its creation." . . .

The commercial and industrial bourgeoisie, therefore, had a keen sense of economic evolution and of the revolutionary force it represented.

At the end of the 18th century, the mass that works with its hands and produces was designated by the propertied, the aristocrats or the upper bourgeoisie, by the rather disdainful title of *people*. Actually, from those that made up the middle bourgeoisie to the proletariat, to use present-day terms, there were many nuances and antagonisms. The artisans were linked to the lower classes by their conditions of life and often by their poverty, but nonetheless had their shop, their bit of equipment and the aspect of independent producers. Having journeymen and apprentices below them heightened their bourgeois mentality. But their attachment to the system of petty production and direct sale set them hopelessly at odds with the industrial bourgeoisie. Hence the absence of a definite social ideal among these artisans and shopkeepers. They were to make up the bulk of the sans-culotte movement and to them the bourgeois Revolution was to owe its success.

The journeymen and proletarians (to the extent to which there was a large scale capitalist industry) had no class spirit. They were scattered in many small workshops; they were not specialized because of the still limited development of technology, nor concentrated in large factories or industrial districts, and often not too clearly set off from the peasantry. Neither workers nor artisans were able to conceive effective remedies for their wretchedness.

Only the bourgeoisie, by reason of its economic position and its intellectual power, had a coherent program, and it alone was ready to take the lead in the revolutionary action.

The peasant world was at once kept together and torn apart by the same unity and the same contradictions. All the peasantry was under the heavy burden of seigneurial rights, ecclesiastical tithes and royal taxes; that alone was enough to unite it against the feudal aristocracy and the monarchy of the ancien regime. But the shock given to traditional society by the attack of the bourgeoisie was required before the peasantry rushed into the assault. Once the movement had been unleashed, they followed their own aims, which were not always those of the bourgeoisie.

The capitalist movement which renovated industrial production also tended to transform the rural districts, bringing into them elements of differentiation and antagonism. Ever since the middle of the century (and the development of the physiocratic school had been the clear sign of the fact) the application of capital and its characteristic methods to agricultural production, with a view to scientific and intensive cultivation, had obvious repercussions on the state of the peasants in the regions of large-scale farming. At the end of the ancien regime a new class of big farmers, capitalists of agricultural exploitation, developed on a wide scale. In their hands was concentrated more and more the exploitation of the land, if not yet its ownership, while an increased mass of production transformed the traditional market of agricultural products. The traditional antagonism between the peasantry and the landed aristocracy was reinforced in the regions of large-scale farming by the antagonism between agricultural capitalism and a more and more proletarianized peasantry. Lacking land, and deprived of their collective rights as private property and large-scale capitalist farming took hold, the peasants swelled the ranks of a poverty-stricken and unstable rural proletariat, and were as ready to rise against the big farms as against the chateaux.

These conditions of course should not be generalized so as to apply to all France. On the eve of the Revolution, the largest part of the country remained the scene of the traditional petty cultivation. But here too elements of dissociation were at work, the source of future antagonisms. Inequality had come into the rural community, once unified by seigneurial domination. Collective ownership and farming of the common lands, and collective restrictions on private property (prohibition of enclosure, compulsory rotation), customary rights in the fields (common pasture, gleaning and straw) and the woods, all constituted, up to the middle of the 18th century, solid economic bases of the rural community, and cemented its social unity. Even though various levels of life coexisted there, the seigneurial regime and feudal rights gave rise to the basic antagonism of rural France under the ancien regime, that between the rural community and the land-holding aristocracy. In the second half of the 18th century economic evolution brings to the fore in the regions of small-scale farming the class of working proprietors, the "village cocks" on whom day-laborers and small peasants depend for their work, and who take over local administration. They were a prosperous peasantry, a rural bourgeoisie, different from the class of capitalist farmers but already producing for the market to a certain extent, and ready to adopt the new agriculture.

This prosperous peasantry is against the rural community almost as much as it is against the feudal aristocracy, for it aims to free property from all collective and seigneurial rights.

Thus the interplay of social antagonisms in the rural areas became complex and diversified. It could already be seen that the basic conflicts between the peasantry and the landed aristocracy would be supplemented by the latent antagonism between owner peasants and poor peasants, once the landed aristocracy had been cut down.

II

The real complexity, under a seeming simplicity, of the social structure of the ancien regime, accounts for the vicissitudes of the class struggles under the Revolution.

The essential cause of the Revolution was the power of a bourgeoisie arrived at its maturity and confronted by a decadent aristocracy holding tenaciously to its privileges. The result was the legal enactment of that power. In this sense, the French Revolution, an episode (but the most resounding one) in the general rise of the bourgeoisie, was a single thing; we cannot follow Mathiez, who distinguishes, after the "revolt of the nobility" of 1787–88 and the bourgeois revolution of 1789, a third revolution, democratic and republican, on August 10, 1792, and then a fourth one, May 31– June 2, 1793, leading to a rough sketch of social democracy. August 10 and June 2 were indeed crucial stages in the Revolution; but what we had there was a deepening of the struggle between the bourgeoisie and the aristocracy, marked by the entrance on the stage of the middle and lower classes. The change was not in the nature of the struggle of classes. In 1793 as in 1789 the aim was still to strike down the aristocracy. In this sense we can not speak either of a "change of front" on the part of the bourgeoisie after the fall of Robespierre, for after the 9th Thermidor as before it, the essential enemy remained the aristocracy, which did not lay down its arms. The Thermidorians thought they could get along without the alliance with the people. Their calculations proved to be false. Though the partisans of Bonaparte continued to fear the sans-culottes, they feared still more the peril of the aristocracy, and to get rid of it had to resort to military dictatorship. Bonaparte was indeed the soldier of the bourgeois revolution.

Yet, under this essential unity, the Revolution is a complex fact. It had various stages, reflecting the fluctuations forward and backward of the battle against the aristocracy. The Revolution also had various currents which were complementary to the main stream. Without the peasantry and the sans-culottes the bourgeoisie could never have brought down the aristocracy; nonetheless, the sans-culottes and the peasantry pursued goals that were not those of the bourgeoisie.

The revolution was marked by stages, as the struggle of classes became sharper and more complicated. We shall not go over them here, but merely raise some problems, which are organically bound together: the problem of the failure of the compromise policy, the problem of the Girondins' "failure of nerve" when confronted with the necessities of the war, and the problem of the Jacobin dictatorship.

The ruling sections of the bourgeoisie would have accepted a compromise which, in the image of the English revolutions of the 17th century, would have set up over the subdued lower classes the domination of the *notables* and the moneyed class. The aristocracy would have none of it, thus rendering inevitable recourse to the popular masses in order to break its resistance. Only a minority, symbolized by the name of La Fayette, understood that it stood to lose nothing in this compromise; the example of England proved that. Compromise was possible in the spring of 1789; but the monarchy would have had to take the initiative boldly. Its attitude showed instead that it was no longer anything more than the instrument of domination by one class. The decision of Louis XVI at the beginning of July to appeal to the soldier seemed to indicate the end of the nascent bourgeois revolution. The force of the people saved it.

Was compromise still possible after July 14 and the October days? There were those who thought so among the bourgeoisie as well as among the aristocracy, and had plans for bringing it about. But the majority of the nobility, and the aristocratic upper clergy, both refused to accept the initial reforms of the Revolution.

Whether for ambition or lack of political understanding, La Fayette persisted for a longer time. Being a great lord, a "hero of two worlds," he had what was needed to attract the upper bourgeoisie. His policy was, within the framework of constitutional monarchy, to conciliate the landed aristocracy with the industrial and commercial bourgeoisie. He failed because the aristocracy stubbornly resisted. Even more, the disorders due to the persistence of the food crisis, and the agrarian revolts caused by the obligation of redeeming the seigneurial rights, hardened the resistance of the aristocracy. From the summer of 1790 on, the compromise policy was ruined.

Alarmed by the progress of the democrats and by the popular agitation, the upper bourgeoisie tried to put a stop to the Revolution. The passive or disfranchized citizens were excluded from the national guard and collective petitions prohibited. On June 14, 1791 the Loi Le Chapelier proscribed "coalitions" and strikes. The resistance of the aristocracy, however, made this policy impossible. The appeal to foreign intervention, evidenced by the flight of the king on June 21, 1791, showed that class interest made the bourgeoisie prefer to betray the nation rather than yield.

The crisis brought forth from among the bourgeoisie a second and socially different revolutionary generation. It was in part recruited from the cultivated middle bourgeoisie of lawyers and journalists, who were in contact with the commercial bourgeoisie. Their most representative figure was Brissot.[1] This commercial bourgeoisie and the politicians in their service wanted to liquidate the counter-revolution in order to restore the value of the assignats, if business was to thrive. As for war, which the aristocracy wanted in order to bring about an end to the revolution, the commercial bourgeoisie was not against

[1] Jacques Pierre Brissot (1754–1793) was a journalist who played an important role in shaping opinion in the early stages of the Revolution; his circle of associates and followers eventually emerged as the so-called "Girondins"; he was guillotined in 1793 along with the other "Girondins." [Editor's note].

it—had not army orders always been a considerable source of profits? The Girondins, or the party of the commercial bourgeoisie, started the continental war in April 1792, but did not declare war on England until February of the following year. War at sea endangered trade with the islands and the prosperity of the maritime cities.

The continental war served both the economic and political interests of the Girondin bourgeoisie. It meant carrying to a climax the struggle against the die-hard aristocracy, unmasking it and destroying it beyond the frontiers where it had sought refuge in emigration, intensifying the class struggle on the scale of the European ancien regime.

The war spoiled the calculations of the Girondin bourgeoisie. A new cleavage took its place among the social antagonisms. The Gironde, under the pretext that the war required unity, had already stood warrant for La Fayette and supported Narbonne, the minister of foreign affairs. Here was an anticipatory sketch of that government of notables . . . which conciliated the interests of that part of the landed aristocracy that had made its peace with the commercial bourgeoisie. The reverses of Spring 1792 made the Gironde realize it needed an alliance with the popular classes to make victory sure. But it showed hesitancy and duplicity. It consented to appeal to the people, on June 20, 1792, only to the extent that the people would keep to the objectives the Gironde assigned them. The Girondin bourgeoisie, unreservedly devoted to economic liberty, was disturbed to see the sans-culottes demand fixed prices on foodstuffs. On August 10, 1792, the monarchy, pillar of the aristocracy and obstacle to an effective policy of national defense, was brushed away by the sans-culottes and the Jacobin middle class. The insurrection of August 10, made without the Gironde, was its death sentence.

The foreign policy of the Girondin Bourgeoisie was the logical consequence of this initial attitude toward the people. In order to obtain peace, the Gironde, in fear of the people, was getting ready to drop into a compromise with the aristocracy and the counterrevolution. The upper bourgeoisie also reunited behind it. Once more class interests got the better of the interests of the nation. This is what the historians call modestly the "failure of nerve" of the Gironde. Like the monarchy on August 10, the Girondin bourgeoisie was an obstacle to the national effort and was eliminated by a popular movement

disciplined by the petty and middle bourgeoisie. Jaurès has denied the class character of the days of May 31–June 2, 1793. To be sure, if we confine ourselves to the parliamentary aspect of these days, or to the political conflict between the Mountain and the Gironde: both derived from the bourgeoisie (and yet the nuances would have to be noted) and had the same conception of property. But the re-entrance of the sans-culottes into the scene now complicated the interplay of the class struggles. The Girondin Pétion was not mistaken when as early as April 1793, in his *Letter to the Parisians*, he sounded the alarm to the bourgeois: "Your property is menaced, and you close your eyes to the danger!"

The internal and external aristocratic menace in 1793–94 required the unity of the Third Estate. The sense of the class struggle was clearer than ever. The energy of the sans-culotte masses was more necessary than ever in this struggle. The Gironde denied itself this aid out of class selfishness, but another section of the bourgeoisie undertook to recruit and discipline the popular ardor in the organization of the revolutionary government and Jacobin dictatorship. This saved the Revolution.

In this coalition, on which the revolutionary government was to rest, the Jacobin middle bourgeoisie that Robespierre incarnated was undoubtedly the leading element, the necessary link between the living forces of the sans-culottes and that section of the bourgeoisie that planned to push the bourgeois revolution to completion. The position did not lack its contradictions and accounted in large measure for the ultimate failure of Robespierre's policy. It was a position that followed from the social condition of the Jacobin middle bourgeoisie that would have to be spelled out by many detailed studies, but was symbolized well by the "cabinet-maker" Duplay, a good Jacobin if there ever was one. He still engaged in the world of labor but got ten to twelve thousand livres of rent from his houses just the same.

The rapid ruin of the revolutionary government is accounted for by the contradictions of the sans-culottes, even more than by the ambiguous position of the Jacobins. But here we touch upon one of those secondary currents of the French Revolution that add to its complexity.

Nothing is clearer than that the sans-culottes fought against the aristocracy first and foremost. July 14 proves that, as well as the ardor of the volunteers. The sans-culottes furnished the bourgeoisie that revolutionary mass that was indispensable for bringing down the old society. For all that, the fact remains that the position of the sans-culottes in the traditional society made them an autonomous element, opposed to the bourgeoisie on many points.

There is thus an autonomous sans-culotte current within the French Revolution, of which the origins would have to be looked for in the deterioration of the conditions of shopkeepers, artisans and workers well before 1789. It is significant that the sans-culottes were set in motion just as much by the foodstuff crises as by the aristocratic plot. The sans-culotte current was autonomous also by virtue of its procedures and organizations, such as general assemblies of the Parisian sections, in which the sans-culottes ruled undisputed in 1793, and people's societies. There was a significant difference between a people's society and the Jacobin Club which the sans-culottes hardly frequented at all. And there was autonomy in certain crises, like the one in early September, 1793, which Mathiez describes as a "Hébertist drive," and which was nothing but a sans-culotte "drive." These days had no strict and precise relationship with the general course of the bourgeois revolution. The sans-culottes demanded fixed prices for foodstuffs and regulation of trade in them, something that the Jacobin bourgeoisie granted only under duress and against its will.

That is where the basic opposition lay between the sans-culottes and the bourgeoisie. The sans-culottes share a pre-capitalist mentality, deeply hostile to the spirit of enterprise that moves the bourgeoisie; the latter demands economic liberty, while the sans-culottes in September 1793 force upon it price-fixing and controls. Beyond this opposition over the organization of economic life, two conceptions clashed: the bourgeois conception of property as a natural, inalienable, total right, and the sans-culotte conception of a property which was controlled, limited and kept within narrow limits which were precisely the limits of the sans-culottes. On September 2, 1793 the sans-culottes of the section of the Jardin des Plantes demanded of the Convention that an upper limit be set to fortunes, that a single citizen should not own more than one workshop or store. It was a position full of contradiction; but there was contradiction too in the position of the revolutionary government that was based on such dissimilar elements as the Jacobin middle bourgeoisie and the sans-culottes. Once victory over the aristocracy was in sight, the dangerous alliance with the sans-culottes seemed less needful. The bourgeoisie, without changing its front, resumed its freedom of action. The revolutionary government did not survive the ninth of Thermidor.

The ambiguous position of the sans-culottes in the French Revolution explains certain errors of perspective with respect to them. . . . Daniel Guérin tried to see the sans-culottes as an advance guard and their attempt of the year II [1793] as an embryonic proletarian revolution: this would confirm the theory of the permanent revolution, according to which the proletarian revolution of the twentieth century was already implicit in the bourgeois revolution of the 18th. Guérin took the sans-culottes for the proletariat. He writes, for example, that the demonstration on September 4, 1793, was specifically *working-class*, . . . This is to make a proletarian advance guard of what was nothing but a rear guard defending the positions of the traditional economy.

The sans-culottes did not form either a party or a class. There were workers among them, especially journeymen; but there were also shopkeepers and artisans who had some property and petty bourgeois of the liberal professions. What united these men was, beyond their hatred of the aristocracy, their common hostility to the capitalist system of production that threatened to reduce them to the rank of proletarians. Hence their utopian equalitarianism and their desire not to suppress the property that many of them already enjoyed, but to limit it to their own measure. The sans-culottes were at once hostile to capitalism because it tended to push them down into the ranks of the proletariat, and attached to the bourgeois order because they had property or hoped to get it. They demanded price-fixing, but at the same time were attached to the independence of the shop, the artisanate, and the small country holding. On this point they were devotees of economic liberalism. Certainly, on the political plane they were the most advanced democratic element. . . . But on the economic plane their positions were reactionary: they were doomed to decline with all the traditional system of production based on the artisanate and the shop. It is a contradiction that gives the dialectic movement of history all its dramatic quality.

The peasant current is not without analogy with the sans-culotte current in some aspects (especially with respect to the poor peasantry), for it too developed within the framework of the bourgeois revolution without getting beyond it. Hatred of feudalism linked the peasantry with the bourgeoisie, and its destruction was one of the Revolution's most important reforms.

The peasant current also developed autonomously, without organic connection with the bourgeois revolution. Upon hearing of the fall of the Bastille, the peasants revolted spontaneously and often despite the bourgeoisie which in many localities, in its quality as landowner, took strong repressive measures. The agrarian revolts continued until the total abolition of seigneurial rights in 1793.

The poor peasantry was marked by the same pre-capitalist mentality as the sans-culottes of the cities; it was attached to collective rights and controls; and in the course of the Revolution it was equally opposed to the seigneurs and to the agencies of the capitalist transformation of agriculture. This is proved by the numerous petitions against large farms and for the maintenance of collective rights. The strength of this peasant current was so great that the bourgeoisie had to come to terms. The Revolution, triumphant in other respects, brought about merely a compromise in the rural districts.

III

If we now try to draw up the balance sheet of the Revolution from the point of view we have taken here, we see how unreal any schematism is. The Revolution destroyed the feudal aristocracy; it still has to be made clear to what extent. At the same time it also ruined those sections of the bourgeoisie that were integrated in one way or another into the society of the ancien regime. The Revolution made certain the triumph of capitalist economy based on economic liberty; in this sense, it hastened the ruin of the social categories that were attached to the traditional system of production. But in the realm of agricultural production, the resistance of the poor peasantry was such that capitalism could not win a definitive victory.

The nobility as a social order disappeared. Distinctions between nobles and commons were done away with. The personal seigneurial rights on which the dependence of the peasants was based were abolished after the night of August 4, 1789. Above all the aristocracy was hit in its economic basis. Other feudal rights were finally terminated by the

Convention on June 17, 1793. The Revolution attacked the landed property of the nobility. The former seigneurs had to return the communal lands that they had seized and the property of the emigres was put on sale in June 1793. As the crisis grew deeper the nobles were gradually excluded from all public positions, civil or military. Exaggeration should be avoided here, however. The nobility was not stripped of its lands altogether nor irrevocably. Only the emigres had their property confiscated. Many nobles went through the Revolution without great loss and kept their landed properties. Furthermore, fictitious divorces and purchases by straw men enabled some emigres to save or recover their lands. In this way a certain section of the old aristocracy held on, and during the 19th century merged with the upper bourgeoisie.

The bourgeoisie of the ancien regime shared the fate of the aristocracy in large measure. The bourgeois who lived "nobly" on their income from the land saw their seigneurial dues and rights vanish. Office holders were ruined by the abolition of the sale of offices. The financial upper bourgeoisie received a mortal blow when stock companies and the farming-out of indirect taxes were abolished. It was hard hit too by the disappearance of the Bank of Discount as well as by the resumption of price-fixing and controls. Finally, as a measure of the blows the bourgeois revolution struck at certain sections of the bourgeoisie, we must consider the considerable repercussions of inflation on settled fortunes. The traditional bourgeoisie invested its savings in mortgage loans or the public debt rather than in commercial and industrial enterprises. In 1794, the depreciation of the assignats led debtors to get rid of their mortgage debts at little cost. The consolidation of the perpetual and annuity debts under the Convention, and the two-thirds bankruptcy under the Directory were additional blows. All these facts account for the rallying of the bourgeoisie of the ancien regime to the counter-revolution. It shared the fate of the aristocracy, whose cause it had taken up.

Just as much as the revolutionary bourgeoisie strove for the destruction of the aristocracy, it obstinately sought the ruin of the traditional economic system, which was incompatible with the expansion of capitalist enterprises. After the Ninth of Thermidor, economic liberty was inaugurated triumphantly on the ruins of the sans-culotte movement.

This had grave consequences for the traditional

lower classes. The abolition of guilds by the Constituent Assembly might have seemed democratic, but it hurt the interests of the master artisans. Thus, at the same time that the material conditions of social life were being transformed, the structure of the traditional lower classes was changing. All the conditions were now present for a broad development of capitalist economy, which would necessarily transform the sans-culottes into a proletariat. The artisans and journeymen had a foreboding of their fate. The latter knew that machinery would increase the chances of unemployment, the former that capitalist concentration would mean the closing of their workshops and make wage earners of them. The Le Chapelier law of 1791, prohibiting "coalition" and strikes, was an effective means of development for the industrial bourgeoisie.

In the realm of agricultural production, where the resistance of the poor peasantry was more desperate, the bourgeois revolution was less radical in its consequences. It made possible the development of a predominant rural bourgeoisie, but it could not completely destroy the rural community and thereby give free rein to the development of capitalist modes of production.

All the peasantry, whether owners or not, profited by the abolition of seigneurial dues and ecclesiastical tithes. The other agrarian reforms of the Revolution served primarily to strengthen those who were already proprietors. Leaving out the city bourgeoisie, who got into their hands a considerable portion of the national property, the conditions under which it was sold, particularly the auctions, favored the big farmers and the prosperous peasants. The rural bourgeoisie was strengthened and the moat deepened between them and the poor peasantry.

But the last-named did not emerge from the Revolution as badly disarmed in the face of the triumphant bourgeoisie as the urban sans-culottes were. The poor peasantry did not get from the revolutionary assemblies the restoration or reinforcement of the traditional rural community, as it had desired. But the bourgeois revolution did not destroy it beyond repair; it did not brutally do away with the communal properties and collective customs that formed its economic basis. Both lasted throughout the 19th century and have not entirely disappeared yet. The law of 1892, still in force, requires the consent of the peasants of the village for the abandonment of common pasture. The rural community has thus survived, going through a slow disintegration.

Here some distinctions are necessary. In the regions of large-scale farming, where the farmers were active agents in the capitalist evolution of agriculture, the rural community broke up rapidly, not by dissociating into antagonistic classes (the big farmers were generally city capitalists who were strangers to the rural community) but by losing its substance, as it were. The poor peasants who were proletarianized were to furnish the labor force needed for capitalist agriculture and big industry. In small-scale farming regions the evolution was slower. The rural community was sapped from within by the antagonism between the rural bourgeoisie and the poor peasantry desperately defending its customary rights to use fields and woods. Thus two forms of economy clashed, one archaic, the other new and asserting the individualism of the capitalist producers. The struggle was covert but bitter, marked during the 19th century by agrarian disorders of the traditional type, the last of them, in 1848–51, being by no means the least violent nor the least typical.

The bourgeois revolution was consequently unable to eradicate the traditional forms of agricultural production. It could only enact a compromise whose full significance can be measured by comparing the development of French and English agriculture. Undoubtedly the bourgeois revolution accelerated the capitalist transformation of agriculture; but that development was considerably slowed up by the maintenance of collective customs and by the subdivision of ownership and cultivation. The autonomy of the small producers was kept up for a long time, giving the political development of France, especially under the Third Republic, some of its characteristic traits. If enclosure and concentration had been imposed in France as they were in England, capitalism might have triumphed as completely in the realm of agricultural production as in that of industrial production. The obstinate resistance of the landed aristocracy to any compromise with the bourgeoisie forced the latter to deal gently with the peasantry, even with the poor peasantry.

If we now consider the class which led the Revolution, and basically profited from it, we note that it has been radically changed. The traditional predominance within it of the settled fortunes has been replaced by that of those who direct production and exchange; the internal equilibrium of the bourgeoisie has been modified. The bourgeoisie of the ancien regime was not totally destroyed, since those of its representatives who had not emigrated kept their lands; but it lost its primacy. A new money bourgeoisie appeared in the forefront, made up of industrial leaders, and the directors of commerce and finance. Equipping, arming and supplying the armies, sale of the national property, exploitation of the conquered countries afforded business men new chances for developing their enterprises. Speculation gave rise to immense fortunes. The bourgeoisie renewed itself by incorporating those "nouveaux riches" who set the tone for the "society" of the Directory. True adventurers of capitalist society, they gave new life to the traditional bourgeoisie by their enterprising spirit and their flair for taking chances. On a lower rung of the bourgeois ladder, circumstances had allowed many tradesmen or artisans to rise into the ranks of the bourgeoisie. It was from this middle level that the new dominant class was soon to recruit the public servants and the members of the liberal professions. The traits of the new bourgeoisie hardened during the Napoleonic period that fused these diverse elements.

ALFRED COBBAN

PLUS ÇA CHANGE OR THE MYTH OF THE BOURGEOIS REVOLUTION

Alfred Cobban, who has held the chair of French History at the University of London since 1953, has served as head of the History Department there since 1961, and is editor of *History: The Journal of the Historical Association*. He is the dean of British historians of the French Revolution. Professor Cobban, who was educated at Cambridge University, has also taught at the University of Durham, and as Visiting Professor at the University of Chicago, at Harvard, and at the University of California, Berkeley. His numerous publications have dealt with Edmund Burke, Rousseau, eighteenth-century diplomacy, public opinion, and political theory, as well as the problems of modern dictatorships and nationalism. More recently, his *In Search of Humanity: The Role of the Enlightenment in Modern History* (1960) has surveyed the ethical and political thought of the eighteenth century and its relevance to the problems of the contemporary world; and his *The Social Interpretation of the French Revolution* (1964) has criticized what Cobban calls the "social" school of Lefebvre, Soboul, Rudé, and Cobb. He is best known to the general public for his three-volume Penguin paperback *History of Modern France* and for the expanded hardback version published more recently by Jonathan Cape (1962–1965).

. . . The French eighteenth century is not a period of great, dominating political figures. Yet if no one man counted overmuch, more men—and women—counted for something than possibly at any other time. The great mass forces of the modern world had not yet been born, while the individual . . . had at last emerged from the anonymity of the Middle Ages. If it was not a century of greatness, for the student of *l'homme sensuel moyen* there is no more fruitful field. The eighteenth century was also . . . the nursery of the modern world. Ideas and social forces, the seeds of which

From Alfred Cobban, "Eighteenth Century Balance Sheet," and "Plus Ça Change," *A History of Modern France* (London: Jonathan Cape, 1962–1963), I, 254–60, II, 211–21. Reprinted by permission of Jonathan Cape Ltd. and George Braziller, Inc.

were doubtless sown much earlier, can be seen now pushing above the surface, not in the neatly arranged rows of the careful gardener but in the haphazard tangle of nature. Yet they *can* be seen and distinguished: . . .

The basic pattern of the age was inherited from the immediate past. French society and government bore the impress of the personality of Louis XIV throughout the century which witnessed his decline and death. If Louis XV and Louis XVI failed and were to be hissed off the stage, it was in part because they were mere understudies, and not very good ones at that, trying to fill the role of the greatest actor of majesty that France had known. Only Napoleon, and he only for a short period, could successfully play the part that had been created by the grand monarch. Failing a great king, a great minister, supported by the king, could have given France the government that she needed; but the intrigues of a court were not breeding ground for greatness, . . . The ministers of the eighteenth century deserve all the condemnation that has been lavished on them by historians who only admire success. There were among them many able and honest men who could provide efficient administration: what they could not provide was a united government and a consistent policy. And when eventually, for lack of a policy, the absolute monarchy collapsed, the revolutionary régime which followed seemed to be attempting to push the weakness of the *ancien régime* to its logical conclusion by turning anarchy into a form of government. In a sense, therefore, the dominant factor throughout was a negative one: the void left at the centre of the machine of state by the death of Louis XIV.

It was for the very reason of lack of central control that French society was able to develop so rapidly and freely and at the same time in such contradictory directions. First, when the king had become the prisoner of a court, instead of the court being the mere decorative background for the king, the way was open for aristocracy to reemerge from the political insignificance into which it had been thrust in the shadow of the bureaucratic colossus erected by Louis XIV, to recapture the highest offices of state, and in the end perish in a bid to gain control of the state itself. . . . The *noblesse de l'épée* drew closer to that *noblesse de robe* which in its parlements had for centuries past upheld the authority of the crown against a turbulent *noblesse* of the sword, but now itself aspired to usurp the authority of

which it had formerly been the docile guardian. The parlements renewed on a more permanent basis the alliance with the aristocracy that they had momentarily consummated during the Fronde. The Church, reduced to subservience to the crown by the Concordat of Francis I and kept in obedience by the Gallican liberties, its wealth and its higher offices put in the hands of the king to be given as rewards or taken away as punishments for the loyalty or disloyalty of the great houses of France, in the eighteenth century looked rather to its allies and relations of the aristocracy than to the crown. The higher Church posts had either by long use become practically hereditary in great families, or else were distributed, as the prize of court intrigues, not to maintain the authority of the crown, but to bolster up ministerial or aristocratic factions. Thus by 1788 the *noblesse* of the sword, robe, and church, which throughout the century had waged parallel campaigns against royal authority, had come so close together that they could unite in a single aristocratic revolt.

Yet their combined forces, dominant at Versailles, and with their centres of power in every cathedral, abbey, parlement, great château, or petty manorhouse scattered through provincial capitals and countryside, though they were able to reduce the royal administration to impotence, were themselves to reveal only their weakness when they were challenged by another force which they had never associated, which indeed had never associated itself, with a claim to power. Looking backwards, the theme of eighteenth-century history in France is the rise of the Third Estate, but how many could have guessed this before 1789? Do we yet fully know what it means, for who were the Third Estate? We can give them another name and call them, if we will, the bourgeoisie, but this helps us no more, for what was the bourgeoisie? All that was not *noblesse* or people, we may reply. It may be suggested that the Third Estate consisted largely of officials, professional men, rentiers, and non-noble landowners; but for any more detailed or reliable estimate we shall have to wait until the social history of the period has been written.

However it was constituted, the problem remains why the Third Estate came to have the power to overthrow the combined aristocracies of France. . . . It was not the bourgeoisie, whoever they may have been, who rioted in the market places, sacked the manor-houses and burnt the manorial rolls, dragged cannon to the Bastille, marched to Versailles, or mutinied in the army and fleet. The men who did these things, and constituted the rank and file of the peasant revolts and the great revolutionary *journées*, were peasants, craftsmen, artisans, small shopkeepers, soldiers. It was by making use of their discontents that the Third Estate was able to overcome the resistance of the privileged Orders and divert the Revolution to its own ends. Once this fact is realized a restatement of the problem becomes possible. The grievances of the people in town and country need not be recapitulated, nor the breakdown of social discipline which at least in part followed from the aristocratic revolt. The real problem is how a class of officials, lawyers, financiers, rentiers, landowners, was able to acquire the leadership of a popular movement constituted mainly of peasants and craftsmen. What did such leaders and followers have in common? To ask the question is to go a long way towards answering it. What they had in common was evidently not economic interests, though each group had its own interest which, to the best of its ability and in so far as it understood that interest, it pursued. What they had in common was an enemy, primarily the *noblesse*, but along with it the superior clergy, *noblesse* of the robe, higher officials, and some sections of the wealthy such as the Farmers-General: in other words all those who might be described as belonging to the privileged classes.

Privilege was the enemy, equality the aim, though it must be remembered that the equality desired by the Third Estate was an equality not of property but of status. This was the inspiring motive of a social grouping which possessed talents, education, and at least moderate wealth, and yet was denied the position and status to which it thought these things entitled it. The peasants also found their primary objective in the assault on privilege and played their part in the events of 1789 under this banner. The better-off peasantry having achieved their principal aims, and the remainder lacking the cohesion or consciousness for more than sporadic unrest, they dropped out of political life. The Revolution was henceforth mainly an urban phenomenon, kept alive in the towns, and above all in Paris, by the unrest of a populace which suffered increasingly from the pressure of high prices and shortage of supplies. The undermining of authority, the breakdown of police control, and the disintegration of the army led to a situation in which even a comparatively small popular demonstration could intimidate the Assembly. The political factions of the left naturally took advantage of the weapon they found to their hand and used it to overthrow their opponents; but the alliance of the Mountain with the masses was fortuitous and effected only a temporary diversion of the main stream of the revolution of the Third Estate. The populace gained little from it, except possibly during the period when the war economy of the Committee of Public Safety for a time halted inflation, and then only at the price of the Terror.

When the new revolutionary army was sufficiently professionalized and disciplined to be used in the streets of Paris, the political role of the people was at an end. But as the politicians of the Third Estate, having made use of the populace, had found themselves at the mercy of their own instrument, so the oligarchy which emerged after Thermidor and leant on the army found its policies determined by the generals, until one rose above all the others and became the autocrat of France. Then, and only then, did the logic of Bourbon absolutism finally triumph over the liberal ideals of the Constituent Assembly, and divine-right monarchy find, with Bonaparte, its historical sequel in the sovereignty of force.

Yet, though the later regimes of the revolutionary decade were to leave their mark on France, it was under the Constituent Assembly that the real harvest of the eighteenth century had been gathered in. Its work was lasting because it was built on foundations which had been solidly laid and because it was the culmination of a social revolution which, underneath the formal, juridical structure of society, had been quietly proceeding for centuries. We can call it the triumph of the bourgeoisie if by this term we mean the venal officers, lawyers, professional men, proprietors, with a few financiers and merchants, who invested their money, for the most part, in land or *rentes*, after venal offices were no longer available. The Revolution gave them the opportunity to obtain some of the lands and more of the offices of the privileged classes and to complete the process of rising to become the ruling class in France. They were not, by and large, a commercial or industrial class; their wealth was only to a minor degree derived from trade or industry, and it did not go back to fertilize the economic life of the nation. In their way of life they were the heirs of the obsolescent *noblesse*, and if they were bourgeois their aim was to be "bourgeois vivant noblement." The pattern of life which they copied and gradually made their own was that of the eighteenth century, the graces of which they were to perpetuate, to the best of their ability, into a modern world. Their eyes remained turned to the past in which their ideal had been set.

The victors had no wish to go beyond the social and political victory they had won, nor had they any intention of sharing their gains with the petty shop-keepers, craftsmen and journeymen, and all the *menu peuple* of the towns who had fought their battle for them. Equally, in the countryside, the better-off peasant proprietors were satisfied with what they had gained, indifferent to the grievances of the share-cropping *métayers*, and hostile to the barely conscious demands of the landless labourers. Out of the Revolution, therefore, there emerged a new and even stronger system of vested interests than had preceded it. Perhaps human capacity for change is limited: at any rate, the Revolution seemed to have effected changes so great that for a time they in-hibited further progress. It did not inaugurate but brought to an end a great age of social transforma-tion. The paradox of French history is that a revolu-tionary settlement was to provide the basis for a profoundly conservative pattern of society.

Yet it would be a narrow view to portray the Revo-lution as concerned only with material interests: the eighteenth century was an age of intellectual and moral as well as social development. Humanitarian and utilitarian reforms that had existed only on pa-per, or at best had received only scattered and par-tial expression before 1789, were given fuller effect in the legislation of the revolutionary assemblies. In one field, admittedly, the eighteenth century had sown dragon's teeth: clericalism and anti-clericalism were to bedevil French politics into the twentieth century. The phenomenon of anti-clericalism is, however, far from being understood: to attribute its outburst among the revolutionary masses merely to the influence of the *philosophes* is unsatisfactory, but if its tap-roots went—as they well may have done—deep into the obscure recesses of the popular mind, from what sources they drew nourishment, and driven by what inner urge it pushed its way to the surface, remain unsolved and perhaps insoluble problems. We can only add this to the sum total of all that the Enlightenment bequeathed to the Revo-lution and so to modern France, of which, intellec-tually and morally, as well as socially, the pattern had been already set when, on the eighteenth of Brumaire, Bonaparte made himself First Consul. Undeniably, the Enlightenment set up ideals that the revolutionaries could aspire towards more often

than they could achieve, yet what they did achieve would give the French eighteenth century greatness if nothing else did. . . .

The collapse of the Second Empire [of Napoleon III in 1870] ends the monarchical and Bonapartist phase in French history. . . . Above all, in its basic pattern French society seemed to be, and indeed was, unaffected by the passing of an Empire.

. . . We nevertheless have to end one [section] and begin another in 1871, . . . because there is, after all, something significant in the political calen-dar. The major changes in political institutions that resulted from the fall of the Second Empire were a determining factor in a fundamental though gradual transformation of French society, and without its opening years the history of the Third Republic would be robbed of the political developments that are essential for its understanding. There is another reason why we must make the break here. The dis-aster that befell the army, the unresisted collapse of the political system, the social *stasis* that burst out in the bloody class war of the Commune, all inflicted a psychological shock that, if the first result was to numb the national spirit, in the end stimulated it to new endeavour. Although, therefore, the disappear-ance of Napoleon III from the scene was not like that of a Louis XIV or a Napoleon I—it did not mark an epoch and hardly left a void—there are reasons for accepting the division of French history at this point and pausing to reflect on the significance of the generations that had elapsed between eighteenth brumaire and Sedan.

It is revealing to look back even earlier to 1770, when Louis XV had been making a new political experiment, as Louis Napoleon was in 1870, and consider the passage of an eventful hundred years, in the course of which France had experienced three major revolutions and moved backwards and for-wards between monarchy, republic, and empire. How much during this century had French society really changed? If we imagine a Rip van Winkle who fell asleep in France, and alternatively in En-gland, in 1770, and woke again in 1870, and ask him in which country there had been a series of revolu-tions, there can be little doubt what his answer would be. He would remember eighteenth-century England as a small, rural community of country-towns, villages and hamlets, with sea-ports, but with no great centre of population outside London, its communications by coach on the new turnpike roads where they existed or by packhorse along tracks, its industry mainly carried on, in town or country, in the homes of domestic workers. Much of this could also apply to the France of 1770, except that in England an agrarian revolution was already under way, while in France the ports were finer and urbanization had produced a crop of elegant provincial towns; also that France was a country with a population of over twenty millions, about three times that of Great Britain. Politically and socially there were more significant differences, but in both countries the powers of monarchy were in practice strictly limited by the influence of the aristocracy, which in turn had to respect the interests of a rising middle class.

Waking in 1870, the sleeper for a hundred years would find changes in England such as he would hardly credit. An industrial revolution that had transformed the appearance of large tracts of country, a population multiplied by five, an urgent political life, with two great parties which had brought political consciousness and activity to large sections of the community, an empire spreading to the four corners of the world: this was the England of Queen Victoria and Mr Gladstone. What was the France of Napoleon III . . . ?

It was a country which seemed in many ways never to have left the eighteenth century. There was an emperor who was the effective head of the government, instead of a king who was only its nominal head; a court at Saint-Cloud instead of Versailles, with fewer old names and more *ennoblis*; a parliament, it is true, but one which lacked the independence, for good or ill, of the juridical parlements of the *ancien régime*; there were still great financiers, and they still exercised some political, and even more social, power; the Church was again in alliance with the state, and again used its influence to frustrate national policies and obstruct reforms; Paris was swollen and rebuilt, its poorer population expelled to the periphery, and the city itself even more than formerly the centre of administration and government, art and letters, finance and banking. Provincial France, apart from isolated patches of industrialization, and the railways that had been driven across it under the Second Empire, remained very much as it had been a century earlier, administered in *départements* by prefects instead of in *généralités* by intendants. For the ordinary man the pattern of daily life, the food he ate and the way in which he ate it, his social relations, his interests, his upbringing and his formal education, had changed little; for the peasantry life had changed hardly at all.

If we ask the reason for the intense conservatism of such a politically revolutionary country as France, we must first look at its economy, its ways of earning and spending. The Second Empire, under the inspiration of the Saint-Simonians, had inaugurated a minor industrial revolution, and in particular endowed France with a railway system. This was a sign of new things stirring, like the rebuilding of Paris . . . and of Lyons . . . But it was attributable to the inspiration of Louis Napoleon himself, with a small group of advisers, and forced through against the opposition of the established powers of French society, . . . the main financial and business interests of France seemed to have a vested interest in social conservatism and economic backwardness. The powerful Bank of France, whose two hundred regents formed the central citadel of wealth, had been given the task, from its Napoleonic beginnings, of guarding against social or economic change. A stable currency, unaffected by wars or revolutions, was one proof of its success. Industry was similarly guarded against experiment or change. In the nineteenth century it was impossible to keep technical improvements out entirely, or to prevent the appearance of some large-scale enterprises. But these were exceptional, and until Napoleon III forced through, against bitter opposition, his new commercial policy, a rigid protectionism shielded French industry from competition and the compulsion of progress.

However, industrialists and financiers and commercial men were not a dominant factor in French society. Men of property and rentiers were the main constituents in the structure of the French upper classes. Their ideas were supplied to them by professional men and writers who were equally conservative in their intellectual formation. They were men of property . . . interested in the accumulation of land and houses, or the collection of government bonds, in which they had a pathetic faith, playing for safety as they thought, and content with modest gains so long as no risks were taken. Ordinary business they rather despised. England in these days was still damned, in Napoleonic phrase, as a nation of shopkeepers. . . . The French elite in the nineteenth century was an elite of bourgeois, but their aim was to be, as in the eighteenth century, "bourgeois vivant noblement."

The ideal of a stable, unchanging society seemed one that was capable of achievement at the time. The pressure which, in the eighteenth century and the earlier part of the nineteenth, produced social unrest and forced speculation about ways to remedy it, the pressure of population on a country already over-populated in relation to its productivity, had slackened. Above all, France remained rural, the masses of the nation scattered in small country towns, villages or hamlets, where a class of peasant proprietors, however lacking in worldly goods or the amenities of life they may have been themselves, were acutely conscious of their interests as property owners, intensely suspicious of anything which seemed to offer the threat of change in the pattern of French agrarian society.

Thus a revolution had laid the foundations of an intensely conservative society, nor is this difficult to understand. The classes which consolidated their victory in the Revolution were the peasant proprietors in the country and the men of property in the towns, neither with any vision beyond the preservation of their own economic interests, conceived in the narrowest and most restrictive sense. A Church devoted — apart from an occasional easily crushed rebel — to the interests of the wealthy propertied classes provided the moral justification for their wealth, and spiritual sanctions against those who would attack it. The small Huguenot minority was, if possible, even more devoted to the protection of the interests of property than the great Catholic majority. A powerful, centralized administrative structure and judicial system, recruited almost exclusively from the upper sectors of society, strengthened the defences of the existing order. If this was bourgeois society, it was an economically reactionary and backward bourgeoisie that it represented, having nothing in common with the inventors and entrepreneurs, the ruthless financiers, the cut-throat competition of the builders and makers of industrial capitalism. The society which emerged in France from the revolutionary decade and was stabilized by Napoleon, under whom the pattern was fixed which it was to keep with little change for the next three-quarters of a century, was a far more static society than the one which had entered the Revolution with such high hopes.

It was also a society torn by periodic gusts of violent and bloody political disturbance. The paradox is not in the political instability, but in the fact that this also is evidence of the conservatism of a society stuck with an unfinished revolution on its hands, one which it seemed under the compulsion to try to re-enact periodically, not because of any social necessity, but because it was now part of the national tradition, a set pattern of behaviour that had to be repeated whenever the coincidence of political and economic crises provided the appropriate stimulus. Then, while some took up the traditional revolutionary stances, others dreamed of reviving the counterrevolution. But since the balance of society remained essentially unchanged, when the smoke had cleared away and the turmoil died down, it was seen that nothing fundamental had changed. Different actors might now be in the front of the stage, but they were still performing the same play.

For this reason the revolutions of 1830, 1848, 1870, though not the frustrated revolution of 1871, each in turn gives the impression of being the result of a chapter of accidents. This is in fact what they were, but it does not mean that they were of no importance and had no effect on national history. What they did was successively to remove most of the political, and in some cases even the administrative personnel of the previous regime, sometimes only temporarily, but sometimes permanently. In addition, they destroyed the reputations and prospects of many of the leaders of revolution themselves. Seldom has a great nation been so wasteful of its elites. Regularly, generation after generation, those who had acquired political or administrative experience were thrown on the scrap-heap of a usually remunerative retirement.

What kept France going, apart from the stability of its social structure, was the rigid framework of a centralized administration, staffed in all its higher levels by the sons of the same propertied class that controlled the nation's economy. So long as their property and their jobs were safe, they were prepared to serve any regime. France has often been taken as the awful example of a country whose politics have been blighted by the curse of ideology. . . . Historically, this is the most arrant nonsense. The interplay between rational political thinking and empirical politics, which was a dominant feature of British political life for four centuries, was lacking in France. The influence of Rousseau on the French Revolution is a legend. The theocrats may have been too lunatic, and the doctrinaires too rational, but the failure of the Restoration was nothing to do with either, any more than the July Monarchy or the Second Republic were influenced by the Utopian Socialists. . . .

In nineteenth-century France political life was the expression of the most blatant materialism. France between 1799 and 1871 was a working model of the instability of a political system without moral and ideological bases. The Napoleonic Empire naturally had none; it was a war dictatorship, . . . The Restoration came to a nation which had already made many compromises with the revolutionary and Napoleonic state, and could not return to the *ancien régime*, which anyhow had already lost its intellectual justification before it met its violent end. The revolution of 1830 merely demonstrated that France could not recover an age that was lost, and that 1789 was irreversible. The raison d'être of the July Monarchy was to protect the interests of property, and when Louis-Philippe was no longer able to do so, after a brief interval Louis Napoleon took up the task. . . . The Second Empire came a little closer to grips with the problems of French society. If it had not been for the disaster of the Franco-Prussian War, the Liberal Empire might have survived and merged into a parliamentary regime not so very different from that of the Third Republic. But it could only have done this by giving some real content to the principle of the sovereignty of the people to which it paid lip service, and this meant in effect the Republic.

If the Revolution had any ideological basis it was the sovereignty of the people; and if this idea had any honest meaning (which is doubtful) it was universal suffrage. . . . In France politics and economics were curiously separated. The case for universal suffrage was argued as a political right of the individual, a sort of magical gesture. Sovereignty of the people became an incantation, a secular religion. It had its prophets, chiefly concerned with their own spiritual sanctity, its dervishes, prepared to suffer or inflict any pain in the service of the cult, and a political priesthood, anxious above all that no doctrines should be taken so seriously as to endanger vested interests.

Electoral management for a time succeeded in controlling the popular vote, but even in a restricted franchise the electorate sometimes refused to be managed, as the history of the Restoration and the July Monarchy showed. The only alternative, since the one-party state had not yet been invented, was the Bonapartist plebiscitary dictatorship. Beyond this we need not ask what Bonapartism was: it was the party of the men with property and jobs, . . . There was no Bonapartist, . . . ideology. French politics between 1815 and 1870 was a . . . model machine for the demonstration of politics as a self-sufficient activity.

The trouble is that real life will keep breaking in, disturbing the happy meaninglessness of the . . . political game, . . . Unfortunately, . . . it cannot always be kept on the level of a game. So the history of nineteenth-century France showed. There were vital issues, which politicians and *fonctionnaires* might try to ignore, but which periodically took charge of the players; . . .

The instability of French politics did not just arise out of the throw of the dice. There were real issues at stake. One of these was religion. To what extent religion in the West has ever been a cement of society is a matter of doubt. In France it certainly was not so in the century of the religious wars, or in that of the persecution and destruction of the Huguenots, or when the Jansenist controversy was bedevilling Church and state. The Revolution created a new religious schism which was dangerous because the anti-clerical minority was large and influential. The constant attempts of the Church to use the machinery of the state to recover its influence over society, to interfere in secular matters and especially to control education, built up an anti-clerical opposition, which was not conciliated by the rise of a proselytizing spirit and a militant ultramontanism which aroused national and Gallican hostility as well. Although many unbelievers in the propertied classes were prepared to accept the power of the Church as a means of keeping the lower orders in the station to which God had called them, they could not enthusiastically support clerical influence over government. They were glad enough to have their daughters brought up in purdah and general ignorance by nuns, but they wanted a better education for their sons. As for the lower orders, whom religion was supposed to be keeping in a state of proper respect, they were steadily being alienated by a Church which seemed to be devoted exclusively to the protection of the interests of the rich. After 1794, however, anti-clericalism never offered a serious threat to the Church in this period, while clericalism was never strong enough to put the clock back to the seventeenth century as it might have liked. This conflict, therefore, produced tension in society, but no dangerous cleavage as yet.

The Age of Revolutions

The class conflict, which was not unconnected with this one, was more immediately alarming. Its nature must not be misunderstood. It was not the class conflict of a modern industrial society, with organized labour waging war for improved conditions and higher wages. Only in Lyons was there, on a small scale, something like this pattern. In the country — and France remained overwhelmingly rural — the peasant proprietors, with no vision beyond their commune, were more concerned to guard their own petty privileges against the rural proletariat than to envisage anything better for themselves. As men of property they could always be called on to rally to the defence of property against the "anarchists" of Paris. Only in the capital was there a sufficiently large proletariat to offer a real threat to the established order and here it was in the form of an unorganized horde, living in depression and degradation, capable — as in 1789 — of being called out by political leaders in the interests of a change of regime, but not capable of conceiving or fighting for a programme of economic reform to better its own conditions. The Parisian populace was a threat, in fact, not to the social system, which seemed irrefrangible, but to political stability.

It is true that in this intensely conservative society ideologies proliferated. Their numbers and their wildness bore witness to their remoteness from practicality. An ineffective left-wing now acquired the tradition of irresponsibility which comes from the divorce from political power, and which the right had inherited from the frondeur aristocracy of the ancien régime; while the various parties of the centre, sunk in a squalid defence of their vested interests, squabbled, and sometimes fought, for power and places and the rewards that went with them.

The picture is a depressing one, of a society which had forgotten most of the ideals inherited from the age of the Enlightenment and the earlier days of the Revolution and from which all who held to these, or to newer ideals, felt themselves alienated. Despairing of political and economic life, finding little solace in religion, they turned to art and literature and inaugurated the tradition of a divorce between these and society, the mutual contempt of the artist and the bourgeois. Instead of a mirror in which were reflected the highest values of contemporary civilization, the arts in France became a protest against a society which rejected them and which they rejected. Victor Hugo with the victims of justice and property in Les Misérables, Daumier in his drawings of the Orleanist bourgeoisie — lawyers and men of affairs, with greed, envy, malice and all uncharitableness written in their countenances, Flaubert and the empty life of the Paris rentier or the provincial lady of fashion, Courbet painting the cold, pinched faces of poverty or the leer of success in Church and state — in these there was conscious social comment; in Gautier and others a turning away from contemporary society to art for art's sake, a rejection of bourgeois values, of the moral and religious phrases that provided the alibi for unfeeling hearts, and of the repetition of stereotypes that was a substitute for thought in obtuse heads. To those who could not accept gross and philistine standards the life of the rich was a spiritual void and that of the poor a material hell. In a sordid cult of dirt, drugs, and debauchery, the artist sought an artificial paradise, which yet in a Baudelaire could reach to the heights of poetry.

The vie de Bohème was a conscious protest against bourgeois values, but it was a pathetically unavailing protest. The aristocracy and bourgeoisie of the eighteenth century had kissed the rods that chastised them: Montesquieu, Voltaire, Rousseau, the Encyclopedists were their idols. Orleanists and Bonapartists just ignored their critics. The age enclosed by the two Napoleons, looked at from the point of view of the high hopes of the Enlightenment and 1789, is bound to seem disappointing and disillusioning. The achievements of the Frenchmen of that age were unimpressive even to themselves, and they remain unimpressive in retrospect. The exciting new developments of the nineteenth century passed France by. In an age of change the French nation appeared to have chosen stagnation without stability. The more the kaleidoscope of its politics changed, the more France remained the same.

Yet, looking forward, it will be seen that this could not have been the whole story. The First Republic succeeded to a great age of reform, and sadly misused its heritage. The Third Republic was to come into a much less promising inheritance and great things were to be made of it. But if this can be said, then there must be a different way from that which I have adopted of summing up the France of the monarchies and the empires. Under the frozen surface of sterile egoism we should detect the early shoots of the creative achievements of the Third Republic. These beginnings have been passed over slightly or not mentioned in this volume. They can be brought in more appropriately later, when they were coming to fruition. For the moment, in 1871, there was little enough evidence of a more hopeful future. It was the end of an unattractive chapter in the history of France. It was not the end of the whole story.

GEORGES LEFEBVRE

REVOLUTION IN ITS WORLD CONTEXT

Georges Lefebvre (1874–1959) was undoubtedly the most admired and respected historian of the French Revolution of the last two generations. Born in the north of France in 1874, he established his scholarly reputation in 1924 with his pioneering doctoral dissertation on the peasants of the French department of the Nord. This was based on twenty years of archival research and inaugurated that study of the Revolution at the "grass roots level" which has been continued, as has been noted earlier, by his students. Lefebvre's enormous erudition, his amazing productivity, his warm personality, his varied interests, and his broad point of view and tolerance of the views of others marked him for a position of leadership among the scholars in his field. After the premature death in 1932 of Albert Mathiez, Lefebvre became the president of the Société des Etudes Robespierristes and Managing Editor of the *Annales historiques de la Révolution française*; five years later he succeeded Philippe Sagnac in the Chair of the History of the French Revolution at the Sorbonne. The author of enumerable monographs, documentary studies, source collections, articles, and reviews, Lefebvre was best known to the international public by his magisterial one-volume treatments in the *Peuples et Civilisation* series on the French Revolution (1951), and on Napoleon (1935).

On the eve of the French Revolution, almost all of Europe was governed by what we now call the *ancien régime*. The prince enjoyed absolute power. The Church looked upon him as God's viceroy and in return he upheld the Church's authority by imposing his religion on his subjects. He had cast aside the concept of natural law, originating with the Stoics and developed during the Middle Ages by theologians like Thomas Aquinas, which assumed a society founded on free contract between governor and governed. Indeed, power had then been conceived only in terms of community welfare and was justified as a guarantee of the inviolable and legitimate rights of the individual.

To achieve absolute power, the prince had undermined seignorial authority and the political authority of the clergy, though allowing them to retain their social preeminence. In becoming subjects, the nobility and the clergy kept their privileges; the king, himself anointed and first gentleman of his realm, did not intend to submerge these orders in the masses. The Old Regime was indeed aristocratic in its structure.

There was a third feature characteristic of France and some other states. In these countries, while the prince had created a territorial and administrative framework, he had not carried this process to its logical conclusion. National unification was therefore incomplete, not only because of the diversity of legal systems, weights and measures, and the customs barriers which impeded the emergence of a national market, but also because the prince had

From Georges Lefebvre, "The French Revolution in the context of World History," *Annales: Économies, Sociétés, Civilisations*, III (1948), pp. 257–66. Translated by Peter Amann in *The Eighteenth Century Revolution: French or Western* (Boston: D. C. Heath, 1963), pp. 83–91. Reprinted by permission of *Annales* and the translator.

granted or [   ] special privileges to provinces and cities. In a dition, he granted similar advantages to groupings, usually organized along professional lines, such as the nobility and clergy, so that society was hierarchical and partly "corporative." These estates implied privilege and therefore inequality. Absolutism, relying on "divide and rule," personified inequality . . . and besides, each estate, united by privilege and jealous of its superiority, demanded submission from those lower in the social scale. Nonetheless, the nation, created by submission to a single leader, by ties of material progress, language, and culture, remained divided territorially and socially. Even so, the French were better off than other nations: elsewhere the state, viewed as the personal property of the prince, took no account of national minorities, many of which were scattered among rival or enemy powers.

This regime faced two internal problems that were both political and social. The aristocracy (in other words, the nobility, since the clergy lacked social unity) resented the political impotence to which it had been reduced by the monarch whose power it dreamed of sharing. The nobleman, himself occasionally a victim of despotism, yearned for a freedom consonant with his dignity. This problem was a legacy from the past.

The other problem looked to the future. Ever since the tenth century there had developed a new class based on commerce, industry, finance, on personal rather than on landed property. This new bourgeois class had emerged from the Third Estate in a society in which land, as sole instrument of production, had entitled its owner to seignorial authority over those who farmed for a living. The king had drawn on these bourgeois both for money and officials, and they came to enjoy not only wealth but education and culture as well. Since the Renaissance, moreover, the new rationalism, exemplified by recent empirical science, provided an intellectual orientation consonant with bourgeois interests. Capitalism, which in its beginning phase had enjoyed mercantilistic state patronage, spread beyond the bounds of commerce to industry. The introduction of machinery opened such unlimited horizons for the bourgeoisie that the profits enticed even aristocrats to join in the exploitation of the world.

The bourgeoisie sought to obtain some share of power and therefore was willing to ally itself with the aristocracy against the king, yet bourgeoisie and aristocracy also were in opposition to each other. For centuries the middle class had striven for nobility; though this objective had not been altogether abandoned, the aristocracy was becoming more exclusive at the very time that the middle class, greatly increased in numbers, could no longer hope for mass ennoblement. The bourgeois, therefore, went beyond the nobles' demand for power and freedom to claim the end of all privileges as well as equality before the law.

At the end of the eighteenth century, because of the unequal pace of economic development, these problems appeared in a different guise in the various parts of Europe. Central and eastern Europe, which had long been backward by west European standards, did not partake in the new maritime trade routes and the exploitation of the New World which the great discoveries of the fifteenth and sixteenth centuries had opened up. The gap between East and West thus tended to widen. In this eastern and central European area newly-formed large states had adopted mercantilist policies and relied on the bourgeoisie for economic development and political organization. These states practiced what has been called "enlightened despotism." The mercantile middle class was, however, small in numbers, and the Enlightenment had more substantial influence on government officials, professors and writers. The prince also confronted a threatening aristocracy. In Poland this nobility had seized power, while in Sweden only the *coup d'etat* of Gustavus III had prevented a similar eventuality. In Hungary and Belgium the aristocracy had fought Joseph II to a standstill. In Prussia and Russia the monarchy had compromised, the aristocracy trading obedience and submission to the ruler for a free hand in dealing with their peasants whose serfdom, as one moved east, approached slavery.

In the countries of the south, particularly in the Iberian peninsula, the Counter Reformation had impeded free intellectual development. While Italy had been bypassed by the great overseas discoveries, Spain, in any case poorly endowed by nature, had been ruined by war. The nobility was somnolent, while the bourgeoisie grew only slowly. The peasant, as in France, did enjoy royal protection.

The maritime nations, Holland, England and a newcomer, the United States, offered a striking contrast to these land-based states. All of the former were Protestant. Holland and England had been the greatest beneficiaries of the rise of the European economy since the sixteenth century. In Holland the bourgeoisie was in control of the republic despite the nobility's support of the monarchist ambitions of the House of Orange. Since in this struggle neither constitutionalism nor liberty was at stake, it may be argued that a compromise between these three forces had either been reached already or was at least within sight.

While Holland had long been regarded as enjoying the greatest degree of freedom, the fame of the English and American revolutions, Britain's power and brilliant intellectual contribution made the Anglo-Saxon countries favorite antitheses to the absolutist regimes.

In England an aristocracy that enjoyed few privileges and no exemption from taxes differed markedly from its counterpart on the continent. Above all, only the lords formed a distinct legal estate, yet even their prerogatives were passed on to their eldest sons only. The younger children were commoners on a level with the gentry and squires who were represented in the House of Commons. The lords themselves could scarcely trace their genealogy beyond the Tudor era, since the nobility had been decimated by the massacres of the Wars of the Roses; hence they were not far removed from their middle class origins. Above all, however, since England was an island, the military character of the nobility had become attenuated or had disappeared altogether, to the point where military service was merely a matter of personal inclination. Consequently nothing stood in the way of the nobleman, even of the peer, going into business, and the distinction between the upper middle class and nobility was only a matter of ancestry and the kind of prestigious distinctions which were even within reach of the bourgeoisie. Nowhere else was there such social mobility: money alone defined class lines. The maritime and colonial expansion had consolidated a community of interest between the aristocracy and the capitalist middle classes. The Reformation, by sanctifying the struggle for naval and world supremacy waged against Spain and France, had heightened this solidarity. After the Catholic and Francophile Stuarts had, in the course of the seventeenth century, succeeded in rousing the whole nation against themselves, two revolutions had insured the final defeat of royal despotism. Yet neither the aristocracy nor the upper middle classes had directed their alliance against the monarchy as such. The Revolution of

1688 was a compromise establishing constitutional government which balanced king, lords, and a combination of gentry and middle class in the House of Commons. The latter was elected by a limited franchise which by its very lack of system insured the absolute control of the wealthy.

History was a source of precedents to be used against royal despotism. More than once the aristocracy had succeeded in extracting concessions from a monarchy that had appeared all-powerful since the Norman conquest, the most famous of these concessions being Magna Carta. English liberties were founded on such precedents and customs, in short, on tradition rather than on philosophical speculation. Even so, natural law had not been forgotten. It inspired Locke's justification of the Revolution of 1688. The importance of his works, which served as bible of all the continental *philosophes* of the eighteenth century, can hardly be exaggerated. However, once the Whig oligarchy had gained power, it gradually abandoned Locke as its intellectual mentor, since the contract theory, the recourse to natural right, could also justify democratic movements which loomed on the horizon threatening its power. On the eve of the French Revolution, Burke agreed with George III in considering the British constitution to be the most perfect imaginable. For Burke the constitution recognized not the rights of man but the rights of Englishmen: only the English had been able to conquer these liberties and they alone had clear title to them.

Not only did English liberty make no claim to universality, but the English state itself did not grant complete freedom of thought. Even though, like Holland, England enjoyed broader toleration than Catholic countries, the state religion was maintained. More important, equality before the law had never become a fighting issue. Because the aristocracy was allied with wealth, the upper middle class had never had to appeal to this equality. Political freedom had never undermined a determination to maintain the existing social hierarchy.

Anglo-Saxon America did not have to become quite so empirically minded. Natural right remained a vital force in these Puritan communities that had left Europe to escape, not only religious intolerance, but the weight of despotism and of aristocratic society. In breaking with the home country, the colonists appealed to natural right to justify their secession, while their declarations proclaimed the rights of man, not merely the rights of Americans. Their public law reflected this universality of natural law. At the same time the Protestant sects sought to safeguard their independence by insisting on religious liberty. There were, however, notable limitations: no one claimed any rights for colored men, and slaves remained slaves. Freedom of thought was not the rule and even though state and church were separated, it was taken for granted that religious liberty was confined to Christians. As in England, there was no insistence on equality. As the United States had never had peers or privileged persons the issue of privilege had never divided gentlemen and rich bourgeoisie. There were gentlemen descended from the British gentry who, living as noblemen on their plantations in Virginia and other Southern colonies, ruled over their enslaved blacks. Among these were the men who, like Washington, led the War of Independence and governed the republic during the first decades of its existence. However, men of a very different social background, such as Jefferson, had also become planters. Nothing prevented a Benjamin Franklin, printer turned merchant and journalist, from taking his place on the outer fringe of the ruling elite. Equality before the law for all whites, irrelevant as an issue in the struggle against Great Britain, had thus never been raised, nor was it ever considered a challenge to a social hierarchy based on wealth. Actually this equality before the law did not extend to politics, since the state constitutions restricted the franchise. What was called "democracy" in France during the first months of the Revolution was a government belonging not to the ruler or the aristocracy but to the nation. The actual procedures allowed, however, for the dominance of the moneyed class.

The English and American examples exercised a profound influence as the birthplaces of freedom. America, moreover, had stressed the universal validity of natural right. In practice this equality of rights, however admitted in principle, was not wholly applied, and in any case was not the basis for these revolutions. It is understandable that the example of these countries should have swayed not only the middle classes but also the continental aristocracy opposing royal power. For both, liberty seemed the pertinent catchword. Since equality had not been one of the consequences of these revolutions, it did not occur to the continental aristocracy that liberty might endanger its social predominance.

The Anglo-Saxon revolutions had been directed against absolutism in behalf of a bourgeois-aristocratic alliance. The French Revolution was to be a very different affair.

From the socioeconomic as well as the geographical point of view our country occupied an intermediate position in Europe. Just as in other continental states, intermittent warfare had helped the nobility to preserve its military character. The very fact that this nobility faced impoverishment only increased its exclusiveness and its tendency to become a closed caste. Yet as a maritime nation France had also participated in European colonial expansion: its commerce was second only to that of Great Britain, while its industrial capitalism, though backward in comparison to the latter, nonetheless enjoyed the most advanced development on the continent. The French bourgeoisie, though closer to the land than the English middle class, was infinitely larger and more influential than that of any other continental monarchy. Perhaps most peculiar to French society was the important role played by saleable offices. The king had tapped middle class wealth by putting many official positions on the auction block. In order to increase their saleability or to gain the support of the officeholders, the king had endowed some of these positions not only with corporate privileges but even with personal or hereditary nobility. Just as in England, the infiltration of bourgeois families meant a renewal of the aristocracy. By the eighteenth century few nobles could produce a genealogy going back to the Crusades. This new nobility of the robe was establishing an increasingly intimate relationship to the military nobility. Nonetheless the nobility of the robe was not only businesslike in the management of its own affairs, but also kept up contact with other officeholders who had not graduated to the nobility. It also maintained ties with a socially less prestigious group, namely the lawyers. An intermediate class had thus developed which included these nobles at the top with officeholders in the middle, and commoners at the bottom. As a result of common professional outlook it shared the concept of law, of a legal order, of a monarchy whose prerogatives were limited by the sovereign courts' privilege of registration and remonstrance. Within this class a quite Cartesian rationalism and a tradition of the monarchy governing in cooperation with the wellborn and the well-to-do found special favor. Locke's ideas of natural right had fallen on fertile ground. In this respect, too, France occupied an intermediate position. While the absolute monarchy did cooperate with the Church in thought control, in contrast to Spain, Italy and Belgium, the Counter Reformation had not succeeded in stifling the development of philosophy and scientific inquiry. Finally, the French king had not had to yield power to the nobles; unlike England where a dominant aristocracy had uprooted the peasantry by enforcing enclosure, the majority of France's peasants were for all practical purposes free landowners.

Down to the time of the Fronde, the French nobility had often countered royal power with armed resistance. Even at that time the judicial officeholders had shown that they too could resist the monarch's authority. This reappeared once the hiatus imposed by Louis XIV was over, although its nature had altered as society had evolved. By the eighteenth century, armed outbreaks had become obsolete: the sovereign courts relied instead on a bourgeois appeal to public opinion, to constitutional tradition, to natural right. At the same time the aristocratically-dominated provincial estates played an increasingly important administrative role, particularly in Languedoc and Brittany. The office of intendant was preempted by nobles, as were the bishoprics. Commoners, already excluded from the sovereign courts, in 1781 were barred from becoming professional officers, though they could still be promoted from the ranks. Aristocratic theorists, among whom Boulainvilliers and Montesquieu stood out, justified seignorial power by claiming that the aristocracy was descended from the Germanic conquerors of Gaul. Peasants complained over what historians have called the "feudal reaction," namely the increasingly exacting collection of manorial dues. It is clear, in any case, that some great land proprietors benefited from royal ordinances permitting them to enclose land and to divide the commons. It is customary to concentrate on the eighteenth century growth of the bourgeoisie and the rise of the Enlightenment which reflected its aspirations. This period, however, was equally notable for the growing influence of the aristocracy, who attacked royal authority and successfully resisted all reform attempts that would have undermined their privileges, particularly exemption from taxation.

The French Revolution, in its first phase a revolution of the nobles, represented the climax of this rebirth of aristocratic opposition. By September 1788 when Louis XVI had been forced to call the Estates General, an aristocratic triumph seemed in sight. If, as anticipated, the Estates were to meet in three separate orders with the clergy dominated by the aristo-

cratic episcopate, the nobility would be in control. This nobility was willing to help the king bring order out of financial chaos, but only at the price of certain concessions.

What were these concessions? The aristocrats demanded what they called liberty, that is, a constitutional government relying on regular meetings of an Estates General dominated by the nobility. In the provinces they would displace the intendant.

The nobility had no inkling that it was undermining the bulwark of its own privileges by weakening royal power. The nobility did not foresee that once the Estates had been called, the bourgeoisie would find its voice. Much as in England, the price of their cooperation was likely to be equality of rights. When this price was demanded the French nobility refused to make this concession. As a result the Estates General, intended as a battering ram against royal authority, saw the nobility thrown back on the defensive. A second phase of the Revolution had begun — the bourgeois revolution.

When Louis XVI accepted both freedom and constitutional government on June 23, 1789, some of the national objectives seemed to have been met. When, however, he threw his support to the nobility and clergy, this was tantamount to rejecting equality which henceforth became the crux of the struggle.

Actually the king, by means of his army, seemed capable of ending the conflict on his own terms. The artisans and peasants, however, whose own interest was unmistakable, supported the bourgeoisie. The popular and peasant revolutions, culminating in the night of August 4, broke the power both of the monarchy and the nobility. Unlike the bourgeoisie which had not aimed for the ruin of the aristocracy, the popular revolution wiped the slate clean and soon completed the social revolution by nationalizing church property.

In practice the consequences of this social revolution were not carried to their logical conclusion in 1789. A part of the manorial dues had to be redeemed; the Catholic clergy retained its monopoly of public religious services, its state financial support, its control of marriage, education and welfare work. When the aristocracy and the monarchy looked abroad for support, civil war broke out. This civil war persuaded some of the middle classes to throw in their lot with the lower classes to complete the destruction of the aristocracy by confiscating the *emigrés'* property and by seeking to crush the clergy's influence. In these circumstances the revolution turned democratic: it adopted manhood suffrage, proclaimed a republic, freed the slaves, separated State from Church, and secularized education, welfare and personal status.

This is the way in which the French Revolution gained its distinctive place in the history of the world. Although the revolution appealed to natural law (as the American Revolution had also done), its achievements left a universal imprint quite alien to British liberty. Its sheer momentum, moreover, was much greater. Not only did the revolution establish a republic but it insisted on manhood suffrage. Freedom for whites was not enough: the slaves were freed. Not content with toleration, the revolution admitted Protestants and Jews to full citizenship and, by secularizing personal status, recognized the individual's right not to belong to any religion.

All this, however, was secondary to the real mission of the revolution which was to be the revolution of equality. While in England and America the alliance of aristocracy and upper middle class had precluded a stress on civil equality, in France the bourgeoisie had been forced to emphasize it by the unbending attitude of the nobility. Indeed, by abolishing manorial rights, the peasants initiated equality with a vengeance. Since by revolutionary definition liberty was tantamount to obedience to lawful authority alone, liberty and equality were complementary in that liberty by itself would lead to privilege for the few.

In gaining freedom and equality, the French had become the Nation One and Indivisible. This new interpretation of national sovereignty is a third outstanding characteristic of the revolution from which grew France's claim that nations, like individuals, should be liberated. Thus France claimed Alsace, Avignon and Corsica by appealing to free consent rather than to conventional treaties between rulers. International law was being revolutionized just as internal civil law had been. In this early phase the revolution looked forward to peace and cooperation among free nations united by the ideal of a society of nations, even of a universal Republic.

These characteristics explain the French Revolution's impact on the world and its long-range significance. At the same time, although these principles have since registered gains, it would be a mistake to attribute their dissemination solely to the revolution. The example of England and the United States had certainly not been forgotten. It would be equally false — and this is a widespread idea — to credit this ideological expansion solely to the magnetism of ideas: in areas adjoining France, the *ancien régime* fell victim mainly to the revolutionary armies led by Napoleon. Since that time capitalism has become the chief vehicle by which these new principles have conquered the world. These principles, as historians have sought to show during the last several decades, reflected the interests of the middle class who championed them. In granting economic freedom, abolishing serfdom, freeing the land from the burden of tithe and manorial dues, bringing church property back into the dynamic channels of the economy, the bourgeoisie was paving the way for capitalism. Wherever capitalism has penetrated — and thanks to its inner dynamic it has become ubiquitous — the same kinds of transformations have occurred. By strengthening or creating a middle class, capitalism has helped the triumph of liberty and civil equality as well as the development of nationalism, in our own day even among colonial peoples once dominated by the white man.

Nonetheless the French Revolution has retained an emotional drawing power unrelated to any selfish interest. It is associated with popular insurrection symbolized by the storming of the Bastille and the wars of liberation which the *Marseillaise* commemorates. This is the work of those who died for the revolution. To ignore the influence of class interests and economics on a movement of ideas would be a mutilated history. To forget that the bourgeoisie was convinced that its rise was identified with justice and the welfare of all mankind would be no less of a distortion. The fighters of July 14 and August 10, the soldiers of Valmy, Jemmapes and Fleurus risked their lives not from self-interest but because they enthusiastically embraced a universal cause.

Nonetheless this equality of rights, this essential principle of the French Revolution by which the bourgeoisie of 1789 rationalized the abolition of aristocratic privilege based on birth, had some unexpected consequences. The middle class, confident in its ability, power and prospect, had ignored the ill-tempered warnings of its opponents in this respect.

For this middle class, as for the Anglo-Saxons,

equality meant equality of opportunity. Although everyone was free to take advantage of these opportunities, obviously not everyone had the requisite ability. What significance could freedom of the press or free access to public office have for someone who was illiterate? Yet public instruction was contingent upon being well-off if not actually wealthy. The bourgeoisie of 1789 interpreted the right to vote and to be elected in a similar spirit. This right, like others, required certain prerequisites, in this case the payment of a given amount of taxes as evidence of a certain standard of economic independence. Thus the rights of man and of the citizen, formulated by the bourgeoisie, were to remain largely academic and theoretical. There was little doubt, and none after Thermidor, that in the eyes of the middle class only property owners were entitled to actual, as against theoretical, power. Property being hereditary meant that privilege due to birth had not, as counterrevolutionaries observed, been eliminated after all. Democrats were soon to point out that private ownership of the means of production led to the subjection of the wage earners. Private property in workshops, the sole source of employment, made illusory the rights of the propertyless.

The lower classes, aware of these implications, had always opposed economic freedom which led to capitalism and the triumph of big business. Their ideal was a nation of peasant proprietors and independent artisans. In any case they sought state protection for the wage earner from the omnipotence of the rich. In order to gain power and organize the defense of the revolution after August 10, 1792, the republican bourgeoisie had accepted universal suffrage and continued its alliance with the so-called "sans-culottes." This alliance resulted in a compromise between the middle class aspirations of 1789 and the masses who called for government intervention to secure a more widespread distribution of property, public education for all, economic controls to keep prices and wages in balance, and a minimum social security system. This policy of "social democracy," initiated by the Mountain during the Year II, horrified and frightened the bourgeoisie and seemed to be banished forever after 9 Thermi-

dor. When, however, republicanism reappeared after 1830, some of its followers took up Montagnard principles. With the re-establishment of universal suffrage in 1848, the application of these principles became one of the facts of political life.

Even during the revolutionary period, however, some groups had gone even farther by calling for the abolition of the private ownership of the means of production and the creation of a communist democracy intended to fulfill the promise of equality. This same intention has, in the final analysis, also made socialist theoreticians, particularly in France, present their systems as the completion of the French revolutionary achievements left unfinished by the middle classes. This is not to claim that the tradition of the French Revolution is the sole element in this development. Religious and humanitarian feelings have also been instrumental in aiding social progress. Above all, the transformation of the economy has had a powerful influence on the broad extension of equality of rights. The victories of capitalism led to trade union and political organization of the proletariat made possible by the concentration of business and labor, which defined and accelerated the class struggle. These organized elements could not be ignored. At the same time, the phenomenal productive growth engendered by capitalism, by increasing the resources available to human society, has brought a variety of welfare services, such as education and social security, within the realm of feasibility, whereas during and long after the revolution the cost of such services relegated them to Utopia.

Leaving aside differing approaches to history, the fundamental problem of our contemporary world appears to be the problem of equality within each nation and equality among nations. It is not the historian's job to prophesy how mankind will resolve such a problem; yet the historian can attest that the French Revolution not only raised this issue but also indicated various directions in which a solution might be sought. One may conclude, therefore, that, admired or loathed, the name of the French Revolution will long remain on men's lips.

3

THE VARIETIES OF NATIONALISM

For the last century or more, nationalism has been one of the basic forces molding the history of the world. It is characterized by great complexity, because it has evolved its forms and its consequences over the generations, according to varying historical circumstances. While its implications and meaning are still debated by scholars, nationalism may be defined as "a state of mind in which the supreme loyalty of the individual is felt to be due to the nation-state" in which "the most essential element is a living and active corporate will" (Hans Kohn).

Although English nationalism apparently began in the seventeenth century, the first great manifestations of nationalism have been associated with the late eighteenth-century revolutions, and the wars which accompanied them, which have been discussed in the first two problems. During the period 1770–1871, it was believed by an ever-increasing number of people that the nation-state was the best means for assuring the individual of freedom and social justice at home and of guaranteeing world peace and cooperation abroad. In our own time, now that nationalism is being manifested in Africa and Asia as well as in Central and Eastern Europe, it is not at all certain that the "liberation" of peoples and the establishment of new nation-states inevitably guarantees individual freedom and equal rights.

In the selections which follow, we have tried to show characteristic examples of some of the varieties of nationalism which appeared between 1770 and 1870. As an example of "cultural nationalism," the quotation from J. G. Herder, who developed the idea of the folk-soul or folk-spirit (*Volksgeist*) rooted in primitive national cultural traditions, has been included. While Herder did not call for the creation of a nation-state, and hence was not a nationalist in the strict sense of the Kohn definition quoted, he did emphasize German cultural nationalism as a moral and spiritual concept. Students should compare Herder's abhorrence of Prussian militarism and the type of German nationalism which triumphed with Bismarck with the sentiments expressed in the Baumgarten essay in the Liberalism Problem. Herder had an immense influence on later, more sinister, aspects of German nationalism. He was also enormously influential with the awakening Slavic peoples in the late eighteenth and early nineteenth centuries, who sought national identity through exploring their *folk* traditions and developing their national literatures.

Historians generally agree that the first major expression of modern nationalism was the French Revolution and the wars (1792–1815) which accompanied it. Certainly the French adopted the doctrine of self-determination of nationalities, which later became part of the Liberal creed, national festivals, a national flag (the blue-white-red tricolor), a national anthem ("La Marseillaise"), national systems of civic and other education, and pride in the French fatherland *(la patrie)*. The

Italians, Belgians, and other neighbors of the French developed similar nationalist symbols and concepts. Even where French "liberation" met with counterrevolutionary and hostile movements, there are instances of nationalism as a negative response to the abhorred French example, as in the Russian "Great Patriotic War" of 1812, the German "War of Liberation" in 1813, The Peninsular War in Spain, 1808–14, and elsewhere. As a not untypical instance of French revolutionary patriotism, we have included a speech by Bertrand Barère.

Romanticism touched and colored nationalism, not only in the Germanies, in Poland, in Russia, and in France, but in Italy as well, as is shown by the selection from Mazzini, the apostle of Italian national spirit and expansion. Mazzini's "Young Italy" movement, founded in 1831, inspired similar secret revolutionary movements among Polish, German, and other political émigrés in Switzerland. Mazzini tried to organize these diverse movements into an association, "Young Europe," which would lead to fraternal organizations of peoples and to international peace. As with many other romantic nationalists, Mazzini was a democrat who hoped to mobilize the popular masses, including the peasantry, in his new religion of the fatherland.

The revolutions of 1848, particularly those in Italy and in Central Europe, were inspired in large measure by nationalism (as well as by liberalism), but the clash of rival national aspirations helped the monarchs to regain control of their former subjects. Undoubtedly Lord Acton, an acute aristocratic observer of European history and institutions, saw many of the weaknesses and dangers of nationalism with great clarity. The student should note that he was writing in 1862, so Europe had not yet experienced the Bismarckian revolution of 1866. The reading of Lord Acton's critique of nationalism in the light of Baumgarten's essay on German liberalism, which is so intimately tied up with German national aspirations, is extremely interesting and significant.

No one selection of various documents by European nationalists, 1770–1870, can illustrate and illuminate all of the complexities and varieties of nationalism, but those presented here may serve as a point of departure for further study.

J. G. VON HERDER

GERMAN CULTURAL NATIONALISM

The social philosopher and historian, Johann Gottfried von Herder (1744–1803), was one of the truly seminal minds in the intellectual history of Germany. He was not only a precursor of Romanticism, but he also provided a conceptual framework for the political philosophy of German nationalism. Herder's variety of nationalism was cultural. It was based on the notion that the human race is a unit in which all nations can live together in harmony for the common good of humanity. His nascent brand of nationalism stressed the concept of national character and of national individuality and can be described as "cultural" or "humanitarian nationalism."

He tried to awaken and to strengthen national feeling in Germany through the creation of a patriotic academy, whose purpose was to foster a national consciousness and to stimulate a common spirit. This plan was prepared at the request of Carl Friedrich, Duke of Baden, in the year 1788. Carl Friedrich was a German patriot who longed to see Germany become a political unity. He was one of the earliest and strongest advocates of the notion of a league of princes, which would create a politically unified Germany. He believed that a society of scholars would contribute greatly toward the spiritual unification of the German people. Therefore he asked Herder, as the person whom he believed was most qualified for the task, to draw up a plan for his proposed academy. Before it could be put into effect, the French Revolution broke out, and the plan remained a dream. The selection which follows was published shortly after Herder's death in 1803.

Herder demonstrated a fervent national feeling which was almost unique in eighteenth-century Germany. The gospel of nationality which he preached proved to be a major driving force in the closing years of the eighteenth century and throughout the nineteenth century, in Germany and elsewhere. Since "Germany" still fragmented into 360 odd states, did not yet possess economic or political foundations for national unity, Herder tried to make the Germans conscious of their cultural bonds and to realize a spiritual unity. "In a word, Herder formulated the idea of German nationalism."

From the time when Germany was the tilting-ground for the tribes and nomadic peoples, through the centuries during which the different territories and provinces fought, worked and invented, to the present time, our fatherland was a political body which did not always know its own powers and therefore could not use them for a common end with any degree of constancy. On the contrary, it often employed them for purposes harmful to itself. In the present state of our organization all efforts are laudable which spread light, but especially those which seek to unite the light so that it may become a common flame. All efforts therefore which tend to aid the different peoples and provinces of Germany in knowing and in understanding one another more intimately, and which aim to assist in uniting all to work for the common welfare so that one law of reason and fairness may reign and blind partisanship be enfeebled, will render immortal service to the whole nationality. It should be the earnest concern of every sovereign and his country to put an end to the unfriendly relations of the German provinces. It must be of importance to them that whoever lives in Germany should belong to Germany and should speak and write a pure German.

Our language, whether it be considered as a learned or a political tool, deserves a center of union for the different provinces which might become the center for the development of this indispensable tool. Our nationality can boast that since the most ancient times of which we know its language has remained unmixed with others, just as our people were not conquered by any other national group and in their wanderings carried their language into different parts of Europe. Hence it is just that this language

From Johann Gottfried Herder, "Plan for the First Patriotic Institute to Foster a Common Spirit in Germany", trans. by Robert R. Ergang in his *Herder and the Foundations of German Nationalism*. (New York, 1931), pp. 129–33. Reprinted by permission of Columbia University Press.

German Cultural Nationalism

not only be preserved as long as the nationality exists but that it also be clarified and strengthened just as the organization of the national group is strengthened. A purified language, regulated by definite rules, contributes incredibly much toward a set mode of thought. History shows that all the ruling peoples of the different periods of world history have ruled not with arms, but especially with reason, art and a highly developed language, often for thousands of years; nay, even after their political power had passed, the highly developed tool of their thoughts and organization remained as an example and sanctum for others. The Greek, Latin and Arabic languages are examples of this in the ancient and middle period; in the modern period, first the Spanish, then the French language have proved what advantages, nay what a secret superiority a nationality whose language has become a dominant one may attain. Just it is, therefore, that the German language be the prevailing one at least within the confines of the nationality, that the German sovereigns understand it, speak it correctly and love it, that the German nobility and every cultured social group, spurred on by their example, endeavor to give it the elasticity and elegance which distinguishes the French language. This will come to pass when our purest book language seeks to become ever more the language of polite society and of every public discourse. To the present it has been far removed from such common use. It is a known fact that our book language, taken in the best sense of the word, is spoken hardly anywhere. Since the taste of our fatherland is anything but established and certain, every person of culture must welcome the establishment of a public institution which, without despotism, would promote the welfare of our fatherland. The exaggerated imitation of other nationalities of which we are accused would then be curbed and transformed into emulation which, with the united support of all, must produce good results.

These and other causes have moved several sovereigns of Germany to reflect upon the idea of establishing and supporting a German academy in which some and perhaps all of the German provinces are to be represented. Our immortal Leibniz already attempted to establish German academies in different provinces and then to unite them. In Berlin he was successful; but the state of affairs at that time and finally his death thwarted the completion of the venture. Since that time diverse academies have been established in various provinces, but there is a great need for a place where the diverse and scattered efforts of the academies can be united for the common welfare. The academy will concern itself with anything that aims to effect this. All petty partisanship, every disdain of other provinces and religions will be rigorously excluded; for everyone who lives in Germany will and must work and think for Germany. No divided political interest of the sovereigns or of the classes shall knowingly disturb the peace of its circle, the clarity of its judgment or the zeal of its efforts; for Germany has but one interest, the life and happiness of all Germans.

Several lines of endeavor would be:

1. Language. The members of the academy will not only endeavor in their writings to give examples of the purity, strength and that unaffected simplicity which are most becoming to the character of our nationality; but they will also, each in his province, name and denote with due honor the writings which bear this stamp. The academy hopes thereby, and especially through its common efforts, to promote the dissemination of these writings. With the greatest care it will avoid all despotic laws concerning language; and it will sedulously endeavor, through observations, suggestions and critical rules, gradually to provide that security which in comparison with other languages it sadly lacks. The academy will attach importance to everything that belongs to the history of the language, to its development in the different provinces, its grammar, its style and its dictionaries, and it will consider no product of the German mind and industry, be it poetry or prose, translation or original work, unworthy of its attention.

2. History of Germany. Although the learned men of our fatherland have applied much diligence to the elucidation of individual points and periods of German history, it is a matter of common opinion that, disregarding several of the important newer works, we are far behind our neighbors in the study of the history of the individual provinces as well as the general history of Germany, at least in the fact that the patriotic study of this history is far from being a common interest of this nationality. And yet this study is indispensable for the creation of a common spirit. The superb examples of the writers who have prepared studies of the history of provinces and also portions of the general history of Germany permit us to hope that the missing parts will soon be supplied and the whole can be brought to an irreproachable perfection as soon as the public of the whole fatherland turns its eyes upon it. Compared with other

The Age of Revolutions

national groups we may appear tardy, but we are better prepared and more thoroughly tested. The auxiliary sciences of history, the antiquities, natural history, geography, legislation and political philosophy of the different periods have already been elaborated in part. With its eyes fixed upon the patriotic history of the entire fatherland, the academy will endeavor to promote further development of the auxiliary sciences. The more unpartisan the spirit in which this work is done, the more it will contribute toward the extirpation of the sectional spirit.

3. Everything that belongs to the active philosophy of national development and national happiness will be the ultimate and highest purpose of the academy; and nothing which might in any way contribute thereto will be excluded. Every clear truth which decreases or puts an end to ruling prejudices and bad habits; every practical attempt and suggestion for the improvement of the education of the rulers, the nobility, the peasants and the burghers; improvements in all public institutions in allotting justice, in the mutual relations of the classes, in the organization of churches and schools, in a rational political economy and human political wisdom, will become matters for consideration, deliberation and practical knowledge in the academy. It cannot be denied that in our fatherland prejudices and follies hold sway which in the neighboring lands are openly recognized as such. It cannot be denied that the division into many states, sects and religions has retarded the development of human reason in general, of the common prudence and reasonableness whose principles have long been the moral and political calculus in other countries. The members from the different provinces will at each meeting present an accurate report concerning the efforts of each province in behalf of the common welfare. The strong will inspire the weak, the experienced will teach the well-meaning and the different provinces and different religions will learn to know, tolerate and love one another.

BERTRAND BARÈRE

FRENCH REVOLUTIONARY PATRIOTISM

Bertrand Barère (1755 – 1841) was a French prophet of European nationalism. Born in Tarbes at the foot of the French Pyrenees, he came from a middle-class family of lawyers and clergymen. When he was elected to the Estates General in 1789, he was at the peak of a brilliant career as a lawyer. His eloquence and analytical talent served him well then and later as a member of the National Convention and of its powerful Committee of Public Safety during the so-called "Reign of Terror." Barère was an eloquent orator, and, according to Leo Gershoy, his leading biographer, he spoke "the language of totalitarian, revolutionary patriotism."

Known throughout the country for his "flowery bulletins of military victories" which he addressed to the National Convention and to the civilian population, his "carmagnoles," as they were called, were exceedingly popular in revolutionary France. They undoubtedly stimulated republican ardor and kept up courage in the face of defeat, treason, incompetence, and shortages of all the indispensable materials of war. Among the demands of the sans-culottes (see the selection by Soboul) was a levée en masse (levy-in-mass), the demand for which was reflected in and stimulated by the revolutionary festival of August 10, 1793, organized by the painter Louis David. The members of the Committee of Public Safety could not afford to let the popular movement get out of hand. Though they were dismayed at the idea of a mass upheaval, they constructed their own plan to organize the defense of the fatherland in such a way as to retain control over the revolutionary enthusiasm of the French masses. When their decree creating the *levée en masse* was voted on August 23, 1793, it was Barère who read the following report couched in epic terms. The speech had a tremendous emotional impact upon his listeners and is a characteristic example of French revolutionary (or patriotic) nationalism.

REPORT ON THE CIVIL REQUISITIONING OF YOUNG CITIZENS FOR THE DEFENSE OF OUR COUNTRY

Barère, in the name of the Committee of Public Safety: Citizens, after the difficulties which for the past week have interrupted your deliberations on the means of carrying out a great plan for finally chasing our enemies from the territory of the Republic, each one of us, attached to the destiny of the Revolution and to the well-being of his fellow citizens, has had to search his heart and his mind for the best method of levying troops, for the best plan for civil requisition, in order to put an end, during the current military campaign, to the attack which Europe's ancient despotism has made against the dawning freedom of France.

To decide hastily about such a serious and important matter is to expose oneself to military reverses, to compromise the safety of the Republic and the existence of its citizens, and to wear down the national spirit with immoderate demands. So let us examine our needs and our resources cooly. Let us know, above all, what we want, what we mean by the calling into service of the entire populace for the defense of the Constitution and of liberty.

What do you want? A contingent furnished by each departmental or territorial division?

Let us leave to the German Corps, let us leave to the federations of Germany, and to the imperial edicts the venal usage of seignorial or federalistic methods. The contingent for the liberty of France comprises all her population, all her industry, all her effort, all her genius. The contingent is only a contribution levied on men, as though they were abject cattle, and this word does not belong to the French language. Therefore, no contingent. The departments which have an abundance of patriots, the districts which are republican in sentiment or are threatened by the enemy, have they asked you to fix by decree the number of their battalions, the degree of their patriotism, the measure of their sacrifices, the quota of their armed citizens? Look at the Department of Aude, and so many others, even more animated by love of their country or hatred of her enemies, competing in generosity and devotion with the departments around them.

What do you want? Another recruitment? The aristocracy is there, hiding in the sections[1] and spying on us. It, too, votes for the recruitment of the empire, that aristocracy which is both incorrigible and avaricious, because it holds in reserve gold to tempt weak or indigent citizens, deserters to dishonor our army, royalists to corrupt its spirit, those who shout "every man for himself!" in order to disband and defeat our troops in the midst of victory, and money with which to speculate on the funds of the very defenders of our country.

Have you forgotten all the troubles, all the machinations and the intrigues to which the counter-revolutionaries have resorted in order to prevent recruitment? Have you lost sight so soon of the deep intrigues and innumerable discussions, the violent altercations which tend to use the national defense as a means of stirring up civil war, on the one hand by sowing discord in the Sections on the means of recruitment, on the other by restoring the practice of drawing lots to recruit the militia, or having a popular election by ballot? Above all, could you fail to recognize such a frequent violation of the principle that in free countries *every citizen is a soldier?* This violation, which goes unpunished, has been committed by rich men who had themselves replaced for money, or by foreigners, or by men who do not

[1] The 48 sections of Paris and those of other large cities were internal political divisions of the municipalities. [Editors note.]

From Bertrand Barère, "Report on the Civil Requisitioning of Young Citizens for the Defense of Our Country," *Le Moniteur ou Gazette universelle*, Vol. VIII, No. 237 (August 25, 1793), pp. 1007–09. [Translated by the editor.]

support our present legislative regime. Take care. By using the method of recruitment, too often you transform wealthy egoists into military recruiters, you give to evil-wishers ways of stirring up trouble, to the rich you give instruments of anarchy and disorder, to the Revolution, men who despise it enough to bring about its ruin, and to our country, soldiers who do not love her enough to defend her.

Therefore, no recruitment.

What do you want? A levy-in-mass?

At this word, all the aristocrats of varying shades of opinion, all the frivolous and light-minded men who do not belong to any country nor to any regime, all the egoists who are neither citizens nor foreigners, all the parasites of revolution who, like the traitors and conspirators whom you have placed outside the law, have placed themselves outside the nations of the world, all the useless people have gladly seized upon this expression, levy-in-mass, and have tried to turn it to ridicule. As though they did not know that a mere wish on the part of this nation fully mobilized would make them return to the dust from which they ought never to have come. As though they could conceal from themselves the fact that the French people have only to say the word, and the entire aristocracy ceases to exist.

This term, levy-in-mass, has nevertheless been understood by the nation, and every citizen has seen in this energetic expression all the nation's strength and resources ready to be deployed at the first signal in proportion to the perils and to the needs of our country.

I repeat it here, because the words have been taken in the wrong sense, even by patriots. I repeat: They are counterrevolutionaries by deed or by intent, they are allies of Pitt or of Coburg, those who want a nation of twenty-seven million men, an entire people, to be called up at the same moment in all parts of the Republic. Who can doubt that this simultaneous commotion, if it could occur, would only produce frightful disturbances, enormous needs, incalculable disorders, and precious opportunities for the aristocracy? Who can doubt that this suspension of work, of commerce, of communication, this electrification of the minds of all, this friction of so many interests, was rather a plan of our enemies than a means of national defense?

Such levies-in-mass are not idle fancies, but they are brought about only by great needs, and imminent dangers. Are we then in that great extremity which necessitates such an extraordinary commotion? Six hundred thousand men who fight under the banners of the Republic—have they then disappeared? Are all our strongholds in the power of the Austrian? Do the honored fortresses of Lille and Thionville no longer exist? Has the Englishman already committed all the crimes? Does the Spaniard mark up nothing but victories? Has fanaticism enlarged the Vendée, and has the royalist added to his success along the Rhône and the Loire?

No, no, citizens. France, which under the races of tyrants has not needed a general insurrection during the sad days of Poitiers, Crécy, and Agincourt, has still less need of it today, when free citizens have replaced feudal serfs, and when each man, in addition to fighting for his family's sake, fights also for his rights. The general and simultaneous levy would be a gigantic effort, and the tyrants of Europe who have had to band together to threaten us, to devastate us, do not yet necessitate the gathering together of the last efforts of a great people.

The requisition of all our forces is necessary, without doubt, but a progressive and gradual use of them is sufficient. That is the spirit and the meaning of the levy of the whole population. All are required, but all can not march nor fulfill the same function. Liberty has become the creditor of all the citizens; some owe her their industry, others their fortune; some their counsel, others their arms. All owe her the blood that flows in their veins.

Thus all Frenchmen, all sexes, all ages, are called by our country to defend liberty. All physical or moral faculties, all political or industrial means are devoted to her. All metals, all elements are in her power. Let each man occupy his place, let each man take his position in the national and military effort that the goal of the campaign necessitates, and all will congratulate themselves before long for having cooperated in the salvation of our country.

Let a minister, a general, an administrator, a regiment, or a province of a monarchy, or a despotic court have the exclusive vanity of defending the State. That is the cold recompense of monarchists and gilded slaves of royal courts. But in a free country all is fused in an irresistible and common need, the need of not allowing one's country to be enslaved, of not letting one's land be dishonored—the need to conquer. Here, we are all bound together: the metallurgist like the legislator, the physician like the blacksmith, the scientist like the laborer, the gunsmith like the colonel, the armaments manufacturer like the general, the patriot and the banker, the poor artisan and the rich proprietor, the artist like the cannon maker, the fortifications engineer like the industrialist, the inhabitant of the country and the city-dweller, all are joined together, all are brothers, all are useful, all will be honored.

You see already, in the rapid rapprochement occasioned by the needs of the war, the whole theory of the truly national movement which you have charged us with organizing, with that wisdom which does not exclude enthusiasm, and with that judgment which does not weaken republican energy.

All France must stand up against the tyrants; but only a part of the citizenry needs to be set in motion.

Thus, all are needed, but all do not march. Some fabricate arms, others use them; some prepare the provisions for the combatants, others make ready their clothing and their basic needs. Men, women, children, the national requisition calls upon all of you, in the name of Liberty and Equality, to devote yourselves, each one according to his means, to the service of the armies of the Republic. Young men will fight and young men will be summoned to prevail. Married men will forge arms, transport equipment and artillery, and prepare the food supplies. Women, who at long last must take their place and arrive at their true destiny during revolutions, will forget their useless occupations. Their hands will sew the soldiers' uniforms, make tents, and administer nursing care in the shelters where the defender of the fatherland receives the aid that his wounds require. Children will make surgical dressings from old clothing. It is for them that we fight. Children, destined to gather all the fruit of the Revolution, will raise their pure hands toward heaven. Old men, taking up again the mission that they had in antiquity, will be carried into the public squares; they will inflame the courage of the young warriors, stir up hatred for kings, and preach the unity of the Republic. By thus enclosing the young citizens, within the two extremities of life, between the praises of the old men and the gratitude of the children, we will have already done a great deal for the defense of the people.

The Republic is no longer anything but a great city under siege. France must no longer be anything other than a vast camp. Public buildings, the unsold houses of the émigrés, will be converted into barracks, and public places into factories. The floors of cellars will serve for the preparation of gunpowder. There is a shortage of saltpeter. There were very severe penalties for those who were opposed to the gathering or to the production of this raw material so necessary to the artillery. The floors of cellars must be washed with lye in order to extract the saltpeter from them. The floors of all the cellars in Montpellier are used for the production of a subtle poison, but one which is useful in the arts. Let all the cellars be used also for the production of saltpeter, which is the poison of the aristocrats and royalists.

All guns of regulation calibre must pass into the hands of those who will march against the enemy. For civil use it will be sufficient to count and collect hunting and luxury guns, side arms, and pikes.

All saddle horses must be requisitioned without exception, without regard to particular circumstances, in order to complete the cavalry corps. That is the secret of our enemies' strength. They count on their horses more than on their men, just as they count on betrayals more than on bravery. Very well, if the cavalry is the strong point of the Austrian and the Englishman, let us too create a large cavalry! And we will have more than the foreign hordes, we will have our infantry with their invincible bayonets, our skillful and courageous artillery, the love of our country, and the courage of freedom.

The horses who dragged around opulent masters or useless commanders must pull cannons and carry provisions. The luxury of horses must become the tributary of the artillery, and the art of war must be enriched by all these trappings that do not impoverish the rich.

So much for our present situation, and for that which we can calculate in a positive manner.

But in organizing this great operation for the service and reinforcement of our armies, we must give the greatest attention to the army of materials which must precede the soldiers and assure their armament, as well as their food supplies. It is not enough to have men. They will never be lacking in the defense of the Republic. Arms! Arms and provisions!

That is the cry of need. It is also the constant object of our concern.

First, in regard to arms. Within a few days Paris is going to see a huge manufacture of arms of all types spring up in her midst. As a depositary of all the arts, this city has immense resources which the Committee of Public Safety has put to work, in collaboration with very capable and very energetic patriots.

The Paris of the Old Regime sold ridiculous fashions, numerous baubles, bright frippery, and comfortable furniture to all France and a part of Europe. The Paris of the Republic, without ceasing to be the theater of taste and the storehouse of agreeable inventions and artistic productions, is going to become the arsenal of France.

The Committee has been engaged in establishing in Paris a large armaments establishment which will soon be able to produce progressively up to 500, 700, and 1,000 arms per day. It will employ 6,000 workers. Eight of the most skilled and experienced engineers are visiting the factories of the nation to examine all their techniques and to bring back to Paris samples of all the parts necessary to the manufacture of muskets. Each factory in the country will hasten to furnish several workers, who are needed to supervise the others. We are taking recognized artisans, such as ironsmiths, and we will still be able to use a great number of clockmakers, a specialty which is a bit neglected at the present time.

In a few days, two hundred fifty forges for the fabrication of musket barrels are going to be located along the periphery of the Luxembourg Gardens and at the extremities of the Square of the Revolution. Since there are as yet no artistic monuments in our public squares, we shall decorate them splendidly by having forged in them the arms against tyrants and aristocrats.

Ten large drilling-shops will be set up in boats on the river.

Sixteen national buildings will be used as large workshops for a hundred twenty to a hundred fifty workers each, making the different musket parts. All the other workers will be employed in their homes and shops, doing piece work according to a set price.

A simple and active administrative system will oversee the work. One unit will distribute the material to the workers; a second will receive and pay for everything that pertains to the manufacture of musket barrels; another will be charged with receiving and paying for all the small parts that are made by workers outside the factories.

Already capable workers are assembled. Already construction workers and mechanics are preparing their materials, and the chiefs of this administration said yesterday evening that they have made sure of all means of execution.

This administration will be under the direction of the war minister, under the supervision of the Committee of Public Safety.

This establishment will not be any obstacle to the other national industries, nor to private manufacturing. It will even extend them. Arts and artisans ought to help, not destroy, one another.

Let the men who hate Paris, who wanted at one time to destroy her and at another to starve her, suspend for a moment that inveterate hatred that the city of the Revolution has never deserved. Paris is the city common to all. Paris is the city of everyone. Well, Paris needs for the employment of her population a diligent organization. France needs new industry for the preservation of her artisans. The Republic needs to have a large number of arms manufactured immediately. Only in Paris can we assemble this valuable multitude of skillful workers which is going to produce in one day up to a thousand muskets, when the organization is completed.

The goal of the present levy is to terminate everything during this military campaign. But the most efficient means of achieving this is to assemble an immense quantity of matérielle.

Let no one think that this manufacture is to benefit Paris alone. Here we can only rifle, weld, and drill cannons. The ramrods will be prepared in the departments of Allier, Nièvre, Cher, Doubs, and Upper Saône, and these are the departments that will also be enriched by furnishing iron fittings for muskets, as well as the large amount of charcoal necessary to this industry. Thus, there will be no monopoly here. Let us even hope that the example of Paris will be imitated, and that this general emulation will deliver us from the aggressors against liberty.

It would be a very short term investment to fabricate

combat weapons at one time and in one place. Despotism, always fearful, disarmed the countryside. Its manufacturers worked only for its satellites, for its assassins in uniform. Freedom, on the contrary, arms every hand, fills the arsenals, and defies all tyrants with imposing security.

Arms, the manufacture of muskets and of cannon, that is what we need. For ten years let our arsenals be multiplied a hundredfold, let our military depots be filled, and let every French citizen have a weapon for the defense of his life and his rights.

It will be a splendid era, and one not far off, when the Republic, after having chased away the bloodthirsty despots who beseige her, will reduce the fortified places to nothing but military towns with only the artisans and workers necessary to her defense, to nothing but camps enclosed by walls. She will set up on the boundaries of her territory columns on which will be engraved the decree which repels any idea of conquest, and which abolishes royalty. We shall write there, as at Rome, the inscription of Brutus. . . . And next to these columns will be impregnable fortresses, full arsenals and free men.

Excuse this digression, caused by the awareness of our needs.

We ask that the Committee of Public Safety be expressly authorized to take all the measures necessary for establishing an extraordinary manufacture and preparation of arms of every type, and to requisition throughout the Republic the artisans and workers who can contribute to their success. A sum of thirty million has seemed necessary for this enterprise, for Paris and for the departments, and these will not be the most badly used funds of the Republic. A large stock of arms is a durable asset. The assiduous work of the citizens is a great treasure for a nation. There are, moreover, departments in which you have established the manufacture of arms and others in which older industries of this type are neglected. You should authorize the representatives of the people whom you are going to send out to speed up this production, and to take, in concert with the Committee and with the Executive Council, all appropriate measures for reviving and accelerating this valuable fabrication.

It is not enough to have men and arms. We must also have provisions. That is the basis of all the operations of war. The representatives already have a law which requires the threshing of grain. Funds will be placed at the disposition of the administrations in charge of provisions, and everything will be arranged so as not to have the provisioning of the regular armies and naval squadrons coincide with that of the newly requisitioned troops. If there were no evilly disposed persons and conspirators, the rich harvests, of which Nature has made a present this year to liberty, would even give us a surplus.

But since it is here a question of extraordinary needs, methods appropriate to these needs are required. Renters and managers of government properties must deliver to the capitals of the respective grain districts the produce of these domains. Citizens who are behind in the payment of their taxes, even those of two thirds of the year 1793, must be obliged to pay them at the rate of the *maximum* of the present month, and taxes will be paid on the basis of the tax rolls which were used to carry out the latest collections.

How could anyone find these measures severe? They are just. One's first debt is to his country. Society has the right to demand even property, when the need is imperative. What must be the case when it is only a matter of produce? Let us even hope that the citizens will hasten in the present crisis, to offer a part of their harvest in kind to the republican armies, for which part the nation will pay them at the market rate. And if it were necessary to recall the course of American history, every possessor of grain would learn what he ought to do for liberty. Washington had his army, pressed by want, between New Jersey and Pennsylvania. He asked the inhabitants of those beautiful regions for help in the form of grain. He encountered delay, rather than resistance. Then the American general demanded, in the name of the nation, that the inhabitants and farmers furnish all the grain necessary for his army. Give them in accordance with the requisition of the army of freedom, said Washington, and Congress will pay you the legitimate price for them. If you refuse, the army will take its provisions—it is fighting for you—and you will not be paid for them. The army of Washington was supplied with provisions—let it be a lesson to aristocratic landowners, constitutional monarchists, moderates, or misers.

After having anticipated the needs of the armies and of their food supplies, let us return to that which touches the citizens most closely, to the manner in which the requisition for the further defense of the Republic will be carried out.

I return to the plan which is proposed to you: It is well that the aristocrats hear it.

All citizens are needed. All ages from eighteen to fifty can pursue a good military career; but all cannot go into action at the same time. Who will be the first to have the honor of dashing to the frontiers? Who will take part first in the conquest of liberty? An imperious voice, the voice of nature and of society answers:

"Young men will go first. It is for them that liberty is founded. It is they who are to gather the fruits of revolution. It is they who have the fewest needs and the most strength. It is they who have the most devotion and the fewest ties. French youth will leave first."

The bachelor and the young man are not as obviously necessary to society as the married citizens who have given children to our country. The first age must therefore fill the first requisition.

Therefore, all French citizens from eighteen to twenty-five are called to the common defense,—this age presents to the hopes of the country the greatest number of vigorous and unattached defenders. It is thought that this age group may comprise more than 400 thousand citizens, and we do not need such a great number. But if still more were needed, if this first column were ineffectual, the second age group, from twenty-five to thirty, would be required, and so on from five years to five years, up to fifty.

But all this is only enumerating the immense resources of freedom. Let us occupy ourselves with gathering them together.

The first idea of the Committee was to place with each army and in each center of civil war, a body of armed citizens, called up from several departments.

This idea had serious drawbacks:
1. Too many musters;
2. Musters that are too far off;
3. Too many diversions, positions under attack, or positions to reinforce;
4. Provisioning too large to accomplish in the capital of several departments;

5. Troublesome and unnecessary traveling for too great a number of citizens.

It has therefore been necessary to look for another procedure for mobilization.

To muster in the capitals of departments would be a federalistic method, and would recall lines of demarcation that must be erased or at least weakened as much as possible.

To assemble in the capitals of districts has appeared to be easier, more convenient, and above all more useful. You will easily appreciate the advantages of it. Each district capital has enough facilities to feed a small muster group. Thus provisioning is easier; there is less waste and less transport.

The district capital presents the advantages of a greater facility in clothing each citizen, and especially in feeding him, since it is closer to his commune.

Finally, the requisition will affect companies, instead of battalions, and their march as well as their destination will be more easily determined.

Do not forget, moreover, that your Constitution gives a great role to the districts. Through the departments, freedom almost perished. Small territorial divisions are more appropriate to the conduct and to the needs of liberty. Arbitrary power agglomerates; republican power disseminates.

We propose, by this means, few commanders, few military ranks. The priority of age will determine the rank for the command of a company or a battalion. General staffs are the brilliant baggage of despotism. General staffs have aristocracy in their manners even when they do not have it in their intentions. And besides, who has not shuddered to see that frightful multiplication of officers of every rank? There was a time at Rome when there were so many statues in all the public squares that historians say that there was in Rome another Roman people, of marble and stone. We could say, without looking for comparisons, that it seems that we have another nation of high-ranking officers, and of commissioners of the executive power.

Here is the bill that the Committee has authorized me to present to you.

I. Henceforth, until its enemies have been driven

from the territory of the Republic, the French people are in permanent requisition for military service.

The young men shall go to battle; the married men shall forge arms and transport food supplies; the women shall make tents and uniforms, and shall serve in the hospitals; the children shall convert old cloth into surgical dressings; the old men shall proceed to the public squares, to stimulate the courage of the soldiers and to preach the unity of the Republic and the hatred of kings.

II. National buildings shall be converted into barracks; public squares into armament workshops; the cellar floors shall be washed in lye in order to extract saltpeter.

III. Arms of uniform calibre shall be exclusively reserved for those who march against the enemy; the service of internal defense shall be carried out with shotguns and sabers.

IV. Saddle horses shall be turned over to supply the cavalry corps; draft horses, other than those required by agriculture, shall haul artillery and food supplies.

V. The Committee of Public Safety is charged with taking all necessary measures to establish, without delay, a special manufacture of arms of all kinds, in accord with the status and the energy of the French people. Accordingly, it is authorized that all establishments, manufactures, workshops, and factories which are judged necessary for the execution of these works shall be constituted, as well as to requisition throughout the entire Republic, the artisans and workers who may contribute to their success. To this end a sum of thirty million livres, taken from the 498,200,000 livres in *assignats* in reserve in the "Fund of the Three Keys," shall be placed at the disposal of the Minister of War. The central headquarters of this special manufacture shall be located at Paris.

VI. The representatives of the people sent out to execute the present law shall have similar authority in their respective districts, acting in concert with the Committee of Public Safety; they are invested with unlimited powers comparable to those of the representatives of the people assigned to the armies.

VII. No one may obtain a replacement in the service to which he is called. Public officials shall remain at their posts.

VIII. The levy shall be general. Unmarried citizens or widowers without children from 18 to 25 years of age shall go first; they shall muster without delay, in the chief town of their districts, where they shall practice the manual of arms daily, while awaiting the order to depart.

IX. The representatives of the people shall regulate the roll calls and the marches so that the armed citizens shall arrive at the points of assembly only in so far as supplies, munitions, and all that constitutes the material part of the army is available in sufficient proportion.

X. The muster points shall be determined by circumstances, and designated by the representatives of the people sent out to execute the present decree, upon the advice of the generals, in cooperation with the Committee of Public Safety and the Provisional Executive Council.

XI. The battalion to be organized in each district shall be united under a banner inscribed with the words: *The French People on their feet against tyrants.*

XII. Battalions shall be organized according to established decrees; their pay shall be the same as that of the battalions at the frontier.

XIII. In order to collect a sufficient quantity of supplies, the farmers and managers of national property shall deposit the produce of that property, in the form of grain, in the chief town of their respective districts.

XIV. Farm owners and others owning grain shall be required to pay, in kind, taxes in arrears, even the two thirds of those of 1793 on the rolls which have served to effect the last payment. . . .

XVII. The Minister of War is charged with taking all measures necessary for the prompt execution of this decree; a sum of 50,000,000 livres from the 498,200,000 livres in *assignats* in the "Fund of the Three Keys," shall be placed at his disposal by the National Treasury.

XVIII. The present decree shall be distributed to the departments by special messengers.

This bill is adopted.

The Age of Revolutions

GIUSEPPE MAZZINI

ITALIAN ROMANTIC NATIONALISM

The Italian patriot, Giuseppe Mazzini (1805–1872), was in many respects typical of the "liberal nationalists" of the mid-nineteenth century. Italian patriots who preached the *Risorgimento,* the resurrection of Italy through the establishment of a republic, one and indivisible, believed that a united Italian Republic would regenerate their people and create a nation-state by freeing them from domestic tyranny and liberating them from foreign domination. This regenerated Italian Republic would join with other national republics organized on liberal political lines in order to live in peace with other nation-states throughout the world and would participate in a broad movement to unite humanity according to God's own plan.

Mazzini participated in the creation of the ill-fated Roman Republic of 1848, of which he was elected President, but which was put down by French troops in June 1849. The rest of Mazzini's life was spent in exile, plotting the expulsion of the Austrians from Italy and propagandizing the Italian people. Though in the immediate sense his work was a failure, a large part of the moral fervor of Italian nationalism was a reflection of Mazzini and his passionate doctrines.

The Duties of Man was part of a series of essays, published 1844–58, designed to be read by Italian workingmen and to guide them in their actions. In it you should notice Mazzini's conception of the basic duties of Italians, the role of God and the means He had given Italians to achieve this duty, the factors which Mazzini believes will create a national sentiment, his comparison of Humanity with an army and the nation with a family, his definition of a country, the form of government essential to the creation of a legitimate fatherland, the emphasis on Italian history as a factor in Europe, and the emotional fervor which characterizes the entire document. Mazzini was a fervent Italian nationalist, strongly imbued with Romanticism, and a republican devoted to the idea of popular sovereignty and of national self-determination.

ON THE DUTIES OF MAN

Your first duties—first as regards importance—are, as I have already told you, towards Humanity. You are men before you are either citizens or fathers. If you do not embrace the whole human family in your affection, if you do not bear witness to your belief in the Unity of that family, consequent upon the Unity of God, and in that fraternity among the peoples which is destined to reduce that unity to action; if, wheresoever a fellow-creature suffers, or the dignity of human nature is violated by falsehood or tyranny—you are not ready, if able, to aid the unhappy, and do not feel called upon to combat, if able, for the redemption of the betrayed or oppressed—you violate your law of life, you comprehend not that Religion which will be the guide and blessing of the future.

From Giuseppe Mazzini, "On the Duties of Man" in Emilie A. Venturi, *Joseph Mazzini: A Memoir* (London, 1875).

But, you tell me, you cannot attempt united action, distinct and divided as you are in language, customs, tendencies, and capacity. The individual is too insignificant, and Humanity too vast. The mariner of Brittany prays to God as he puts to sea: Help me, my God! my boat is so small and thy ocean so wide! And this prayer is the true expression of the condition of each one of you, until you find the means of infinitely multiplying your forces and powers of action.

This means was provided for you by God when he gave you a country; when, even as a wise overseer of labour distributes the various branches of employment according to the different capacities of the workmen, he divided Humanity into distinct groups or nuclei upon the face of the earth, thus creating the germ of Nationalities. Evil governments have disfigured the divine design. Nevertheless you may still trace it, distinctly marked out—at least as far as Europe is concerned—by the course of the great rivers, the direction of the higher mountains, and other geographical conditions. They have disfigured it by their conquests, their greed, and their jealousy even of the righteous power of others; disfigured it so far that, if we except England and France—there is not perhaps a single country whose present boundaries correspond to that design.

These governments did not, and do not, recognize any country save their own families or dynasty, the egotism of caste. But the Divine design will infallibly be realized. Natural divisions, and the spontaneous, innate tendencies of the peoples, will take the place of the arbitrary divisions sanctioned by evil governments. The map of Europe will be redrawn. The countries of the Peoples, defined by the vote of free men, will arise upon the ruins of the countries of kings and privileged castes, and between these countries harmony and fraternity will exist. And the common work of Humanity, of general amelioration and the gradual discovery and application of its Law of life, being distributed according to local and general capacities, will be wrought out in peaceful and progressive development and advance. Then may each one of you, fortified by the power and the affection of many millions, all speaking the same language, gifted with the same tendencies, and educated by the same historical tradition, hope, even by your own single effort, to be able to benefit all Humanity.

O my brothers, love your Country! Our country is our Home, the house that God has given us, placing therein a numerous family that loves us, and whom we love; a family with whom we sympathise more readily, and whom we understand more quickly than we do others; and which, from its being centred around a given spot, and from the homogeneous nature of its elements, is adapted to a special branch of activity. Our country is our common workshop, whence the products of our activity are sent forth for the benefit of the whole world; wherein the tools and implements of labour we can most usefully employ are gathered together: nor may we reject them without disobeying the plan of the Almighty, and diminishing our own strength.

In labouring for our own country on the right principle, we labour for Humanity. Our country is the fulcrum of the lever we have to wield for the common good. If we abandon that fulcrum, we run the risk of rendering ourselves useless not only to humanity but to our country itself. Before men can associate with the nations of which humanity is composed, they must have a National existence. There is no true association except among equals. It is only through our country that we can have a recognized collective existence.

Humanity is a vast army advancing to the conquest of lands unknown, against enemies both powerful and astute. The peoples are the different corps, the divisions of that army. Each of them has its post assigned to it, and its special operation to execute; and the common victory depends upon the exactitude with which those distinct operations shall be fulfilled. Disturb not the order of battle. Forsake not the banner given you by God. Wheresoever you may be, in the centre of whatsoever people circumstances may have placed you, be ever ready to combat for the liberty of that people should it be necessary, but combat in such wise that the blood you shed may reflect glory, not on yourselves alone, but on your country. Say not I, but we. Let each man among you strive to incarnate his country in himself. Let each man among you regard himself as a guarantee, responsible for his fellow-countrymen, and learn so to govern his actions as to cause his country to be loved and respected through him. Your country is the sign of the mission God has given you to fulfill towards Humanity. The faculties and forces of all her sons should be associated in the accomplishment of that mission. The true country is a community of free men and equals, bound together in fraternal concord to labour towards a common aim.

The Age of Revolutions

You are bound to make it and to maintain it such. The country is not an aggregation, but an association. There is therefore no true country without an uniform right. There is no true country where the uniformity of that right is violated by the existence of castes, privilege, and inequality. Where the activity of a portion of the powers and faculties of the individual is either cancelled or dormant; where there is not a common Principle, recognized, accepted, and developed by all, there is no true nation, no People; but only a multitude, a fortuitous agglomeration of men whom circumstances have called together, and whom circumstances may again divide. In the name of the love you bear your country you must peacefully but untiringly combat the existence of privilege and inequality in the land that gave you life.

There is but one sole legitimate privilege, the privilege of Genius when it reveals itself united with virtue. But this is a privilege given by God, and when you acknowledge it and follow its inspiration, you do so freely, exercising your own reason and your own choice. Every privilege which demands submission from you in virtue of power, inheritance, or any other right than the Right common to all, is a usurpation and a tyranny which you are bound to resist and destroy.

Be your country your Temple. God at the summit; a people of equals at the base.

Accept no other formula, no other moral law, if you would not dishonour alike your country and yourselves. Let all secondary laws be but the gradual regulation of your existence by the progressive application of this supreme law. And in order that they may be such, it is necessary that all of you should aid in framing them. Laws framed only by a single fraction of the citizens, can never, in the very nature of things, be other than the mere expression of the thoughts, aspirations, and desires of that fraction; the representation, not of the Country, but of a third or fourth part, of a class or zone of the country.

The laws should be the expression of the universal aspiration, and promote the universal good. They should be a pulsation of the heart of the nation. The entire nation should, either directly or indirectly, legislate.

By yielding up this mission into the hands of a few, you substitute the egotism of one class for the Country, which is the union of all classes.

Country is not a mere zone or territory. The true country is the Idea to which it gives birth; it is the Thought of love, the sense of communion which unites in one all the sons of that territory.

So long as a single one amongst your brothers has no vote to represent him in the development of the national life, so long as there is one left to vegetate in ignorance where others are educated, so long as a single man, able and willing to work, languishes in poverty through want of work to do, you have no country in the sense in which country ought to exist—the country of all and for all.

Education, labour, and the franchise, are the three main pillars of the nation. Rest not until you have built them strongly up with your own labour and exertions.

Never deny your sister nations. Be it yours to evolve the life of your country in loveliness and strength; free from all servile fears or sceptical doubts; maintaining as its basis the People; as its guide the consequences of the principles of its Religious Faith, logically and energetically applied; its strength, the united strength of all; its aim, the fulfilment of the mission given to it by God.

And so long as you are ready to die for Humanity, the life of your country will be immortal.

LORD ACTON

A CRITIQUE OF NATIONALISM

The historian and writer, Sir John Emerich Edward Dalberg-Acton, 1st Baron Acton (1834–1902), born in Naples, the son of the 7th English Baronet Acton and of the daughter of the Duke of Dalberg, a German noble in the service of Napoleonic France, grandson of a Neapolitan admiral who, though born in France, had been commander in chief of all armed forces and Prime Minister of the kingdom of Naples, and nephew of the Archbishop-Elector of Mainz, Archchancellor of the Holy Roman Empire and then Primate of the Napoleonic Confederation of the Rhine, was the very figure of a cosmopolitan aristocrat. Educated in France, England, Scotland, and Germany, Lord Acton spoke the languages of these and most other European countries, was personally familiar with almost all Europe, and had traveled even in Russia and the United States. Equally at home in England, France, and Germany, he divided his residence between these three countries. He therefore was in a position to study and to criticize the rising force of nineteenth-century nationalism. Acton was a devout but liberal Roman Catholic and in politics an ardent Gladstonian Liberal. As will be seen in the following selection, Lord Acton was as critical of nationalism as he was of religious persecution and bigotry.

As an historian, Lord Acton is best known for his assistance in establishing the *English Historical Review* (1886), his position as Regius Professor of Modern History at Cambridge University (1895), and his editorship of the *Cambridge Modern History* (1899–1900). An assiduous reader, he never wrote a book himself, though he gathered immense quantities of research material for monumental works on the History of Freedom and on the French Revolution. During his lifetime he published a handful of valuable essays (including the article on Nationality which follows), suggestive fragments, and his inaugural address on the study of history (1896). After his death in 1902, four volumes of his lectures and essays were published, as well as selections from his voluminous correspondence. As editor of the *Cambridge Modern History*, he announced that "nothing shall reveal the country, religion, or party to which the writers belong."

In the old European system, the rights of nationalities were neither recognised by governments nor asserted by the people. The interest of the reigning families, not those of the nations, regulated the frontiers; and the administration was conducted generally without any reference to popular desires. Where all liberties were suppressed, the claims of national independence were necessarily ignored, and a princess, in the words of Fénelon, carried a monarchy in her wedding portion. The eighteenth century acquiesced in this oblivion of corporate rights on the Continent, for the absolutists cared only for the State, and the liberals only for the individual. The Church, the nobles, and the nation had no place in the

From John Emerich Edward Dalberg-Acton, First Baron Acton, "Nationality" in *Home and Foreign Review;* Vol. I (July 1862), pp. 169–174.

popular theories of the age; and they devised none in their own defence, for they were not openly attacked. The aristocracy retained its privileges, and the Church her property; and the dynastic interest, which overruled the natural inclination of the nations, and destroyed their independence, nevertheless maintained their integrity. The national sentiment was not wounded in its most sensitive part. To dispossess a sovereign of his hereditary crown, and to annex his dominions, would have been held to inflict an injury upon all monarchies, and to furnish their subjects with a dangerous example, by depriving royalty of its inviolable character. In time of war, as there was not national cause at stake, there was no attempt to rouse national feeling. The courtesy of the rulers towards each other was proportionate to the contempt for the lower orders. Compliments passed between the commanders of hostile armies; there was no bitterness, and no excitement; battles were fought with the pomp and pride of a parade. The art of war became a slow and learned game. The monarchies were united not only by a natural community of interests, but by family alliances. A marriage contract sometimes became the signal for an interminable war, whilst family connections often set a barrier to ambition. After the wars of religion came to an end in 1648, the only wars were those which were waged for an inheritance or a dependency, or against countries whose system of government exempted them from the common law of dynastic States, and made them not only unprotected but obnoxious. These countries were England and Holland, until Holland ceased to be a republic, and until, in England, the defeat of the Jacobites in the forty-five terminated the struggle for the Crown. There was one country, however, which still continued to be an exception; one monarch whose place was not admitted in the comity of kings.

Poland did not possess those securities for stability which were supplied by dynastic connections and the theory of legitimacy, wherever a crown could be obtained by marriage or inheritance. A monarch without royal blood, a crown bestowed by the nation, were an anomaly and an outrage in that age of dynastic absolutism. The country was excluded from the European system by the nature of its institutions. It excited a cupidity which could not be satisfied. It gave the reigning families of Europe no hope of permanently strengthening themselves by intermarriage with its rulers, or of obtaining it by request or by inheritance. The Hapsburgs had contested the possession of Spain and the Indies with the French Bourbons, of Italy with the Spanish Bourbons, of the empire with the house of Wittelsbach, of Silesia with the house of Hohenzollern. There had been wars between rival houses for half the territories of Italy and Germany. But none could hope to redeem their losses or increase their power in a country to which marriage and descent gave no claim. Where they could not permanently inherit they endeavoured, by intrigues, to prevail at each election, and after contending in support of candidates who were their partisans, the neighbours at last appointed an instrument for the final demolition of the Polish State. Till then no nation had been deprived of its political existence by the Christian Powers, and whatever disregard had been shown for national interests and sympathies, some care had been taken to conceal the wrong by a hypocritical perversion of law. But the partition of Poland was an act of wanton violence, committed in open defiance not only of popular feeling but of public law. For the first time in modern history a great State was suppressed, and a whole nation divided among its enemies.

This famous measure, the most revolutionary act of the old absolutism, awakened the theory of nationality in Europe, converting a dormant right into an aspiration, and a sentiment into a political claim. "No wise or honest man," wrote Edmund Burke, "can approve of that partition, or can contemplate it without prognosticating great mischief from it to all countries at some future time." Thenceforward there was a nation demanding to be united in a State,—a soul, as it were, wandering in search of a body in which to begin life over again; and, for the first time, a cry was heard that the arrangement of States was unjust—that their limits were unnatural, and that a whole people was deprived of its right to constitute an independent community. Before that claim could be efficiently asserted against the overwhelming power of its opponents,—before it gained energy, after the last partition, to overcome the influence of long habits of submission, and of the contempt which previous disorders had brought upon Poland,—the ancient European system was in ruins, and a new world was rising in its place.

The old despotic policy which made the Poles its prey had two adversaries,—the spirit of English liberty, and the doctrines of that revolution which destroyed the French monarchy with its own weapons; and these two contradicted in contrary ways the theory that nations have no collective rights. At the present day, the theory of nationality is not only the most powerful auxiliary of revolution, but its actual substance in the movements of the last three years. This, however, is a recent alliance, unknown to the first French Revolution. The modern theory of nationality arose partly as a legitimate consequence, partly as a reaction against it. As the system which overlooked national division was opposed by liberalism in two forms, the French and the English, so the system which insists upon them proceeds from two distinct sources, and exhibits the character either of 1688 or of 1789. When the French people abolished the authorities under which it lived, and became its own master, France was in danger of dissolution: for the common will is difficult to ascertain, and does not readily agree. "The laws," said Vergniaud,[1] in the debate on the sentence of the king, "are obligatory only as the presumptive will of the people, which retains the right of approving or condemning them. The instant it manifests its wish the work of the national representation, the law, must disappear." This doctrine resolved society into its natural elements, and threatened to break up the country into as many republics as there were communes. For true republicanism is the principle of self-government in the whole and in all the parts. In an extensive country, it can prevail only by the union of several independent communities in a single confederacy, as in Greece, in Switzerland, in the Netherlands, and in America; so that a large republic not founded on the federal principle must result in the government of a single city, like Rome and Paris, and, in a less degree, Athens, Berne, and Amsterdam; or, in other words, a great democracy must either sacrifice self-government to unity, or preserve it by federalism.

The France of history fell together with the French State, which was the growth of centuries. The old sovereignty was destroyed. The local authorities were looked upon with aversion and alarm. The new central authority needed to be established on a new principle of unity. The state of nature, which was the ideal of society, was made the basis of the nation; descent was put in the place of tradition, and the French people was regarded as a physical product: an ethnological, not historic, unit. It was assumed that a unity existed separate from the representation and the government, wholly independent of the past, and capable at any moment of expressing or of changing its mind. In the words of Siéyès, it was no longer France, but some unknown country to which the nation was transported. The central power possessed authority, inasmuch as it obeyed the whole, and no divergence was permitted from the universal sentiment. This power, endowed with volition, was personified in the Republic One and Indivisible. The title signified that a part could not speak or act for the whole, — that there was a power supreme over the State, distinct from, and independent of, its members; and it expressed, for the first time in history, the notion of an abstract nationality. In this manner the idea of the sovereignty of the people, uncontrolled by the past, gave birth to the idea of nationality independent of the political influence of history. It sprang from the rejection of the two authorities, — of the State and of the past. The kingdom of France was, geographically as well as politically, the product of a long series of events, and the same influences which built up the State formed the territory. The Revolution repudiated alike the agencies to which France owed her boundaries and those to which she owed her government. Every effaceable trace and relic of national history was carefully wiped away, — the system of administration, the physical divisions of the country, the classes of society, the corporations, the weights and measures, the calendar. France was no longer bounded by the limits she had received from the condemned influence of her history; she could recognise only those which were set by nature. The definition of the nation was borrowed from the material world, and, in order to avoid a loss of territory, it became not only an abstraction but a fiction.

There was a principle of nationality in the ethnological character of the movement, which is the source of the common observation that revolution is more frequent in Catholic than in Protestant countries. It is, in fact, more frequent in the Latin than in the Teutonic world, because it depends partly on a national impulse, which is only awakened where there is an alien element, the vestige of a foreign dominion, to expel. Western Europe has undergone two conquests — one by the Romans and one by the Germans, and twice received laws from the invaders. Each time it rose again against the victorious race; and the two great reactions, while they differ according to the different characters of the two conquests, have the phenomenon of imperialism in common. The Roman republic laboured to crush the

---

[1] Paul Vergniaud (1753–1793) was a member of the National Assembly and a leader of the so called "Girondins." He voted for the execution of Louis XVI but was later guillotined himself as a result of his opposition to more radical revolutionary forces. [Editor's note.]

The Age of Revolutions

subjugated nations into a homogeneous and obedient mass; but the increase which the proconsular authority obtained in the process subverted the republican government, and the reaction of the provinces against Rome assisted in establishing the empire. The Caesarean system gave an unprecedented freedom to the dependencies, and raised them to a civil equality which put an end to the dominion of race over race and of class over class. The monarchy was hailed as a refuge from the pride and cupidity of the Roman people; and the love of equality, the hatred of nobility, and the tolerance of despotism implanted by Rome became, at least in Gaul, the chief feature of the national character. But among the nations whose vitality had been broken down by the stern republic, not one retained the materials necessary to enjoy independence, or to develop a new history. The political faculty which organises states and finds society in a moral order was exhausted, and the Christian doctors looked in vain over the waste of ruins for a people by whose aid the Church might survive the decay of Rome. A new element of national life was brought to that declining world by the enemies who destroyed it. The flood of barbarians settled over it for a season, and then subsided; and when the landmarks of civilisation appeared once more, it was found that the soil had been impregnated with a fertilising and regenerating influence, and that the inundation had laid the germs of future states and of a new society. The political sense and energy came with the new blood, and was exhibited in the power exercised by the younger race upon the old, and in the establishment of a graduated freedom. Instead of universal equal rights, the actual enjoyment of which is necessarily contingent on, and commensurate with, power, the rights of the people were made dependent on a variety of conditions, the first of which was the distribution of property. Civil society became a classified organism instead of a formless combination of atoms, and the feudal system gradually arose.

Roman Gaul had so thoroughly adopted the ideas of absolute authority and undistinguished equality during the five centuries between Caesar and Clovis, that the people could never be reconciled to the new system. Feudalism remained a foreign importation, and the feudal aristocracy an alien race, and the common people of France sought protection against both in the Roman jurisprudence and the power of the crown. The development of absolute monarchy by the help of democracy is the one constant character of French history. The royal power, feudal at first, and limited by the immunities and the great vassals, became more popular as it grew more absolute; while the suppression of aristocracy, the removal of the intermediate authorities, was so particularly the object of the nation, that it was more energetically accomplished after the fall of the throne. The monarchy which had been engaged from the thirteenth century in curbing the nobles, was at last thrust aside by the democracy, because it was too dilatory in the work, and was unable to deny its own origin and effectually ruin the class from which it sprang. All those things which constitute the peculiar character of the French Revolution, —the demand for equality, the hatred of nobility and feudalism, and of the Church which was connected with them, the constant reference to pagan examples, the suppression of monarchy, the new code of law, the breach with tradition, and the substitution of an ideal system for everything that had proceeded from the mixture and mutual action of the races, —all these exhibit the common type of a reaction against the effects of the Frankish invasion. The hatred of royalty was less than the hatred of aristocracy; privileges were more detested than tyranny; and the king perished because of the origin of his authority rather than because of its abuse. Monarchy unconnected with aristocracy became popular in France, even when most uncontrolled; whilst the attempt to reconstitute the throne, and to limit and fence it with its peers, broke down, because the old Teutonic elements on which it relied —hereditary nobility, primogeniture, and privilege —were no longer tolerated. The substance of the ideas of 1789 is not the limitation of the sovereign power, but the abrogation of intermediate powers. These powers, and the classes which enjoyed them, come in Latin Europe from a barbarian origin; and the movement which calls itself liberal is essentially national. If liberty were its object, its means would be the establishment of great independent authorities not derived from the State, and its model would be England. But its object is equality; and it seeks, like France in 1789, to cast out the elements of inequality which were introduced by the Teutonic race. This is the object which Italy and Spain have had in common with France, and herein consists the natural league of the Latin nations.

This national element in the movement was not understood by the revolutionary leaders. At first, their doctrine appeared entirely contrary to the idea of nationality. They taught that certain general principles of government were absolutely right in all

States; and they asserted in theory the unrestricted freedom of the individual, and the supremacy of the will over every external necessity or obligation. This is in apparent contradiction to the national theory, that certain natural forces ought to determine the character, the form, and the policy of the State, by which a kind of fate is put in the place of freedom. Accordingly the national sentiment was not developed directly out of the revolution in which it was involved, but was exhibited first in resistance to it, when the attempt to emancipate had been absorbed in the desire to subjugate, and the republic had been succeeded by the empire. Napoleon called a new power into existence by attacking nationality in Russia, by delivering it in Italy, by governing in defiance of it in Germany and Spain. The sovereigns of these countries were deposed or degraded; and a system of administration was introduced which was French in its origin, its spirit, and its instruments. The people resisted the change. The movement against it was popular and spontaneous, because the rulers were absent or helpless; and it was national, because it was directed against foreign institutions. In Tyrol, in Spain, and afterwards in Prussia, the people did not receive the impulse from the government, but undertook of their own accord to cast out the armies and the ideas of revolutionised France. Men were made conscious of the national element of the revolution by its conquests, not in its rise. The three things which the Empire most openly oppressed —religion, national independence, and political liberty—united in a short-lived league to animate the great uprising by which Napoleon fell. Under the influence of that memorable alliance a political spirit was called forth on the Continent, which clung to freedom and abhorred revolution, and sought to restore, to develop, and to reform the decayed national institutions. The men who proclaimed these ideas, Stein and Görres, Humboldt, Müller, and De Maistre,[2] were hostile to Bonapart-

ism as to the absolutism of the old governments, and insisted on the national rights, which had been invaded equally by both, and which they hoped to restore by the destruction of the French supremacy. With the cause that triumphed at Waterloo the friends of the Revolution had no sympathy, for they had learned to identify their doctrine with the cause of France. The Holland House Whigs in England, the Afrancesados in Spain, the Muratists in Italy, and the partisans of the Confederation of the Rhine, merging patriotism in their revolutionary affections, regretted the fall of the French power, and looked with alarm at those new and unknown forces which the War of Deliverance had evoked, and which were as menacing to French liberalism as to French supremacy.

But the new aspirations for national and popular rights were crushed at the restoration. The liberals of those days cared for freedom, not in the shape of national independence, but of French institutions; and they combined against the nations with the ambition of the governments. They were as ready to sacrifice nationality to their ideal as the Holy Alliance was to the interests of absolutism. Talleyrand indeed declared at Vienna that the Polish question ought to have precedence over all other questions, because the partition of Poland had been one of the first and greatest causes of the evils which Europe had suffered; but dynastic interests prevailed. All the sovereigns represented at Vienna recovered their dominions, except the King of Saxony, who was punished for his fidelity to Napoleon; but the States that were unrepresented in the reigning families— Poland, Venice, and Genoa—were not revived, and even the Pope had great difficulty in recovering the Legations from the grasp of Austria. Nationality, which the old *regime* had ignored, which had been outraged by the revolution and the empire, received, after its first open demonstration, the hardest blow at the Congress of Vienna. The principle which the first partition had generated, to which the revolution had given a basis of theory, which had been lashed by the empire into a momentary convulsive effort, was matured by the long error of the restoration into a consistent doctrine, nourished and justified by the situation of Europe.

The governments of the Holy Alliance devoted themselves to suppress with equal care the revolutionary spirit by which they had been threatened, and the national spirit by which they had been restored. Austria, which owed nothing to the national

[2] Heinrich Friedrich Kare, Baron vom Stein (1757–1831) was a Prussian reformer and nationalist who as secretary of trade introduced political, economic, social, and military reforms which laid the basis for Prussia's rise to greatness in the nineteenth century. Johann Joseph von Görres (1776–1848) was a German writer who contributed to German nationalism and reforming spirit. Karl Wilhelm von Humboldt (1769–1835) was a statesman and scholar who fostered German science and learning and, as minister of public instruction, promoted education; he played a key role in strengthening Prussia after the Napoleonic wars. Wilhelm Müller (1794–1827) was a lyric poet who took part in the War of Liberation against Napoleon and whose poetry sounded the call for freedom in Germany. Joseph de Maistre (1753–1821) was a French philosopher and man of letters who left France during the Revolution and always remained a severe critic of the Revolution. [Editor's note.]

The Age of Revolutions

movement, and had prevented its revival after 1809, naturally took the lead in repressing it. Every disturbance of the final settlements of 1815, every aspiration for changes or reforms, was condemned as sedition. This system repressed the good with the evil tendencies of the age; and the resistance which it provoked, during the generation that passed away from the restoration to the fall of Metternich, and again under the reaction which commenced with Schwarzenberg and ended with the administrations of Bach and Manteuffel,[3] proceeded from various combinations of the opposite forms of liberalism. In the successive phases of that struggle, the idea that national claims are above all other rights gradually rose to the supremacy which it now possesses among the revolutionary agencies.

The first liberal movement, that of the Carbonari in the south of Europe, had no specific national character, but was supported by the Bonapartists both in Spain and Italy. In the following years the opposite ideas of 1813 came to the front, and a revolutionary movement, in many respects hostile to the principles of revolution, began in defence of liberty, religion, and nationality. All these causes were united in the Irish agitation, and in the Greek, Belgian, and Polish revolutionists. Those sentiments which had been insulted by Napoleon, and had risen against him, rose against the governments of the restoration. They had been oppressed by the sword, and then by the treaties. The national principle added force, but not justice, to this movement, which in every case but Poland, was successful. A period followed in which it degenerated into a purely national idea, as the agitation for repeal succeeded emancipation, and Panslavism and Panhellenism arose under the auspices of the Eastern Church. This was the third phase of the resistance to the settlement of Vienna, which was weak, because it failed to satisfy national or constitutional aspirations, either of which would have been a safeguard against the other, by a moral if not by a popular justification. At first, in 1813, the people rose against their conquerors, in defence of their legitimate rulers. They refused to be governed by usurpers. In the period between 1825 and 1831, they resolved that they would not be misgoverned by strangers. The French administration was often

better than that which it displaced, but there were prior claimants for the authority exercised by the French, and at first the national contest was a contest for legitimacy. In the second period this element was wanting. No dispossessed princes led the Greeks, the Belgians, or the Poles. The Turks, the Dutch, and the Russians were attacked, not as usurpers, but as oppressors,—because they misgoverned, not because they were of a different race. Then began a time when the text simply was, that nations would not be governed by foreigners. Power legitimately obtained, and exercised with moderation, was declared invalid. National rights, like religion, had borne part in the previous combinations, and had been auxiliaries in the struggles for freedom, but now nationality became a paramount claim, which was to assert itself alone, which might put forward as pretexts the rights of rulers, the liberties of the people, the safety of religion, but which, if no such union could be formed, was to prevail at the expense of every other cause for which nations make sacrifices.

Metternich is, next to Napoleon, the chief promoter of this theory; for the anti-national character of the restoration was most distinct in Austria, and it is in opposition to the Austrian Government that nationality grew into a system. Napoleon, who, trusting to his armies, despised moral forces in politics, was overthrown by their rising. Austria committed the same fault in the government of her Italian provinces. The kingdom of Italy had united all the northern part of the Peninsula in a single State; and the national feelings, which the French repressed elsewhere, were encouraged as a safeguard of their power in Italy and in Poland. When the tide of victory turned, Austria invoked against the French the aid of the new sentiment they had fostered. Nugent[4] announced, in his proclamation to the Italians, that they should become an independent nation. The same spirit served different masters, and contributed first to the destruction of the old States, then to the expulsion of the French, and again, under Charles Albert, to a new revolution. It was appealed to in the name of the most contradictory principles of government, and served all parties in succession, because it was one in which all could unite. Beginning by a protest against the dominion of race over race,

[3] Felix Ludwig Johann Friedrich Schwarzenberg (1800–1852) and Baron Alexander von Bach (1813–1893) were conservative prime ministers and ardent supporters of reaction in Austria. Baron Otto von Manteuffel (1805–1882) was a conservative Prussian statesman who served as prime minister and minister of foreign affairs from 1850 to 1858. [Editor's note.]

[4] Laval Nugent (Count Nugent von Westmeath) (1777–1862) was an Irishman who rose to the position of field marshal in the Austrian army and became a prince of the Holy Roman Empire. He led several Austrian campaigns in Italy, including the one in 1859 when the Italians succeeded in ending Austrian domination. [Editor's note.]

its mildest and least-developed form, it grew into a condemnation of every State that included different races, and finally became the complete and consistent theory, that the State and the nation must be co-extensive. "It is," says Mr. Mill, "in general a necessary condition of free institutions, that the boundaries of governments should coincide in the main with those of nationalities."

The outward historical progress of this idea from an indefinite aspiration to be the keystone of a political system, may be traced in the life of the man who gave to it the element in which its strength resides, —Giuseppe Mazzini. He found Carbonarism impotent against the measures of the governments, and resolved to give new life to the liberal movement by transferring it to the ground of nationality. Exile is the nursery of nationality, as oppression is the school of liberalism; and Mazzini conceived the idea of Young Italy when he was a refugee at Marseilles. In the same way, the Polish exiles are the champions of every national movement; for to them all political rights are absorbed in the idea of independence, which, however they may differ with each other, is the one aspiration common to them all. Towards the year 1830 literature also contributed to the national idea. "It was the time," says Mazzini, "of the great conflict between the romantic and the classical school, which might with equal truth be called a conflict between the partisans of freedom and of authority." The romantic school was infidel in Italy, and Catholic in Germany; but in both it had the common effect of encouraging national history and literature, and Dante was as great an authority with the Italian democrats as with the leaders of the mediaeval revival at Vienna, Munich, and Berlin. But neither the influence of the exiles, nor that of the poets and critics of the new party, extended over the masses. It was a sect without popular sympathy or encouragement, a conspiracy founded not on a grievance, but on a doctrine; and when the attempt to rise was made in Savoy, in 1834, under a banner with the motto "Unity, Independence, God and Humanity," the people were puzzled at its object, and indifferent to its failure. But Mazzini continued his propaganda, developed his *Giovine Italia* into a *Giovine Europa*, and established in 1847 the international league of nations. "The people," he said, in his opening address, "is penetrated with only one idea, that of unity and nationality. . . . There is no international question as to forms of government, but only a national question."

The revolution of 1848, unsuccessful in its national purpose, prepared the subsequent victories of nationality in two ways. The first of these was the restoration of the Austrian power in Italy, with a new and more energetic centralisation, which gave no promise of freedom. Whilst that system prevailed, the right was on the side of the national aspirations, and they were revived in a more complete and cultivated form by Manin.[5] The policy of the Austrian Government, which failed during the ten years of the reaction to convert the tenure by force into a tenure by right, and to establish with free institutions the condition of allegiance, gave a negative encouragement to the theory. It deprived Francis Joseph of all active support and sympathy in 1859, for he was more clearly wrong in his conduct than his enemies in their doctrines. The real cause of the energy which the national theory has acquired is, however, the triumph of the democratic principle in France, and its recognition by the European Powers. The theory of nationality is involved in the democratic theory of the sovereignty of the general will. "One hardly knows what any division of the human race should be free to do, if not to determine with which of the various collective bodies of human beings they choose to associate themselves." It is by this act that a nation constitutes itself. To have a collective will, unity is necessary, and independence is requisite in order to assert it. Unity and nationality are still more essential to the notion of the sovereignty of the people than the cashiering of monarchs, or the revocation of laws. Arbitrary acts of this kind may be prevented by the happiness of the people or the popularity of the king, but a nation inspired by the democratic idea cannot with consistency allow a part of itself to belong to a foreign State, or the whole to be divided into several native States. The theory of nationality therefore proceeds from both the principles which divide the political world,—from legitimacy, which ignores its claims, and from the revolution, which assumes them; and for the same reason it is the chief weapon of the last against the first.

In pursuing the outward and visible growth of the national theory we are prepared for an examination of its political character and value. The absolutism which has created it denies equally that absolute right of national unity which is a product of democracy, and that claim of national liberty which be-

[5] Daniele Manin (1804–1857) was a patriotic leader against the Austrians during the 1830's and 1840's and a promoter of liberal opinion in Italy. [Editor's note.]

longs to the theory of freedom. These two views of nationality, corresponding to the French and to the English systems, are connected in name only, and are in reality the opposite extremes of political thought. In one case, nationality is founded on the perpetual supremacy of the collective will, of which the unity of the nation is the necessary condition, to which every other influence must defer, and against which no obligation enjoys authority, and all resistance is tyrannical. The nation is here an ideal unit founded on the race, in defiance of the modifying action of external causes, of tradition, and of existing rights. It overrules the rights and wishes of the inhabitants, absorbing their divergent interests in a fictitious unity; sacrifices their several inclinations and duties to the higher claim of nationality, and crushes all natural rights and all established liberties for the purpose of vindicating itself. Whenever a single definite object is made the supreme end of the State, be it the advantage of a class, the safety or the power of the country, the greatest happiness of the greatest number, or the support of any speculative idea, the State becomes for the time inevitably absolute. Liberty alone demands for its realisation the limitation of the public authority, for liberty is the only object which benefits all alike, and provokes no sincere opposition. In supporting the claims of national unity, governments must be subverted in whose title there is no flaw, and whose policy is beneficent and equitable, and subjects must be compelled to transfer their allegiance to an authority for which they have no attachment, and which may be practically a foreign domination. Connected with this theory in nothing except in the common enmity of the absolute state, is the theory which represents nationality as an essential, but not a supreme element in determining the forms of the State. It is distinguished from the other, because it tends to diversity and not to uniformity, to harmony and not to unity; because it aims not at an arbitrary change, but at careful respect for the existing conditions of political life, and because it obeys the laws and results of history, not the aspirations of an ideal future. While the theory of unity makes the nation a source of despotism and revolution, the theory of liberty regards it as the bulwark of self-government, and the foremost limit to the excessive power of the State. Private rights, which are sacrificed to the unity, are preserved by the union of nations. No power can so efficiently resist the tendencies of centralisation, of corruption, and of absolutism, as that community which is the vastest that can be included in a State, which imposes on its members a consistent similarity of character, interest, and opinion, and which arrests the action of the sovereign by the influence of a divided patriotism. The presence of different nations under the same sovereignty is similar in its effect to the independence of the Church in the State. It provides against the servility which flourishes under the shadow of a single authority, by balancing interests, multiplying associations, and giving to the subject the restraint and support of a combined opinion. In the same way it promotes independence by forming definite groups of public opinion, and by affording a great source and centre of political sentiments, and of notions of duty not derived from the sovereign will. Liberty provokes diversity, and diversity preserves liberty by supplying the means of organisation. All those portions of law which govern the relations of men with each other, and regulate social life, are the varying result of national custom and the creation of private society. In these things, therefore, the several nations will differ from each other; for they themselves have produced them, and they do not owe them to the State which rules them all. This diversity in the same State is a firm barrier against the intrusion of the government beyond the political sphere which is common to all into the social department which escapes legislation and is ruled by spontaneous laws. This sort of interference is characteristic of an absolute government, and is sure to provoke a reaction, and finally a remedy. That intolerance of social freedom which is natural to absolutism is sure to find a corrective in the national diversities, which no other force could so efficiently provide. The co-existence of several nations under the same State is a test, as well as the best security of its freedom. It is also one of the chief instruments of civilisation; and, as such, it is in the natural and providential order, and indicates a state of greater advancement than the national unity which is the ideal of modern liberalism.

The combination of different nations in one State is as necessary a condition of civilised life as the combination of men in society. Inferior races are raised by living in political union with races intellectually superior. Exhausted and decaying nations are revived by the contact of a younger vitality. Nations in which the elements of organisation and the capacity for government have been lost, either through the demoralising influence of despotism, or the disintegrating action of democracy, are restored and educated anew under the discipline of a stronger and less corrupted race. This fertilising and regenerating process can only be obtained by living under one government. It is in the cauldron of the State that the fusion takes place by which the vigour, the knowledge, and the capacity of one portion of mankind may be communicated to another. Where political and national boundaries coincide, society ceases to advance, and nations relapse into a condition corresponding to that of men who renounce intercourse with their fellow-men. The difference between the two unites mankind not only by the benefits it confers on those who live together, but because it connects society either by a political or a national bond, gives to every people an interest in its neighbours, either because they are under the same government or because they are of the same race, and thus promotes the interests of humanity, of civilisation, and of religion.

Christianity rejoices at the mixture of races, . . . It was the mission of the Church to overcome national differences. The period of her undisputed supremacy was that in which all Western Europe obeyed the same laws, all literature was contained in one language, and the political unit of Christendom was personified in a single potentate, while its intellectual unity was represented in one university. . . . Out of the mediaeval period, and the combined action of the German race and the Church, came forth a new system of nations and a new conception of nationality. Nature was overcome in the nation as well as in the individual. . . . [Nations] had many things in common; the old barriers which separated them were removed, and the new principle of self-government, which Christianity imposed, enabled them to live together under the same authority, without necessarily losing their cherished habits, their customs, or their laws. The new idea of freedom made room for different races in one State. A nation was . . . a moral and political being; not the creation of geographical or physiological unity, but developed in the course of history by the action of the State. It is derived from the State, not supreme over it. A State may in course of time produce a nationality; but that a nationality should constitute a State is contrary to the nature of modern civilisation. The nation derives its rights and its power from the memory of a former independence.

The Church has agreed in this respect with the tendency of political progress, and discouraged wherever she could the isolation of nations; . . . she defends national liberty against uniformity and centralisation with an energy inspired by perfect community of interests. For the same enemy threatens both; and the State which is reluctant to tolerate differences, and to do justice to the peculiar character of various races, must from the same cause interfere in the internal government of religion. The connection of religious liberty with the emancipation of Poland or Ireland is not merely the accidental result of local causes; . . . From this influence of religion in modern history has proceeded a new definition of patriotism.

The difference between nationality and the State is exhibited in the nature of patriotic attachment. Our connection with the race is merely natural or physical, whilst our duties to the political nation are ethical. One is a community of affections and instincts infinitely important and powerful in savage life, but pertaining more to the animal than to the civilised man; the other is an authority governing by laws, imposing obligations, and giving a moral sanction and character to the natural relations of society. Patriotism is in political life what faith is in religion, and it stands to the domestic feelings and to homesickness as faith to fanaticism and to superstition. It has one aspect derived from private life and nature, for it is an extension of the family affections, as the tribe is an extension of the family. But in its real political character, patriotism consists in the development of the instinct of self-preservation into a moral duty which may involve self-sacrifice. Self-preservation is both an instinct and a duty, natural and involuntary in one respect, and at the same time a moral obligation. By the first it produces the family; by the last the State. If the nation could exist without the State, subject only to the instinct of self-preservation, it would be incapable of denying, controlling, or sacrificing itself; it would be an end and a rule to itself. But in the political order moral purposes are realised and public ends are pursued to which private interests and even existence must be sacrificed. The great sign of true patriotism, the development of selfishness into sacrifice, is the product of political life. That sense of duty which is supplied by race is not entirely separated from its selfish and instinctive basis; and the love of country, like married love, stands at the same time on a material and a moral foundation. The patriot must distinguish between the two causes or objects of his devotion. The attachment which is given only to the country is like obedience given only to the State — a submission to physical influences. The man who prefers his country before every other duty shows the same spirit as the man who surrenders every right to the State. They both deny that right is superior to authority. . . .

The nationality formed by the State, then, is the only one to which we owe political duties, and it is, therefore, the only one which has political rights. The Swiss are ethnologically either French, Italian, or German; but no nationality has the slightest claim upon them, except the purely political nationality of Switzerland. . . .

. . . When different races inhabit the different territories of one Empire composed of several smaller States, it is of all possible combinations the most favourable to the establishment of a highly developed system of freedom. In Austria there are two circumstances which add to the difficulty of the problem, but also increase its importance. The several nationalities are at very unequal degrees of advancement, and there is no single nation which is so predominant as to overwhelm or absorb the others. These are the conditions necessary for the very highest degree of organisation which government is capable of receiving. They supply the greatest variety of intellectual resource; the perpetual incentive to progress which is afforded not merely by competition, but by the spectacle of a more advanced people; the most abundant elements of self-government, combined with the impossibility for the State to rule all by its own will; and the fullest security for the preservation of local customs and ancient rights. In such a country as this, liberty would achieve its most glorious results, while centralisation and absolutism would be destruction.

The problem presented to the government of Austria is higher than that which is solved in England, because of the necessity of admitting the national claims. The parliamentary system fails to provide for them, as it presupposes the unity of the people. Hence in those countries in which different races dwell together, it has not satisfied their desires, and is regarded as an imperfect form of freedom. It brings out more clearly than before the differences it does not recognise, and thus continues the work of the old absolutism, and appears as a new phase of centralisation. In those countries, therefore, the power of the imperial parliament must be limited as jealously as the power of the crown, and many of its functions must be discharged by provincial diets, and a descending series of local authorities.

The great importance of nationality in the State con-

sists in the fact that it is the basis of political capacity. The character of a nation determines in great measure the form and vitality of the State. Certain political habits and ideas belong to particular nations, and they vary with the course of the national history. A people just emerging from barbarism, a people effete from the excesses of a luxurious civilisation, cannot possess the means of governing itself; a people devoted to equality, or to absolute monarchy, is incapable of producing an aristocracy; a people averse to the institution of private property is without the first element of freedom. Each of these can be converted into efficient members of a free community only by the contact of a superior race, in whose power will lie the future prospects of the State. A system which ignores these things, and does not rely for its support on the character and aptitude of the people, does not intend that they should administer their own affairs, but that they should simply be obedient to the supreme command. The denial of nationality, therefore, implies the denial of political liberty.

The greatest adversary of the rights of nationality is the modern theory of nationality. By making the State and the nation commensurate with each other in theory, it reduces practically to a subject condition all other nationalities that may be within the boundary. It cannot admit them to an equality with the ruling nation which constitutes the State, because the State would then cease to be national, which would be a contradiction of the principle of its existence. According, therefore, to the degree of humanity and civilisation in that dominant body which claims all the rights of the community, the inferior races are exterminated, or reduced to servitude, or outlawed, or put in a condition of dependence.

If we take the establishment of liberty for the realisation of moral duties to be the end of civil society, we must conclude that those states are substantially the most perfect which, like the British and Austrian Empires, include various distinct nationalities without oppressing them. Those in which no mixture of races has occurred are imperfect; and those in which its effects have disappeared are decrepit. A State which is incompetent to satisfy different races condemns itself; a State which labours to neutralise, to absorb, or to expel them, destroys its own vitality; a State which does not include them is destitute of the chief basis of self-government. The theory of nationality, therefore, is a retrograde step in history.

It is the most advanced form of the revolution, and must retain its power to the end of the revolutionary period, of which it announces the approach. Its great historical importance depends on two chief causes.

First, it is a chimera. The settlement at which it aims is impossible. As it can never be satisfied and exhausted, and always continues to assert itself, it prevents the government from ever relapsing into the condition which provoked its rise. The danger is too threatening, and the power over men's minds too great, to allow any system to endure which justifies the resistance of nationality. It must contribute, therefore, to obtain that which in theory it condemns,—the liberty of different nationalities as members of one sovereign community. This is a service which no other force could accomplish; for it is a corrective alike of absolute monarchy, of democracy, and of constitutionalism, as well as of the centralisation which is common to all three. Neither the monarchical nor the revolutionary, nor the parliamentary system can do this; and all the ideas which have exited enthusiasm in past times are impotent for the purpose except nationality alone.

And secondly, the national theory marks the end of the revolutionary doctrine and its logical exhaustion. In proclaiming the supremacy of the rights of nationality, the system of democratic equality goes beyond its own extreme boundary, and falls into contradiction with itself. Between the democratic and the national phase of the revolution, socialism had intervened, and had already carried the consequences of the principle to an absurdity. But that phase was passed. The revolution survived its offspring, and produced another further result. Nationality is more advanced than socialism, because it is a more arbitrary system. The social theory endeavours to provide for the existence of the individual beneath the terrible burdens which modern society heaps upon labour. It is not merely a development of the notion of equality, but a refuge from real misery and starvation. However false the solution, it was a reasonable demand that the poor should be saved from destruction; and if the freedom of the State was sacrificed to the safety of the individual, the more immediate object was, at least in theory, attained. But nationality does not aim either at liberty or prosperity, both of which it sacrifices to the imperative necessity of making the nation the mould and measure of the State. Its course will be marked with material as well as moral ruin, in order that a new invention may prevail over the works of God and the interests of mankind. There is no principle of change, no phase of political speculation conceivable, more comprehensive, more subversive, or more arbitrary than this. It is a confutation of democracy, because it sets limits to the excercise of the popular will, and substitutes for it a higher principle. It prevents not only the division, but the extension of the State, and forbids to terminate war by conquest, and to obtain a security for peace. Thus, after surrendering the individual to the collective will, the revolutionary system makes the collective will subject to conditions which are independent of it, and rejects all law, only to be controlled by an accident.

Although, therefore, the theory of nationality is more absurd and more criminal than the theory of socialism, it has an important mission in the world, and marks the final conflict, and therefore the end, of two forces which are the worst enemies of civil freedom, —the absolute monarchy and the revolution.

4

LIBERALISM: BOURGEOIS SELF-INTEREST OR ROAD TO DEMOCRACY?

One of the major legacies of the Eighteenth Century Revolutions and a major force for change after 1815 was "liberalism." As a political label "liberal," although applied by Napoleon to his own system, was first coined as an epithet for the Spanish rebels against the French. In France, however, it was used after 1815 by the royalists to denote their opponents who advocated political reform and progressive legislation. Englishmen spoke of Guizot as the typical French "liberal" but they also designated Thiers and Odilon Barrot, who opposed Guizot and each other, by the same label. In England by 1850, a Liberal was a member of the party of Gladstone. In Germany and Central Europe, groups of professors, lawyers, and bureaucrats came to be called by the same name. After reading the following extracts, the student should understand what these people and their fellows had in common, as well as how they differed.

The cornerstone of the liberal creed was personal freedom. Liberty, it taught, was the basis of the dignity, value, and moral worth both of the individual human being and of Western civilization. Man, liberals believed, could be free and good if only he had free institutions. While some liberals thought that man was good by nature, all believed that he was moulded by his environment. If the latter consisted of free institutions—political liberty, civil rights, constitutional guarantees, parliamentary government, and social equality—the material and spiritual progress of all men, all classes, and all creeds would result.

The liberal's glorification of the free individual was matched by his distrust of the state. Civil liberties won in the English, American, and French Revolutions included freedom of thought and expression, free speech and a free press, the right of assembly, jury trial, security of property and sanctity of contract. A constitution should guarantee these rights and should strictly limit the power of the executive, guarantee the independence and impartiality of the judiciary, and subordinate all government to a representative legislature. Liberals agreed that government should be responsible to "the people," but in practice many of them at first limited political participation to the well-to-do citizens by means of property qualifications and literacy tests for voters and office holders. Gradually the franchise and office holding were extended during the nineteenth century until, reluctantly, "liberalism" was at last identified with "democracy." Similarly, liberals disagreed on ministerial responsibility. At first, cabinets were answerable to the monarch but finally to the majority party in parliament.

The social tenets of liberalism included equality: Equality of opportunity (though not of wealth), equality in the eyes of the law and in the presence of the judge, equality at the hands of the tax collector, and (though not always and rarely at first) equal access to public office. A privileged, hereditary aristocracy was unthinkable. Wealth gave status but not privileges. For the liberal, religion was a private matter, and thence followed freedom of religious belief and worship, as well as separation of church and state. Generally, even if not systematically anti-clerical, most liberals were hostile to the Roman Catholic Church which eventually (1864) condemned liberalism.

In the economic realm early nineteenth-century liberals, like the Physiocrats and Adam Smith a generation before, worshipped *laissez-faire* and believed that evil rather than good would come of government intervention in the economic process.

Hence they favored the liquidation of age-old mercantilist policies, the liberation of private economic initiative, and free trade — in a word, they were dedicated to "free enterprise." Capitalism was one of their basic assumptions.

Finally, the revolutionary concept of the "sovereignty of the people" was retained in the form of nationalism — the right of a people to create an independent, self-governing state. Eventually liberals in Central Europe had to choose between constitutional reform and national unity, and, as we shall see, many chose nationalism.

The liberals were always a dynamic, never a static, group. They reflected changing interests, adjusted to circumstances, and reflected new forces such as the progress of the Industrial Revolution and the rise of nationalism. Hence liberalism has never been an unchanging system of thought. Rather it is an attitude toward life and its problems which emphasizes the values of freedom for the individual, for minorities, for nations, and for mankind.

The concepts of liberalism were the products of the Enlightenment, of the English Revolution of 1688, of the American Revolution ("life, liberty, and the pursuit of happiness"), and of the French Revolution ("liberty, equality, fraternity"). Because of recent memories of "Jacobin Terror" and "Bonapartist dictatorship" early nineteenth-century liberals tended to play down rationalism, anti-clericalism, militarism, republicanism, equality, the right of rebellion, and democracy, and to stress utilitarianism, reform, secularism, constitutional monarchy, and limitations on popular participation in government. They abhorred the idea of revolution and advocated orderly change through use of the legislative process. Nevertheless, liberals and conservatives alike were conscious of the revolutionary heritage and implications of liberalism. The European Revolutions of 1820–21, 1830, 1848, and 1870 were inspired in part by the "principles of 1789."

From the first, liberalism was found to be congenial by the commercial and industrial middle classes, by skilled technicians and by men of the liberal professions. Their status, wealth, and influence were on the rise. When bourgeois leaders like Guizot became spokesmen for liberalism, it tended to become a conservative, middle-class ideology. As the nineteenth century developed, liberals became alarmed at the social consequences of unregulated industrialization. As the growing proletariat became class conscious and then politically radical and even socialistic, liberals like J. S. Mill modernized their creed and expanded their reform program to advance the interests of all classes.

By 1870 England and Western Europe (though not Central and Eastern Europe) had secured the free institutions desired by liberals. Thereafter they would have to demonstrate that those institutions would indeed lead to spiritual and material progress for all. They found that they were caught between two dangerous opponents — one to the Left, Socialism, the party of Karl Marx — and one to the Right, the party of reaction, now led by men like Bismarck. In at least the case of the German liberals (see Baumgarten), they succumbed to the temptation to climb aboard the victory chariot of the conservatives.

The student should carefully analyze the following documents which have been selected to illustrate the attitudes and points of view of a French bourgeois liberal orator of the 1830's (Guizot), of an English reformed liberal writing in the 1850's (Mill), and a disillusioned German liberal writing in 1866 under the impact of the successful Bismarckian Revolution (Baumgarten). What do they tell us about the nature and meaning of liberalism, "the lessons of history," the significance and value of democracy, the inter-relations of classes, and the processes of government during this period?

FRANÇOIS GUIZOT

FRENCH BOURGEOIS LIBERALISM

The French journalist, author, educator, and historian, François Pierre Guillaume Guizot (1787–1874), was one of the outstanding "liberal" statesmen of nineteenth-century Europe. During the Bourbon Restoration, 1815–1830, he was a leader of the Liberals and a severe critic of the administration. During the reign of Louis Philippe, 1830–1848, he was associated with conservatism and defended the established order.

Born of Protestant parents at Nîmes, in the south of France, he came to Paris in 1805 where he became actively involved in a literary career. He was named Professor of History at the University of Paris in 1812, and he is still widely known for his lectures on the history of civilization in France and in Europe and for his books on the seventeenth-century English Revolution and for a history of France written for his grandchildren.

Guizot served as Minister of Public Instruction, 1832–1836, and organized primary education in France, improved the secondary schools and universities, and founded the Société de l'Histoire de France to encourage historical research and publications, and the Comité des Travaux Historiques to publish original sources at the expense of the government.

During the July Monarchy, Guizot was known as a "bourgeois" liberal, and he advocated rule by the bourgeoisie on the ground that it was they who provided a solid base for political freedom. He was hotly attacked by the democrats and the socialists on the Left and by the royalist reactionaries on the Right. From 1840 to 1848, he served as Prime Minister of France, until the revolution of 1848 overthrew the régime of Louis Philippe and drove Guizot himself into exile.

The excerpt which follows shows Guizot as an advocate of the bourgeoisie as the upholders of freedom. It was a speech which he delivered in the French Chamber on May 5, 1837, after he had resigned as Minister of the Interior and broken with the Prime Minister, Count Molé. In it, he argued that the electorate based on the bourgeoisie could be expanded as a result of greater opportunities to acquire wealth, and that the middle classes were "the best guardians of the principles of 1789; of social order as of constitutional government, of liberty as of order, of civil liberties as of political liberties, of progress as of stability."

Chamber of Deputies, Session of Friday, May 5, 1837.

[During the political debate provoked by the discussion of secret funds on May 3, 1837, Guizot had spoken on the subject of the middle classes and democracy.]

M. Mauguin: I am going to end the discussion quickly. Did not M. Guizot say, (and a little while ago when I repeated it, did you not regard my words as the exact reproduction of his thought?) . . . that he wished to organize the triumph and the victory of the middle classes (*la classe moyen*) in France? (Yes! Yes!) Well! You cannot organize the triumph and the victory of the middle classes except through introducing inequalities and consequently dominators and dominated. . . .

Numerous voices to the center: No! No!

From the Left: Yes! Yes!

M. Guizot: I did not say that.

From the two extremities: Let him speak! Let him speak! . . .

M. Guizot: . . . I had the honor to say, the day before yesterday, that I regarded the French Revolution of 1789 to 1830 as the triumph of the middle class (*la classe moyen*).

M. Odilon Barrot: Let us say of the entire nation.

M. Guizot: I repeat the words that I pronounced: . . . . as the triumph of the middle class over privilege and over absolute power, and it is that which it is a question of organizing. (*Applause on the right center.*)

M. Odilon Barrot: It is not that which must be organized; it is a question of having the entire nation triumph, and not one class. (*Noise and various movements.*) . . .

M. Mauguin: There is in this thought, in this proposal to establish the influence of one class no matter which, something deadly for France; for you alarm all the others, and it is all the others whom you make your enemies.

Do you want me to reply in one word by the lessons of history? France, like all the other countries, is divided into three more or less clearly defined classes: the upper rich, the intermediate rich, and the working classes, the laboring classes.

Well then! Of these three classes one should never dominate the other two. Do you want to recall the memories of the Revolution? In '89 the intermediate class wanted to triumph and have its triumph alone; '93 witnessed its fall. Then the working classes triumphed over the middle class. (*Agitation.*)

After '93, the popular class, which was governing then, was vanquished in its turn, because it was alone. And if we now pass immediately to 1830, the July Revolution was nothing else (*Interruption.*) than the revolt of the two middle and lower classes against the upper class, against the aristocratic class, which wanted to dominate. . . .

M. Odilon Barrot: . . . In our France, national sovereignty places political power, not in a class, but in the nation. . . . Victory was won by all classes, it is the entire nation which carried it off. (*New applause to the left.*)

The victory which we have won is great; I desire that it should be definitive, and that the combat

From Francois Guizot, "Speech during the discussion of the bill on the secret funds for 1837." Chamber of Deputies, Session of May 3 and May 5, 1837, in *Archives Parlementares de 1787 a 1860*, ed. M. Mavidal, E. Laurent, and others, 2nd Series (1800–1860), Vol. CX (Paris: Paul Dupont, 1904), pp. 480–81, 492, 494–97. [Translated by the editor.]

which lasted for fifty years in order to achieve the consecration of our principles of 1789, of our principles of equality and of liberty, I desire that it should be terminated forever, and that it should not begin again; but if it must recommence, if the two principles which come, as the honorable M. Guizot was saying the day before yesterday, are face to face; if this democratic principle which is on the rise in France, which you find everywhere, in the workshop, even in the palaces of the rich, in all classes of society, must one day again defend itself on the field of battle, remember that it would be highly imprudent, that it would be even criminal, perhaps, so far as our Revolution is concerned, to have said a single time without denial: that it is the middle class which won, which triumphed, which profited from the victory. If you do so, you deprive our great and beautiful cause of all that it can win by way of support from the energy of the entire nation.

To the left: Very good! . . .

(M. Odilon Barrot, returning to his seat receives the congratulations of a great number of members.

M. Guizot, who appears at the speaker's tribune, waits for almost ten minutes while calm and silence are re-established.)

M. Guizot: [After denying that his retirement during the ministerial crisis the previous year had been based on personal considerations, Guizot went on to reply to the attacks that had been made against him two days before and earlier during this same debate by M. Odilon Barrot and others.]

M. Guizot: I must say now what I really think. (*Yes! Yes! Speak! Speak!*) For the last six years [that is to say, since the July Revolution of 1830], gentlemen, the country has been put to the test, but it has had a full measure of freedom of the press, freedom of elections. One can attack as one wishes our electoral system, the influences exercised in the elections; but no one can deny that the country has enjoyed for the past seven years in electoral and press matters, a liberty greater than at any other epoch; no one can deny that the government of July has not sought the opinion of the country more profoundly and with infinitely more sincerity than has any other preceeding government. . . . No government that I know of, claims to be infallible; no government pretends that all its projects were adopted by the public powers, that all its ideas were shared by the

majority which supported it. . . . I state this as a generalization without stopping at special exceptions . . . which do not destroy it. I state the fact that the judgment pronounced by the country, by the free and legal country, [i.e. the electorate based on a high property qualification] for the last six years between the opposition and us, that it is to say between the system of the opposition and our own, that this judgment has been constantly in our favor.

Gentlemen, here is the explanation, and I am brought back by the words of the honorable M. Barrot on the middle class. The middle class, he said, as if he would make you think of it as a class apart, constituted separately, and in consequence opposed to the other classes of the nation. It is a lie! It is a danger; you forget all the victories of our Revolution which have been gained by everyone; you forget the blood which flowed at home and abroad for the independence and for the liberty of France! It is the blood of everyone. No, I am not forgetting that! There are in our Charter rights, public rights which have been conquered for everyone, which are the price of the blood of everyone. (*Very good! Very good!*) These rights are equality of public office, equal admissibility to all public employment, freedom of the press, individual liberty. These rights, among us, are those of everyone; these rights belong to all Frenchmen; they are really worth the trouble of being won by the battles that we have fought and by the victories which we have won. . . . But it is understood that at the end of these combats, and in order to guarantee all these liberties, all these rights that it has conquered, victory has evidently meant that it establishes in the midst of itself a regular government, a stable government, a government which is not ceaselessly and perpetually to call in question again by combats analogous to those which we have fought for the last fifty years. Evidently the French nation has not intended to live for ever in [a state of] revolution as it lived during twenty long years. No, certainly not; it has intended to arrive at a state of affairs which is regular, stable, in which the portion of the nation that is truly capable of exercising public power, capable of possessing public powers, should be regularly constituted under the form of a free government, of a government which guarantees liberties, the rights of all, by the active and direct intervention of a certain number of men. I say intentionally "a certain number," to exclude forever, at least in my own thought, the theory of universal suffrage, of the universality of political rights; a theory which is hidden, I repeat, at the bottom of all the revolutionary theories, and which still survives in most of the ideas and the systems which the opposition brings to this rostrum.

From the center: Very good!

M. *Guizot*: That is what I wanted to say when I spoke of the necessity of constituting and organizing the middle class. Have I assigned any limits to the middle class? Have you heard me say where it begins, or where it ends? I have carefully abstained from doing so; I have distinguished neither an upper class, nor lower class. I have simply expressed the generalization that there exists, in the heart of a great country like France, a class which is not devoted to manual labor, which does not live from wages, which has freedom and leisure for thought, which can consecrate a considerable part of its time and its faculties to public affairs, which has not only the necessary wealth for such work, but which has at the same time enlightenment (lumière), independence, without which his work cannot be accomplished.

When I said yesterday that the date of February 5, 1817, which established direct elections in France, had founded the reality of direct representative government, that side of the Chamber (he motions to the Left) made signs of agreement; your signs of agreement yesterday are the most formal condemnation of the system which you have come to support today.

What did the law of February 5, 1817, establish? It commenced precisely this work of which I am speaking to the Chamber, this constitution, this political organization of the middle class; this law posed precisely the bases of the political preponderance of the middle class; it vested political power in the highest part [of society], that is to say in the independent, enlightened, capable part of society. At the same time it made provision for political power to expand downwards to a low enough level so that it arrives at the limit where capacity ends. When, in the course of time, this limit will be changed, when greater knowledge and increase of wealth, all the factors which contribute to social change will have called up a greater number of men and more numerous classes, [have acquired] political capacity, the limit will change. [i.e. The electorate will be expanded]. The very perfection of our [system of] government, consists in the fact that political rights, limited by their nature to those who are capable of exercising them, can extend in pro-

portion as capacity is acquired by more people. At the same time it is the great virtue of our government that it constantly encourages the extension of this capacity by spreading political enlightenment and knowledge of political questions. At the same time that places a limit on political rights, at this moment it works to change this limit, (*Very good! Very good!*), to extend it, to put it off, and thus to raise up the entire nation.

How could you believe, how could anyone in this Chamber believe that it was part of my thought to set up the middle class in a narrow manner, in a privileged manner, to make it something resembling the former aristocracies? But permit me to say it, I would have had to have abdicated the opinions which I have supported all my life, I would have had to have abandoned the cause which I have constantly defended, the task on which, for the last six years, I have had the honor of working under your eyes and with your cooperation. [i.e. as Minister of Public Instruction and educational reformer]. When I applied myself to expand enlightenment of all kinds in this country, when I tried to elevate these laboring classes, these classes which live on wages, to the dignity of man, to give them the knowledge which they need for their situation, it is a continual provocation on my part, on the part of the entire government, to help them to acquire greater knowledge, greater enlightenment, to mount ever higher. It is the commencement of this work of civilization, of this ascending universal movement, which is in the nature of man to hope for with ardor. (*Lively applause.*) . . .

M. *Odilon Barrot*: No doubt it is for that reason that you reject men of ability?

M. *Guizot*: I reject, I reject absolutely, both for the system [of government] which I have the honor to support and for myself, these accusations of [favoring] narrow systems, alien to the mass of the nation and to the general welfare, [and of being] uniquely devoted to the special interests of one or another class of citizens. I reject them absolutely, and at the same time I maintain that there is truth in this system: that the moment has come to discard these outmoded ideas, this ancient prejudice of absolute equality. . . .

M. *Guizot*: . . . I repeat on purpose, that the moment has come, in my opinion, to set aside these old prejudices of equality of political rights, of universality of political rights, which have been not only in France, but in all countries, everywhere where they have been applied, the death of true liberty and of justice, which is true equality. (*Pronounced movement of agreement.*)

They speak of democracy, they accuse me of disregarding the rights, the interests of democracy. Ah! Gentlemen, I tried yesterday to reply in advance to this objection. I tried to demonstrate that what destroys democracy in all countries where it has been ruined, and it often has been [destroyed], it is precisely because it is not conscious of human dignity. Democracy does not know how to raise itself constantly, and instead of admitting the variations in situations and the social hierarchy without which there is no society—and which has no need to be a closed hierarchy, or a privileged one, which freely admits the liberty and the upward mobility of the individual, and the perpetual competition according to the merit of each one. Instead of admitting this fact as I say, it rejects it with arrogant blindness. What has often destroyed democracy, is the fact that it is unable to admit any hierarchical organization of society. Liberty is not sufficient for it; it desires leveling (*le nivellement*), it wants everyone to be equal. That is why democracy perished. (*Very good! Very good!*)

Well, I am one of those who fights against the leveling process in whatever form it may present itself; I am one of those who ceaselessly challenges the entire nation, democracy itself, to raise itself. But at the same time I want to warn that in a given moment everyone is not rising, that everyone is not capable of rising; that elevation has its special conditions, that it requires capacity, intelligence, virtue, hard work, and a host of qualities which everyone does not possess. (*Very good! Bravos!*)

I desire that everywhere where these qualities shall be found, everywhere where there will be capacity, virtue, work, democracy should raise itself to the highest functions of the State, that it should mount this rostrum, to make its voice heard, to speak to the entire country. But you have that; you have no need to ask for it; your government gives it to you. It is inscribed in your Charter, in this official constitution, the legal basis of your society, against which you endlessly excite yourselves. You are ungrateful

men, you constantly misrepresent the benefits you have in your possession; you speak always as if you lived under an oppressive regime, under slavery, as if you were in the presence of an aristocracy like that of Venice, of absolute power. Well! Gentlemen, you live in the midst of the freest society which has ever been seen, and where the principle of social equality is the most consecrated. Never have you seen a similar meeting of individuals raised to the highest rank in all walks of life. We have almost all won our promotions by the sweat of our brow and on the field of battle. (*Prolonged applause*). . . .

. . . But today the battle is over, peace is made, the treaty is concluded; the treaty is the Charter, and the government which proceeds from it. . . . (*Prolonged cheers*)

I do not wish to see my country recommence what it has already accomplished. I accept 1791, 1792; even the years following; I accept them in history, but I do not want to relive them again in the future. . . . (*Very good! Very good!*) And I make it my duty, a duty of conscience, to warn my country every time I see it leaning toward that side.

Gentlemen, one never falls except on the side toward which one leans. (*Sensation*) I do not wish my country to lean on that side [to the Left], and every time that I see it leaning, I hasten to warn it. (*Agitation.*)

There, gentlemen, there is my system, my policy, my only policy; that is the sense in which I mean these words *middle class* and *democracy*, *liberty* and *equality*, that have been repeated so much in this tribune a little while ago. . . .

That is the cause to which I am devoted; that is the confidence that I seek. . . . (*Prolonged bravos in the center. Applause.*)

(Mr. Guizot, descending from the tribune is welcomed by the congratulations of his colleagues belonging to various sections of the Chamber. The discussion of the bill is postponed until next day. The Chamber disperses in the middle of the most lively agitation. The session is suspended at 6:15 in the evening.)

JOHN STUART MILL

ENGLISH REFORMIST LIBERALISM

The English political philosopher and economist, John Stuart Mill (1806–1873), shows an advance beyond the liberalism of Guizot and of his own fellow English liberals of the first half of the nineteenth century. These had for the most part reflected the interests, needs, and beliefs of the "bourgeoisie," that is to say the industrial and commercial middle classes who in England had received the right to vote in 1832 and who had used their power to repeal the Corn Laws in 1846.

Mill's work *On Liberty*, published in 1859, developed the concept of liberalism as a social philosophy and provided arguments to demonstrate that liberty, particularly freedom of thought and expression, was essential for the development of human progress. In reading this classic formulation of English liberal thought, you should attempt to follow Mill's arguments as to the value of liberty in the development of human individuality which he holds to be the highest good. Note also the defense of moral and intellectual freedom for its own sake against the dangers, in Mill's view, inherent in a democracy.

Nevertheless, English Liberals came to accept the necessity for further advances toward democracy in the second Reform Bill of 1867 and the third of 1884. In the period after 1870 liberal thought evolved still more in the direction of State intervention, for every act of liberation involved for some individual group a corresponding act of restraint.

This, then, is the appropriate region of human liberty. It comprises, first, the inward domain of consciousness; demanding liberty of conscience in the most comprehensive sense; liberty of thought and feeling; absolute freedom of opinion and sentiment on all subjects, practical or speculative, scientific, moral, or theological. The liberty of expressing and publishing opinions may seem to fall under a different principle, since it belongs to that part of the conduct of an individual which concerns other people; but, being almost of as much importance as the liberty of thought itself, and resting in great part on the same reasons, is practically inseparable from it. Secondly, the principle requires liberty of tastes and pursuits; of framing the plan of our life to suit our own character; of doing as we like, subject to such consequences as may follow: without impediment from our fellow-creatures, so long as what we do does not harm them, even though they should think our conduct foolish, perverse, or wrong. Thirdly, from this liberty of each individual, follows the liberty, within the same limits, of combination among individuals; freedom to unite, for any purpose not involving harm to others: the persons combining being supposed to be of full age, and not forced or deceived.

No society in which these liberties are not, on the whole, respected is free, whatever may be its form of government; and none is completely free in which they do not exist absolute and unqualified. The only freedom which deserves the name, is that of pursuing our own good in our own way, so long as we do not attempt to deprive others of theirs, or impede their efforts to obtain it. . . . Mankind are

John Stuart Mill, *On Liberty* (Boston: Ticknor and Fields, 1860), pp. 27–29, 35, 56–57, 66–68, 118–19, 124–25, 128–29, 135–40, 213–23.

greater gainers by suffering each other to live as seems good to themselves, than by compelling each to live as seems good to the rest. . . .

Let us suppose . . . that the government is entirely at one with the people, and never thinks of exerting any power of coercion unless in agreement with what it conceives to be their voice. But I deny the right of the people to exercise such coercion, either by themselves or by their government. The power itself is illegitimate. The best government has no more title to it than the worst. It is as noxious, or more noxious, when exerted in accordance with public opinion, than when in opposition to it. If all mankind minus one were of one opinion, and only one person were of the contrary opinion, mankind would be no more justified in silencing that one person, than he, if he had the power, would be justified in silencing mankind. . . .

But, indeed, the dictum that truth always triumphs over persecution is one of those pleasant falsehoods which men repeat after one another till they pass into commonplaces, but which all experience refutes. History teems with instances of truth put down by persecution. If not suppressed for ever, it may be thrown back for centuries. . . . It is a piece of idle sentimentality that truth, merely as truth, has any inherent power denied to error of prevailing against the dungeon and the stake. Men are not more zealous for truth than they often are for error, and a sufficient application of legal or even of social penalties will generally succeed in stopping the propagation of either. . . .

There have been, and may again be, great individual thinkers in a general atmosphere of mental slavery. But there never has been, nor ever will be, in that atmosphere an intellectually active people. Where any people has made a temporary approach to such a character, it has been because the dread of heterodox speculation was for a time suspended. Where there is a tacit convention that principles are not to be disputed; where the discussion of the greatest questions which can occupy humanity is considered to be closed, we cannot hope to find that generally high scale of mental activity which has made some periods of history so remarkable. Never when controversy avoided the subjects which are large and important enough to kindle enthusiasm, was the mind of a people stirred up from its foundations, and the impulse given which raised even persons of the most ordinary intellect to something of

dignity of thinking beings. Of such we have had an example in the condition of Europe during the times immediately following the Reformation; another, though limited to the Continent and to a more cultivated class, in the speculative movement of the latter half of the eighteenth century; and a third, of still briefer duration, in the intellectual fermentation of Germany during the Goethian and Fichtean period. These periods differed widely in the particular opinions which they developed; but were alike in this, that during all three the yoke of authority was broken. In each, an old mental despotism had been thrown off, and no new one had yet taken its place. The impulse given at these three periods has made Europe what it now is. . . .

In our times, from the highest class of society down to the lowest, every one lives as under the eye of a hostile and dreaded censorship. . . . They ask themselves, what is suitable to my position? what is usually done by persons of my station and pecuniary circumstances? or (worse still) what is usually done by persons of a station and circumstance superior to mine? . . . It does not occur to them to have any inclination, except for what is customary. Thus the mind itself is bowed to the yoke: even in what people do for pleasure, conformity is the first thing thought of; they live in crowds; they exercise choice only among things commonly done; peculiarity of taste, eccentricity of conduct, are shunned equally with crimes; until by dint of not following their own nature they have no nature to follow: their human capacities are withered and starved: they become incapable of any strong wishes or native pleasures, and are generally without either opinions or feelings of home growth, or properly their own. . . .

It will not be denied by anybody, that originality is a valuable element in human affairs. There is always need of persons not only to discover new truths, and point out when what were once truths are true no longer, but also to commence new practices, and set the example of more enlightened conduct, and better taste and sense in human life. . . . It is true that this benefit is not capable of being rendered by everybody alike: there are but few persons, in comparison with the whole of mankind, whose experiments, if adopted by others, would be likely to be any improvement on established practice. But these few are the salt of the earth; without them, human life would become a stagnant pool. Not only is it they who introduce good things which did not before exist; it is they who keep the life in those which already exist. . . . There is only too great a tendency in the best beliefs and practices to degenerate into the mechanical; and unless there were a succession of persons whose ever-recurring originality prevents the grounds of those beliefs and practices from becoming merely traditional, such dead matter would not resist the smallest shock from anything really alive, and there would be no reason why civilization should not die out, as in the Byzantine Empire. Persons of genius, it is true, are, and are always likely to be, a small minority; but in order to have them, it is necessary to preserve the soil in which they grow. Genius can only breathe freely in an *atmosphere* of freedom. . . .

No government by a democracy or a numerous aristocracy, either in its political acts or in the opinions, qualities, and tone of mind which it fosters, ever did or could rise above mediocrity, except in so far as the sovereign. Many have let themselves be guided (which in their best times they have always done) by the counsels and influence of a more highly gifted and instructed One or Few. The initiation of all wise or noble things comes and must come from the individuals; generally at first from some one individual. The honour and glory of the average man is that he is capable of following that initiative; that he can respond internally to wise and noble things, and be led to them with his eyes open. I am not countenancing the sort of "hero-worship" which applauds the strong man of genius for forcibly seizing on the government of the world and making it do his bidding in spite of itself. All he can claim is, freedom to point out the way. . . .

The despotism of custom is everywhere the standing hindrance to human advancement, being in unceasing antagonism to that disposition to aim at something better than customary, which is called, according to circumstances, the spirit of liberty, or that of progress or improvement. The spirit of improvement is not always a spirit of liberty, for it may aim at forcing improvements on an unwilling people; and the spirit of liberty, in so far as it resists such attempts, may ally itself locally and temporarily with the opponents of improvement; but the only unfailing and permanent source of improvement is liberty, since by it there are as many possible independent centres of improvement as there are individuals. The progressive principle, however, in either shape, whether as the love of liberty or of improvement, is antagonistic to the sway of Custom,

involving at least emancipation from that yoke; and the contest between the two constitutes the chief interest of the history of mankind. The greater part of the world has, properly speaking, no history, because the despotism of Custom is complete. . . .

It is not progress that we object to; on the contrary, we flatter ourselves that we are the most progressive people who ever lived. It is individuality that we war against: we should think we had done wonders if we had made ourselves all alike; forgetting that the unlikeness of one person to another is generally the first thing which draws the attention of either to the imperfection of his own type, and the superiority of another, or the possibility, by combining the advantages of both, of producing something better than either. We have a warning example in China. . . .

What is it that has hitherto preserved Europe from this lot? What has made the European family of nations an improving, instead of a stationary portion of mankind? Not any superior excellence in them, which, when it exists, exists as the effect, not as the cause; but their remarkable diversity of character and culture. Individuals, classes, nations, have been extremely unlike one another: they have struck out a great variety of paths, each leading to something valuable; and although at every period those who travelled in different paths have been intolerant of one another, and each would have thought it an excellent thing if all the rest could have been compelled to travel his road, their attempts to thwart each other's development have rarely had any permanent success, and each has in the time endured to receive the good which the others have offered. Europe is, in my judgment, wholly indebted to this plurality of paths for its progressive and many-sided development. . . .

The third and most cogent reason for restricting the interference of government is the great evil of adding unnecessarily to its power. . . .

If the roads, the railways, the banks, the insurance offices, the great joint-stock companies, the universities, and the public charities, were all of them branches of the government; if, in addition, the municipal corporations and local boards, with all that now devolves on them, became departments of the central administration, if the employees of all these different enterprises were appointed and paid by the government, and looked to the government for every rise in life; not all the freedom of the press and popular constitution of the legislature would make this or any other country free otherwise than in name. And the evil would be greater, the more efficiently and scientifically the administrative machinery was constructed. . . .

All the enlarged culture and practised intelligence in the country, except the purely speculative, would be concentrated in a numerous bureaucracy, to whom alone the rest of the community would look for all things; the multitude for direction and dictation in all they had to do; the able and aspiring for personal advancement. To be admitted into the ranks of this bureaucracy, and when admitted, to rise therein, would be the sole objects of ambition. Under this *régime*, not only is the outside public ill-qualified, for want of practical experience, to criticise or check the mode of operation of the bureaucracy, but even if the accidents of despotic or the natural working of popular institutions occasionally raise to the summit a ruler of reforming inclinations, no reform can be effected which is contrary to the interest of the bureaucracy. Such is the melancholy condition of the Russian empire, as shown in the accounts of those who have had sufficient opportunity of observation. The Czar himself is powerless against the bureaucratic body; he can send any one of them to Siberia, but he cannot govern without them, or against their will. On every decree of his they have a tacit veto, by merely refraining from carrying it into effect. In countries of more advanced civilisation and of a more insurrectionary spirit . . . when the evil exceeds their amount of patience, they rise against the government, and make what is called a revolution; whereupon somebody else, with or without legitimate authority from the nation, vaults into the seat, issues his orders to the bureaucracy, and everything goes on much as it did before; the bureaucracy being unchanged, and nobody else being capable of taking their place.

A very different spectacle is exhibited among a people accustomed to transact their own business. . . . Let them be left without a government, every body of Americans is able to improvise one, and to carry on that or any other public business with a sufficient amount of intelligence, order, and decision. This is what every free people ought to be: and a people capable of this is certain to be free; it will never let itself be enslaved by any man or body of men because these are able to seize and pull the reins of the central administration. No bureaucracy can hope to make such a people as this do or undergo anything that they do not like. But where everything is done through the bureaucracy, nothing to which the bureaucracy is really adverse can be done at all. . . . The governors are as much the slaves of their organisation and discipline as the governed are of the governors. A Chinese mandarin is as much the tool and creature of a despotism as the humbled cultivator. . . .

To determine the point at which evils, so formidable to human freedom and advancement, begin, or rather at which they begin to predominate over the benefits attending the collective application of the force of society, under its recognised chiefs, for the removal of the obstacles which stand in the way of its well-being; to secure as much of the advantages of centralised power and intelligence as can be had without turning into governmental channels too great a proportion of the general activity — is one of the most difficult and complicated questions in the art of government. It is, in a great measure, a question of detail, in which many and various considerations must be kept in view, and no absolute rule can be laid down. But I believe that the practical principle in which safety resides, the ideal to be kept in view, the standard by which to test all arrangements intended for overcoming the difficulty, may be conveyed in these words: the greatest dissemination of power consistent with efficiency; but the greatest possible centralisation of information, and diffusion of it from the centre. Thus, in municipal administration, there would be, as in the New England States, a very minute division among separate officers, chosen by the localities, of all business which is not better left to the persons directly interested; but besides this, there would be, in each department of local affairs, a central superintendence, forming a branch of the general government. The organ of this superintendence would concentrate, as in a focus, the variety of information and experience derived from the conduct of that branch of public business in all the localities, from everything analogous which is done in foreign countries, and from the general principles of political science. This central organ should have a right to know all that is done, and its special duty should be that of making the knowledge acquired in one place available for others. Emancipated from the petty prejudices and narrow views of a locality by its elevated position and comprehensive sphere of observation, its advice would naturally carry much authority; but its actual power, as a permanent institution, should, I conceive, be limited to compelling the local officers to obey the laws laid down for their guidance. In all things not provided for by general rules, those officers should be left to their own judgment, under responsibility to their constituents. For the violation of rules, they should be responsible to law, and the rules themselves should be laid down by the legislature; the central administrative authority only watching over their execution. . . .

A Government cannot have too much of the kind of activity which does not impede, but aids and stimulates, individual exertion and development. The mischief begins when, instead of calling forth the activity and powers of individuals and bodies, it substitutes its own activity for theirs; when, instead of informing, advising, and, upon occasion, denouncing, it makes them work in fetters, or bids them stand aside and does their work instead of them. The worth of a State, in the long run, is the worth of the individuals composing it; and a State which postpones the interests of *their* mental expansion and elevation to a little more of administrative skill, or of that semblance of it which practice gives, in the details of business; a State which dwarfs its men, in order that they may be more docile instruments in its hands even for beneficial purposes—will find that with small men no great thing can really be accomplished; and that the perfection of machinery to which it has sacrificed everything will in the end avail it nothing, for want of the vital power which, in order that the machine might work more smoothly, it has preferred to banish.

HERMANN BAUMGARTEN

GERMAN LIBERALISM SURRENDERS

The German historian, Hermann Baumgarten (1825–1893), was both a liberal and a nationalist, and this selection from his curious essay on "German Liberalism —A Self Criticism," as has been mentioned, might have been included equally well in the problem of Nationalism. In fact, it provides a vital connecting link between two of the major themes of the Age of Revolutions.

Baumgarten, who was a Professor of History at the University of Karlsruhe in Baden, played a political role in that liberal Duchy, and also gained a solid reputation as an authority in Spanish history. His insights concerning the latter failed to help him to understand Germany and its problems in the 1860's. Like most other German liberals and nationalists, he had opposed the militaristic plans of King William of Prussia and the diplomatic and other machinations of his Chancellor, Count Bismarck. When the "miraculous year" 1866 witnessed the triumph of Prussian military might at the battle of Königgrätz (Sadowa) after Bismarck's successful diplomatic maneuvering had isolated Austria, Baumgarten and many other German liberals not only jubilantly acclaimed King William and his "Iron Chancellor" but they concluded that military and diplomatic matters could be safely confided only to the monarchs and the Junker leaders. Moreover, panegyrics for Prussia and for her aristocratic and militaristic leaders were accompanied by self-abasing statements concerning the political disabilities of middle-class German liberals.

During the Franco-Prussian War (1870–71), Baumgarten reversed himself on the annexation of Alsace-Lorraine by Germany, which he had opposed before the military triumph over France, but then supported. It is evident that Baumgarten's nationalism became progressively stronger than his liberalism as the material success of Bismarck's "Blood and Iron" policy became increasingly apparent. It should be recognized, however, that the "Bismarckian Revolution" also profoundly modified conservative thought.

What does Baumgarten conclude concerning the success of Bismarck's gamble? What revelance does that attitude have for later German history, for example, the Weimar Republic? The complete triumph of Bismarck came on January 18, 1871, when King William of Prussia was proclaimed German Emperor in the presence of the German princes and their soldiers in the Hall of Mirrors at the Palace of Versailles. That Empire—known to its supporters as the Second Reich—was defeated and destroyed by World War I. Hitler's "Third Reich" was smashed in 1945. It was only then that many Germans came to doubt the Bismarckian solution and to question the conversion to it of men like Baumgarten.

. . . In every monarchial state the nobility is the real political class. Not only in England has it been for centuries the nobility in its various classes which has almost exclusively carried the burden of political activity; also in the continental states the nobility has without exception always played a predominant role in the business of the state. And if this role in the modern constitutional history of France and Spain has been an unfortunate one, then there exists a basic reason why these countries up until this time have advanced so little in orderly political freedom, while on the other side Italy owes its undreamed-of success chiefly to the intelligent and patriotic participation of its nobility in the great work of national rebirth. The unalterable nature of the relationships is the cause of this phenomenon which emerges everywhere in the same way; namely, that monarchical states have only the choice either to achieve with the help of the nobility a modernized constitution and parliamentary forms, or to remain under the rule of a bureaucratic, more or less absolute, government.

In all modern states the middle class has elevated itself to a great economic significance and to a proud possession of scientific and industrial knowledge; all modern states rest basically on middle-class labor, all will for that reason also have to concede a meaningful influence in political life to the middle-class powers. Yet nonetheless, the middle class is hardly suited to true political action. It will be a main factor in the life of the state everywhere;

its insight, its activity, its property will be claimed by the state above all, its interests and tendencies will have to be taken into the greatest consideration by every intelligent statesman. But the nature of his position in society, the effect of his professional activity on his manner of living, character, and modes of thought, will only in exceptional cases enable the middle-class man to work successfully in great political business. The middle class will contribute perceptive and knowledgeable members to the [legislative] chambers, but will seldom give leaders who are able to govern the entire situation with a statesmanlike glance and to perform the decisive deed at the decisive moment. It will deliver excellent advice to the ministers, but will seldom deliver good ministers, who are able to deal just as cleverly with the reigning lords as with the deputies.

The Burger is born to labor, but not to rule, and the statesman's basic duty is to rule. The most capable powers of the middle class have worked themselves up from below; their cradle stood in a narrow little room, in narrow and impoverished circumstances their youth was a struggle with needs of all kinds. Only recently did they achieve a position which affords a more unhampered view of the situation of the world, and work and care for their house and business remains, as a rule, their lot in life until their creative power is exhausted. Such a way of life is the most beneficial to human ability that can be conceived; it gives character, freedom, and purity of the soul. But whoever has struggled his way up in this

From Hermann Baumgarten, "Der Deutsche Liberalismus: Eine Selbstkritik," *Preussische Jahrbücher*, Vol. XVIII, No. 5 (November, 1866), pp. 470–72; No. 6 (December, 1866), pp. 594–96, 600–03, 605–06, 617–20, 624–25. Translated by the editor.

manner is in a certain sense too good for politics. He has learned in all things to have faith in his own power and to follow his own conviction, he does not give in on every point, he bears in himself a noble, masculine pride, and at the same time, a shy modesty. He is strong, but also clumsy; he is conscientious, but also arbitrary. Place such a man in a circle of diplomats or place him next to a throne: inwardly he will value them little, yet still be duped by them; the pomp of the castle will soon impress him too much, then soon repel him too much. He will always feel himself in a strange world and will demand to return to the quiet and independence of his middle-class work. The middle class is fundamentally democratic, and fundamental democratic characteristics will always push the middle-class statesman into a certain opposition to the aristocratic beings who surround and bear every monarch. This opposition will have the result that he either, in a denial of his nature, plunges into servility, or wastes uselessly an abundance of the best power in a continuing little friction. . . .

The movement which has seized German Liberalism since 1862 has remained unsuccessful because a very small measure of effective political power was inherent in it, and yet at the same time it wished to bring about a condition for which even the greatest power would have striven in vain. If we inquire about the methods which were used in Prussia and various other states in order to push aside hostile régimes, then we may say in short, they were by nature methods of agitation. In the press, in unions, and in meetings, the questions of daily politics were dealt with in a lively manner; in vast circles of the public a basically harmonious opinion was created, and then this opinion was expressed in proclamations of the most varied sort. If it had dealt with questions of religion or of knowledge, then this activity would doubtlessly have been both practical and effective. For there is the main issue, that a certain conviction or insight be circulated as much as possible. For politics, on the other hand, that signifies a surely important and indispensable beginning, but not more. Indeed, if one remains stationary at this beginning and is unable to draw practical consequences out of it, one has made under the circumstances a beginning not for the better, but for the worst. When the voters of a great state in their great majority repeatedly declare a government to be unconstitutional and destructive to the state, and thereupon acquiesce in the fact that this declaration has no effect, then they inflict a grave injury on public morale and on the healthy development of the state, as if they had resigned themselves to come to a tolerable agreement with such a régime. For through such a procedure, the nature of political life is falsified, the moral power of a people is buried, [and] the dignity of the latter is lowered, particularly when the procedure is bound with such enthusiastic pathos as has become fashionable with us in recent years.

We have experienced a countless number of times the hardly edifying drama that great gatherings, indeed the representatives of our highest political bodies, made demands with such stress, as if the nation would immediately answer the denial with a powerful rebellion, and then accepted the complete failure of the great act with an indifference as though they had indeed expected nothing else. Without doubt, it would not only have been difficult, but highly dangerous, if the Prussian Chamber of Deputies had dared to attempt to call up the force of the people against the violation of the constitution. But if this people was not in a position to hold back the means to the denied expenditures, then one must not just deny the expenditures. If the House, however, had felt it its duty to carry the conflict to this extreme, now indeed it would have had to take care that the voters fought out the dispute with the same unyielding energy which the regime developed on its side, and the leaders in the House had the natural duty to be the leaders in the struggle of deeds as in the struggle of words. In the phrase "with all lawful means," it is a praiseworthy axiom to have in the very beginning a citizenry suited to its strictly lawful meaning; but then one must also take care not to set up goals which now simply cannot be achieved by lawful means. But to bring about cheerfully a situation whose next phase must step out beyond the line of the law, and then when this phase has been entered, to plant the law before oneself like an impregnable rampart, that is an inoffensiveness that is not appropriate to the seriousness of politics. Such a tactic proves not respect for the law, but fear of the natural results of what one has done. It compromises the law as it does him who claims to respect the law above all else. . . .

[The German historian] Gervinius has declared of the nineteenth century that it places the activity and power of the many in the position of the ruling force of individuals; its character is democratic and excludes the aristocratic preponderance. To be sure, that may be said in the highest degree of German

Liberalism of our time. It is only a question of whether that is a praiseworthy and desirable characteristic. I maintain that as long as it operates in this one-sided democratic way under the rule of monarchial forms of government, it will have to give up all claims to ever realizing its own ideas itself; that is to say, to taking hold of political life with full power. Thousands can and must share in the work of propagating certain ideas; but it would be impossible for them ever to share in the executive of a modern state, and only the executive brings political ideas into life. With us until now the course has always been that the Liberals posed certain demands and represented them so far that it was impossible to deny them any longer; then, however, not liberal but conservative regimes took over the practical execution. The one great, shining victory of Liberalism, which our century recognizes was fought for in Italy. However, in Italy, I feel, the many in docile subordination helped the one, and this one, who really conquered, was an aristocrat. The truly decisive impulses went forth not from the Italian people nor from some Italian party, but from Cavour. He had Italy take part in the Crimean War, he created the alliance with France, he brought about the war. Only a single man can prepare and carry out such crises, and they are in politics that which gives the powerful pressure of a people the strength to reach the goal. Certainly our age is in important respects ruled by democratic tendencies, but precisely this democratic character makes its outstanding individual so much the more indispensable. For democracy requires a head. Only aristocracies can allow the mass of chosen ones to exercise collective power. A comparison of the most recent history of France and England shows the truth of this sentence with self-evident clarity.

We saw earlier how the Liberal opposition in the small [German] states, because it was damned to remain opposition, assumed a predominantly negative character. He who can never do anything but say no to what happens, who does not imagine how he might someday say yes, approaches things in a distorted, unnatural position. Such is the case above all in politics, which has a thoroughly positive character. In it negation is justified only insofar as something wrong must be discarded in order to build that which is right in its place. In it, criticism must be absolutely subordinate to creative action. For the most mediocre action is more fruitful for the state than the most admirable, but inactive, criticism. Certainly there is a close danger for a people that has grown great in theory as have the Germans, that it would allow more of its rational intelligence than its active will to have effect even in the world of action. But precisely this danger must become particularly perilous to just such a people. For while it exercises its criticism of ideas on the phenomena of the rough and always unfinished reality, it clears itself of the duty to become active in circumstances which it has recognized as most lamentable. The man of philosophical speculation, scholarly research, artistic pretension, or domestic morality, brings to political facts a criterion which they can actually never satisfy. For a long time our participation in the state consisted basically in remaining aloof from it by our absolute criticism; and if we still allowed ourselves to be seduced into wishing to negotiate within it, we quickly made such discouraging discoveries of the impossibility of realizing in it the noble and pure ideals in our bosoms, that we once more quickly resigned ourselves to experiencing these ideals in the chaste stillness of our homes. Such a nature and custom among us had to give the defensive negation an unfortunate predominance over the improving activity. Our good-natured and devoted manner expressed this inclination for quite some time in the most harmless forms. Up until the end of the forties, this disposition averted the opposition, which could hardly appease us, more than it attacked that which existed. And up until the present, that opposition suffers acutely from doing too much for some and not enough for others, a fact which destines both to prefer to remain passive rather than to take part in an activity with which they cannot agree in the least.

But once the patriotic zeal entered us as in 1848 and 1859, and our most powerful political motive, the rapturous enthusiasm for the greatness and splendor of the Fatherland, hurled us with a powerful blow onto the impoverished nature of our real circumstance, then a strange gift became apparent in us. This was the ability to work over critically everything that happened higher up and everything that existed. This theoretical opposition attained an all the more clever soaring, since the thought was still quite strange to us, ever to test ourselves in creative deeds. . . .

What a fortunate change Prussia had achieved since the fall of 1858! But how much more splendidly had the enthusiasm of the people, glorifying the new regime depicted this new era! The disparity from this image of phantasy became more and more painful and it worked all the more excitingly as the memory of the tests under the [reactionary] Man-teuffel Régime [1849–58] quickly faded. For we are accustomed in days of an ugly reaction to re-treat back into our domesticity. We appear only when a blue heaven beams outdoors: then woe to us, if several light clouds veil the ether! We have almost forgotten that storm and rain were only recently raging, for we took great care to protect our sensitive skin from such injuries. We saw how the voice of opposition grew under the Liberal ministry.

Now even came the Junker régime! Now the govern-ment spoke in expressions and with arguments that deeply wounded every middle-class consciousness. Then came the excesses of the drunken soldiers and the flighty officers. We felt that nothing so unheard-of had ever come to pass. Finally the government took vigorous action on all sides with ruthless power, with a power that often aroused the suspicion that it desired to injure and to irritate. No one can be sur-prised that the public now on its part opposed every-thing that happened, with merciless criticism. The hope of doing away with this abuse soon grew very weak; people allowed themselves more and more the satisfaction of hurting him who had insulted public opinion so feelingly. People took pleasure in the strong words of the parliamentary debates, in the harsh decrees concerning the hated government, and gradually lost the consciousness that this régime still, unfortunately, represented the state, and that they often hit the latter when they intended to strike the former.

In Baden this systematic opposition had once shaken the stability of the state to such an extent that it became the prey of a tragic revolution. Also the op-position of the Prussian Progressive Party came more and more in danger of harming the state in order to damage a hated régime. At least the opinion is wide-spread that this opposition injured important in-terests of the state more than once, because the government which demanded measures for the state was against it. Outside of Prussia, for example, one could not justify that it repeatedly refused money for the fleet. One has most decidedly had to rebuke it, that it held back when the Danish War had become indispensable, because it feared more that the government and the army reform might prove its worth and establish itself in the war than that Prussia might leave an incomparable moment un-used. Finally, this summer it has placed the interest of the [Liberal] party above that of the Fatherland in such a measure that Prussian history will pardon

it with difficulty. Here a Prussian party should cer-tainly not have gone the erroneous path of the small states' opposition. For it was answerable for the greatness and power of its state, upon which even in its opinion the welfare of the entire nation rested. In Baden or Saxony the Liberals in the heat of the struggle might well lose sight of their duty toward the state, for what meaning did it [the state] have? In Prussia, however, it was a serious offence, even just temporarily to follow a tactic which harmed the state and strengthened the enemies. In Prussia, I feel, it should never have been forgotten that next to internal politics stood foreign policy, that the state had great duties to perform in Germany and in Europe, duties in which the party itself had the strongest interest. For the tension with the German opponents grew in the same measure as the inner conflict. Apparently the moment of a great decision over the destinies of Prussia and of Germany was drawing near. In the duchies [of Schleswig and Hol-stein], the gain or loss of an immensely important region rested on the outcome. The internal questions stepped into the background for every unbiased judgment. Certainly then the time had not come to free the opposition from every consideration of these great tasks of power and of existence, and to leave unnoticed how that which one does against the internal enemy works on the foreign one. Un-fortunately, however, it thus came to pass that the language of the Liberal press and the Liberal deputies was received with joy by those on the outside who forged their weapons against Prussia, and that this language in small German states also drove the friends of Prussia more and more into the hostile camp. Here, indeed, the government, for its part, bore the gravest guilt. But the mistakes of a régime do not release the opposition from the responsibility for its own errors. And the Prussian opposition spoke and wrote so of the conditions at home that outside, the general opinion developed that Prussia was succumbing to a terrible decay and at the first blow it would collapse like a rotten building. Each in-habitant of a dwarf state thanked Heaven that it protected him from such horrible conditions. Did this picture drawn by the opposition correspond, even from a distance, to reality? And did it corres-pond to the interest of the liberal middle class in Prussia, that the world was filled with loathing toward Prussia? . . .

It was unmistakable, the Bismarck ministry had elevated the appearance and the meaning of Prussia, since the situation of this state was said to have become the most wretched in the world, to an extent that had been longed for again and again for fifty years, but always in vain. And if one could lessen the fame of the Minister-President in the Schleswig-Holstein affair by the most varied exhibitions, by the allusions to his uncertainty in the beginning, to the serious contradictions in which he became involved, to his disdain for justice, to the basically military character of the undertaking—then the low estimation held by liberals of his truly statesmanlike abilities must nonetheless come into serious difficulty through the consideration that the success in Schleswig-Holstein is in no way isolated, [but] rather that the Minister has succeeded in a similar way in a whole succession of cases. For years the claim of Electoral Hesse [for less arbitrary government] was fought for in vain by the Auerswald ministry and the people's representatives of nearly all German states. Herr von Bismarck sent the famous courier to Cassel and in a few days the arbitrariness of the elector was broken. Because of the Polish insurrection, the alliance of Prussia with Russia had aroused the disgust of liberal opinion in Germany and Europe and the fear of a coalition of three powers: the alliance achieved its goal. As the inner conflict raged with renewed vigor, Austria attempted with the middle states to humble what they thought of as a crippled Prussia at the Frankfurt Assembly of Princes: the pompously staged manoeuver had a pitiful finish. No sooner was Austria feelingly rejected than it was seen, to the astonishment of the whole world, going hand in hand with the same Prussia to Schleswig. That Austria and Prussia traveled the same path had been experienced often enough; however, that not Austria but Prussia led, that gave a completely new appearance. And while Austria worked in Schleswig for the policies and the interests of Prussia, it attempted in the affair of the French trade treaty to cross Prussia's path, here also again heartily supported by the middle states. But the result was no different than in the Assembly of Princes. Prussia conquered in this, as in all other questions, completely. . . .

Today [October, 1866] we stand in a completely new situation. For the fourth time, Prussia has completed its saving labor in Germany; and this time the power of this state, gathered in two centuries of most serious endeavor, has finally had such great success that we can look forward to the future of the Fatherland with secure confidence. The Great Elector, the great king [Frederick II], and the Wars of Liberation . . . had given Prussia a position in Germany which had to direct the glances of perceptive patriots on this state as the bearer of national development. But the great deeds of 1813 and 1815 had only halfway born fruits for Prussia. In Germany it remained subordinate to the Austrian rivalry. It was greater than the other German kingdoms, but it was not so great that they had to submit themselves to it without further ado. Its European position suffered serious weaknesses which forced it to take fearful precautions among less gifted rulers. Its inner development even seemed to remain behind that of the German small states in important respects. Those men who were able to comprehend the overall situation of the nation with a confident view, and who could read their history books, may have secured in themselves more and more the conviction that only Prussia could rescue the Germans from anarchy and impotence. But although their influence in 1849 succeeded in bringing this idea to the attention of the German Reich constitution, although all later discoveries demonstrated the impossibility of every other solution to the German question, the program of the Prussian party remained a theoretical postulate, so to speak.

It would remain so as long as Prussia had not given the actual proof to the German political system which had been created by the Congress of Vienna, that German power and activity, that the ability to complete great things, that health in military and political organization, were to be found in Prussia alone. We might well have demonstrated . . . the senselessness of the triad [the concept of "Three Germanies"], the destructiveness of dualism, the absolute necessity of unitary leadership, and that only Prussia could satisfy this greatest need. We could not convince the nation that Prussia was really what we praised it for, so long as it had not experienced a forceful example. A fifty-year period of peace had spread the strangest illusions concerning the true strength of our German soldiers. The opinion had grown firm, especially in the south, where every direct outlook of the Prussian state was lacking, that Prussia was indeed larger than Bavaria and the other kingdoms, but that the difference in quantitative affairs was diminishing. Bavaria and Hanover were just as valid states as Prussia. Most of them felt it highly problematic that Prussia, who at every attempt to advance in German affairs found Austria and the middle states united against it, would ever be able to defeat this coalition. Indeed, a few dared to hope that it might someday make the attempt. The memories of [the humiliation of Prussia at] Olmütz and Dresden, of the Baden and the first Schleswig-Holstein campaigns, of the wavering of Prussian policies from 1859 to 1862, had deeply shaken the nation's faith in Prussian power. The successes which Bismarck's policies gained since then had appeared in such a dubious light and in connection with such serious symptoms of a grave inner sickness, that ultimately even in Germany, Prussia's credit sank in the same measure as it rose in Europe.

The general assumption was that only with the enthusiastic support of the nation could Prussia rise to the position it had to assume in Germany's and its own interests, and that it could only win this support with a truly liberal régime. Unity through freedom! —so the talk went. It seemed as enlightened as possible, and was nevertheless an obvious chimera. For the ideal of freedom of the Germans in the small states bore fundamental characteristics of statelessness; it was equipped with endless privileges and allotted duties; it alternated the claims of an unfettered individualism, our most dangerous evil, with the demands of a healthy class outlook. In order ever to have been recognized as an example of a liberal state in Germany, Prussia would have been forced to sacrifice important elements of its power as a state: its serious decorum, its military strictness, and its aristocratic foundation. Also we must not forget that quite opposite achievements would have been needed to enthuse the Old Bavarian and the Rhinelander, the Swabian and the Lower Saxon. In 1859, Prussia had the most liberal government of all the German states: did that gain it the sympathies of the south? It was never hated there more than at that time. But let us assume that which, according to all previous experience, is impossible is actually possible; let us suppose that Prussia actually won over liberal opinion: what political power has this opinion displayed up until now? It was powerless in the Schleswig-Holstein affair against the weakest régimes, where even particularism was on its side. It would have been completely impotent if the governments had been able to set in motion against it the ambition of the petty residents, the inertia of men grown up in narrow circumstances, and that infinity of local and provincial antipathies. It seems to me that the National Union [Nationalverein] has made extensive discoveries on this point.

In the circle of previously attempted operations, the German question had to appear as a completely insoluble problem, and with the German question every other serious political task remained in help-less uncertainty. German politics presented itself to other nations as a tangled chaos of fruitless talking and writing. Each year we delivered as many discussions as the rest of Europe together, and as few deeds as a third-rate power. People had become accustomed to marvelling at us as a strange species of man, which along with all possible virtues of private life possessed the absolute inability to achieve corresponding success in public affairs. Even we had gradually lost confidence in ourselves. The defeat of national endeavors in 1850 still left us many a consolation; what we had experienced since 1859 seemed completely hopeless. We revolved in the saddest circle. Even the most sanguine optimism sooner or later would have to convince itself of the fruitlessness of the political drive begun since 1859. Each one of the thousands who from time to time proclaimed high-sounding resolutions had the gloomy feeling that he was doing something of no consequence. And still we knew nothing to do other than try the worn-out methods over and over again. The empty phrase threatened to become an open lie, and political life, which otherwise has the power to toughen weak natures, threatened to demoralize us. The constitutional nature of the small states failed to advance and in Prussia a serious illness seemed to threaten the entire organism. The terrible fact for a state with this past, namely, that the beginning of a war with Austria would be the beginning of a great revolution in Prussia, was considered to be so certain that the policies of Austria and the middle states in May and June [1866] rested fundamentally on this basis.

So things stood on the 14th of June [1866]. Three weeks later the entire German world was completely transformed. The middle-sized states had revealed themselves as small states lacking any independent ability to be effective. Prussia stood over this poverty of small statism like a giant full of robust power. It had shattered boastful Austria in a week. And it stood there, not only as the healthy power next to one sick in every limb, but also as a highly civilized power next to a fundamentally barbarous one. The "German Brother" in Austria had taken it upon itself to completely cure the south German enthusiasts. What shameless lies in their press, what stupid brutality in the dressing stations and in the prison camps, what faithlessness toward allies, what subservience toward the foreign emperer [Napoleon III] ! Now the Great Germans in Bavaria and Swabia experienced the true nature of the Habsburg splendor; now the blind ones saw that the House of Habsburg had poi-

The Age of Revolutions

soned Austria to the core as had once been done to Spain and that the brotherly phrases of the German Austrians were nothing but a clumsy trap for the simpletons in the Reich. The participants in the great alliance for the chastisement of Prussia proved themselves beyond all expectations to be small and poor: poor in ideas, and in knowledge as poor as in actual enthusiasm; small on the field of battle as in the cabinet. And the much abused Prussia stood great and rich beyond all expectations; great in every achievement, rich in every power.

The astonished world did not know what to admire more, the unique organization of Prussia's armed forces or the ethical dedication of its people, the incomparable health of its economy or the solidity of its general education, the greatness of its victories or the modesty of its victory bulletins, the courage of its young soldiers or the devotion to duty of its aged king. Everything, everything in this state, which for years people had learned to look upon as the sure prey of Revolution, showed itself to be wonderfully genuine, and the more this enigmatic appearance was tested, the more that was found to be marvelled at. This Nation [*Volk*] in arms stormed forward with irrepressible force on a victory road without equal, and yet remained a people of peace, entirely untouched by the intoxication of military glory, demanding a return to their quiet labor, almost more mournful over those who had died than jubilant over victory. It developed incomparable courage in a struggle which it had long kept at a distance with all its energy. It placed all of its energies at the service of a régime against which it had waged the most embittered warfare for four years. Was that the same people whose representatives, not yet a year before, had executed the great retreat under Classen-Cappelmann, and whose press even now had found almost no other answer to the infamous provocations of the Vienna newspapers other than sighs for peace? If this people accomplished so much in such an unpopular struggle under such a government, what must be expected of it if it once went forth wholeheartedly with no party opposition to deeply divide the population and cripple its power! . . .

That Prussia is the German power, and that all other states are loose fragments who can secure their own existence only through a sincere, honorable annexation to the former, that is a fact which the arbitrary Swabian can fool only himself into doubting. This beneficial simplification of our situation, this good fortune, that we finally feel firm, secure ground under

our feet, will surely in a short time repel a host of our political bad habits, and allow the robust health, which thank God, we enjoy in other areas of life, to prove useful to our politics. The chatterers who until now have held the entire stage will have no more success in the sharp, clear air in which we now move about. After we actually have experienced in the highest degree what action is, we will find no more pleasure in allowing our ears to be titillated by bombastic phrases. Since the work of the political dilettantes has failed so completely, we will demand that in the great state through which we have entered the life of the world, complete gravity and virile capability be proven, which in other areas we have so long found self-evident. After we have experienced that in a monarchical state the nobility forms an indispensable constituent, and after we have seen that these much despised Junkers know how to fight and die for the Fatherland, in spite of the best Liberal, we will restrict our bourgeois conceit a little and resign ourselves to maintaining an honorable place next to the nobility. We thought that by our agitation we could transform Germany: then we were well on our way simply to sweep ourselves out; I think we will take this experience to heart. The tremendous events which we have witnessed have taught us how very frail these same premises were on which we had built, as if on a foundation of rock, our national liberal policy in the last years. Almost all the elements of our political system have been shown [to be] erroneous by the facts themselves.

It would be difficult for us to accept this new insight if it were accompanied by our misfortune. But we have experienced a miracle almost without parallel. The victory of our principles would have brought misery upon us, whereas the defeat of our principles has brought us boundless salvation. Truly we could not be conscientious, altruistic, and pure if we did not respond to such a blessing from Heaven by sincere self-criticism and by the unshakable determination to start life anew with unassuming dedication and faithful obedience to the great revelations which have come to us this year. . . .

There will perhaps be no lack of those who will call betrayal to the party that which only true devotion to the party could have appointed me to do. If Liberalism were not important to me, I would not have taken so much trouble on its account. I am firmly convinced that a satisfactory solution of our political tasks will succeed only if Liberalism ceases to be preponderantly opposition; only if it succeeds in satisfying certain vastly important desires of the nation, for which only Liberalism has a complete and sincere understanding, in its own governmental activity; only if we succeed in obtaining a beneficial and refreshing succession of liberal and conservative regimes. *Liberälism must become capable of governing* [*regierungsfähig*]. Whoever finds a curtailment of Liberal greatness in a situation where instead of demanding the boundless as a member of the opposition he should accomplish something small as a member of the government, such a man I cannot help.

5

THE INDUSTRIAL REVOLUTION IN ENGLAND—
POVERTY OR PROGRESS OF THE WORKERS?

Our final problem is concerned with the economic, social and political effects of the Industrial Revolution upon the working class in England. There is a large and growing literature concerned with the definition, causes, and characteristics of that vast and Protean economic movement known as "the Industrial Revolution," so that an introductory statement by the editor is difficult to limit to the small space available here.

Applied in the early nineteenth century by French writers (Blanqui, for example, in 1837), popularized in the lectures of an Englishman, Arnold Toynbee (delivered 1880–81, published 1884), the term "Industrial Revolution" has become a wellworn cliché of twentieth-century textbooks. Though disparaged and qualified by economic historians of the last forty years, it can still be used in a meaningful way if we remember that it was not a sudden innovation but a quickening and deepening of technological and related changes in industry which appeared in the sixteenth century and which have transformed the European economy since the middle of the eighteenth century. Beginning in Britain about 1770 or 1780, the "Industrial Revolution" spread to France and Belgium by the 1830's, moved on to Central Europe and the United States in the second third of the nineteenth century, and achieved maturity in most Western European states by the end of the century.

Today industrialization is advocated by Marxists and non-Marxists alike as the road to affluence, in the form of higher standards of living, for the under-developed nations of Asia, Africa, and Latin America. Therefore, the leaders of these new nations, as well as students of history and economics, turn with hope to the study of the "First Industrial Revolution" of late eighteenth-century Britain.

In the selection by A. J. Taylor the student will find a summary of the evidence and arguments concerning the impact of the process of industrialization upon the standard of living of English workers during the period 1780–1850. The positions of recent optimistic "revisionist" historians like T. S. Ashton and of the "orthodox" historians (who tend to be pessimistic revisers of the revisionists) such as Eric J. Hobsbawm, are made clear so that the student can reach his own judgements concerning this controversial aspect of the problem.

Walt Whitman Rostow, well known to the public for his role as an economic and foreign policy adviser to the U.S. State Department and to President Johnson, and to the scholarly world for his theory of the industrial "take-off," has contributed the second selection. It brings out interrelations between price changes, trade cycles, living standards, and movements of political discontent among English workers. It is an excellent illustration of the application of statistical analysis and theory of economic growth to the study of wages, prices, and the business cycle.

The final selection, which is from Edward P. Thompson's *The Making of the English Working Class*, argues that the experience of the Industrial Revolution contributed powerfully to the development of class consciousness among the members of the English working class. Thompson sees the working class not as an econometric "category" or as a sociological "structure" but as a social and cultural formation "arising from historical processes operating over the years 1780 to 1832." Class consciousness was based, he believes, on a feeling of "identity of interests as between themselves and as against their rulers and employers." What evidence does he offer in support of this hypothesis? The student will notice that this selection has brought us back once more to our first two problems, the causes and the character of the political revolutions between 1770 and 1870, and that it too tries to view these movements "from below." The author relates them to social and economic problems as well as to the themes of liberalism and nationalism.

A. J. TAYLOR

INDUSTRIALIZATION AND THE STANDARD OF LIVING

The British economic historian, Arthur John Taylor (1919–   ), has been Professor of Modern History at Leeds University since 1961. Educated at Manchester University, he taught at University College, London, from 1948 until 1961.

In this selection he has summarized the historical evidence and the major arguments offered by economic historians on the highly controversial topic of the effects of the Industrial Revolution upon the standard of living and working conditions of the industrial workers in Britain. Since the early years of the nineteenth century the issue has been hotly debated and is still a historical problem of vital importance.

[Before the Industrial Revolution] the workers enjoyed a comfortable and peaceful existence. . . . Their standard of life was much better than that of the factory worker today. F. Engels, *The Condition of the Working Class in England* (1845).

If we look back to the condition of the mass of the people as it existed in this country, even so recently as the beginning of the present century, and then look around us at the indications of greater comfort and respectability that meet us on every side, it is hardly possible to doubt that here, in

England at least, the elements of social improvement have been successfully at work, and that they have been and are producing an increased amount of comfort to the great bulk of the people. G. R. Porter, *The Progress of the Nation*, 2nd edn. (1847).

Did the condition of the working classes improve or deteriorate during the period of rapid industrial change between 1780 and 1850? The controversy is as old as the Industrial Revolution itself. For men like Andrew Ure and Thomas Carlyle, as for Porter and Engels, the issue was one of contemporary politics. While Ure, a nineteenth-century Dr. Pangloss, so admired the new industrial order that he could compare factory children to "lively elves" at play, Carlyle saw the world of the millhand as "but a dingy prison-house, of rebellious unthrift, rebellion, rancour, indignation against themselves and against all men." Even among the classical economists there was a sharp division of opinion. On the one hand were those like Porter, whose optimism had its roots in the doctrines of *The Wealth of Nations*; on the other those whose pessimism reflected the less sanguine approach of Malthus and Ricardo.

With the marked improvement in national prosperity which Britain experienced in the third quarter of the nineteenth century, the debate lost something of its early vigour and urgency. The statistical investigations of Leone Levi and Sir Robert Giffen tended to confirm what the observation of contemporaries already suggested: that, in common with the nation at large, the working classes were enjoying a perceptibly higher standard of living in 1875 than twenty-five years earlier. The will to resist the tide of industrial growth was declining as its benefits became more apparent, and with the logic of time the controversy was passing from the hands of the publicists and reformers into those of the economic historians.

The transition was, however, by no means an immediate one. Thorold Rogers, an early historian of the Industrial Revolution, in 1884 welcomed the return of the political economist "to his proper and ancient function, that of interpreting the causes which hinder the just and adequate distribution of wealth." To Rogers the years of rapid industrial change were a "dismal period" for the working classes, and the quarter century after 1790 "the worst time in the whole history of English labour." Arnold

Toynbee's verdict echoed that of Rogers. "We now approach," he said, "a darker period—a period as disastrous and as terrible as any through which a nation ever passed; disastrous and terrible because side by side with a great increase of wealth was seen an enormous increase of pauperism." In both these interpretations the voice of the social reformer mingles with that of the historian: and the view thus firmly expressed commanded general acceptance for more than a generation. It is to be found as much in the writings of Ashley and Cunningham as in those of the Webbs and the Hammonds.

It was not until after the first world war that a new and less dismal note was struck. Then within the short space of little more than a year the pessimists' interpretation was four times put to serious question. In her *London Life of the Eighteenth Century*, Mrs. Dorothy George argued, largely on the basis of mortality statistics, that the standard of life of the London labourer had improved considerably in the course of the eighteenth century. This thesis was reinforced and extended a year later in the work of Miss M. C. Buer and G. Talbot Griffith. Each found evidence of a declining death-rate in the country as a whole between 1750 and 1850, and from this drew the general conclusion that living standards were rising. At the same time an even more powerful "optimist" entered the lists. From the evidence of nineteenth-century wage statistics and commodity prices, Sir John Clapham concluded that the purchasing power of the English labourer in town and country had risen substantially between 1785 and 1850.

This new turn in the controversy not only redressed the balance of forces, but, by reintroducing the statistical weapon, revived methods of argument largely disused since the days of Rogers and Giffen. Where the Hammonds, like Engels before them, turned to the evidence of the blue books and the pamphleteers, Mrs. George and Griffith appealed to the bills of mortality, and Clapham to the wage books. Faced with so great a display of statistical force, J. L. Hammond conceded—though not uncritically—this part of the field. He was content to rest his case on the written and verbal testimony of contemporaries to the physical and spiritual suffering which, he contended, had been the inevitable concomitant of the new order. Men might

From A. J. Taylor, "Progress and Poverty in Britain, 1780–1850: Its Reappraisal," *History*, New Series, Vol. XLV, No. 153 (February 1960), pp. 16–31. Reprinted without footnotes by permission of *History*.

have more food for their bellies and cheaper clothing for their backs but the price exacted for these benefits was out of all proportion to the gains. "The spirit of wonder . . . could not live at peace in treadmill cities where the daylight never broke upon the beauty and the wisdom of the world."

As a *via media* between two hitherto irreconcilable viewpoints, Hammond's compromise was readily accepted by writers of general histories, and it has retained an unshaken place in their affections; but it could be no final settlement of the debate. Thirty years now separate us from the work of Clapham and Hammond. In those years discussion has continued sporadically but vigorously. Most recently T. S. Ashton and E. J. Hobsbawm, in particular, have opened up new fields of evidence and lines of enquiry. It is appropriate to ask how far their findings have changed the broad pattern of argument and interpretation.

Of the twin sides of the debate that which relates to the qualitative aspects of the labourer's life has, not surprisingly, made least progress. The bleakness and degradation of much urban life in the early nineteenth century needs no underlining. The mean streets and insanitary houses still surviving in many industrial towns, and the mute desolation of large areas of South Wales and the West Midlands are as eloquent testimony to the drabness of nineteenth-century life as are the pages of the parliamentary reports. This was an England "built in a hurry" and with little thought for the health and wellbeing of its rapidly growing multitudes. But, as J. D. Chambers has observed: "Whatever the merits of the preindustrial world may have been, they were enjoyed by a deplorably small proportion of those born into it." If the industrial towns carried the seeds of physical and spiritual death for some, they also brought new life and opportunity to others. Not only did the towns ultimately give enhanced possibilities of physical health and enjoyment to the many; they also provided those widening cultural opportunities which, side by side with more debasing attractions, have come to distinguish the urban societies of the modern world. The older generation perhaps suffered most in the upheavals and disorders of early industrial development: for the younger and more adaptable the transition may not all have been disenchantment. But at this point argument comes close to dogmatism, for the historian's assessment of gain and loss must inevitably be coloured by his personal value judgements and predilections.

This overriding difficulty is not entirely absent from the parallel controversy about material living standards; but here at least the historian can appeal to the statistics. Although this particular oracle is in no sense infallible—too often it is mute or, when vocal, ambiguous—it offers some firm foundations for argument. It is essential, therefore, at this point, that we examine, however briefly, the main types of statistical evidence available to the historian.

The most direct route to the assessment of changing living standards lies through the measurement of the movement of real wages. Real wages relate money earnings to retail prices, and their movement, therefore, reflects the changing purchasing power of the consumer. Clapham's calculation of the movement of real wages suggests that the purchasing power of the industrial worker rose by some 16 per cent between 1790 and 1840, and by 70 per cent over the slightly longer period from 1790 to 1850. In the same periods the real earnings of farm-workers increased by 22 per cent and 60 per cent. These assessments were based on the wage statistics assembled at the beginning of the present century by A. L. Bowley and G. H. Wood, and on a cost-of-living index computed by N. J. Silberling. Since Clapham's guarded findings were published, however, Silberling's index has been tested and found wanting, and its rejection has inevitably invalidated the conclusions which Clapham based upon it.

Where Silberling failed, others have ventured with little greater success. But even were a satisfactory cost-of-living index established, and in the nature of things this would seem unlikely, it would still leave unsolved the equally complex problem of devising a satisfactory general index of working-class earnings. Here, as in the case of prices, the fundamental obstacle is the insufficiency and unreliability of the surviving evidence; but additional difficulties arise from the changing structure of the labour force—there were virtually no factory operatives in cotton in 1780, for example, and few surviving domestic workers in the industry seventy years later—and the problem of assessing the incidence of rural and urban employment. Our knowledge of the extent and nature of mid-nineteenth-century unemployment remains limited, notwithstanding the light thrown upon the subject by recent investigations. For the eighteenth century even this modicum of evidence is lacking, and a basis for comparison between the two periods in consequence hardly exists.

It seems, therefore, that despite its attractiveness, the approach to the standard of living question through the measurement of real wages must be abandoned. The movement of real wages can be determined within acceptable limits of error only in the case of certain restricted occupational groups: for the working class as a whole the margin of error is such as to preclude any dependable calculation.

A more promising approach is provided by attempts to establish changes in the pattern of working-class consumption. This method has a long and respectable ancestry—it was employed, for example, by both Giffen and Levi—but its application to the period before 1840 has only recently been attempted. It is perhaps primarily on the basis of their investigations in this field that Professor Ashton reaches the conclusion that towards the end of the eighteenth century "in some important respects the standard of living was rising," and that Dr. Hobsbawm arrives at the precisely opposite conclusion for the early nineteenth century. We may usefully investigate the basis of these generalizations.

Let us first consider food. In the middle of the nineteenth century, as half a century earlier, bread and potatoes were the staple items in the diet of every working-class family. It is impossible, on the evidence available to us, to calculate the changing levels of consumption of these commodities with any degree of accuracy; but it seems possible, as Dr. Hobsbawm suggests, that bread consumption was declining in the early decades of the nineteenth century. The implications of the development, however, are far from clear. In 1847 G. R. Porter noted that "a large and increasing number [of the population] are in a great measure fed upon potatoes"; but at the same time he observed that "unless in years of scarcity, no part of the inhabitants of England except in the extreme North, and there only partially, have now recourse to barley or rye bread." It has been usual among dieticians and economic historians to interpret a shift from rye to wheaten bread as evidence of improvement, and a shift from bread to potatoes as evidence of deterioration in general living standards. Here the two processes are seen working themselves out side by side. How, if at all, is this seeming contradiction to be resolved?

The potato was still a relative newcomer to the diet of the average Englishman at the end of the eighteenth century. Its advance represented a minor dietetic revolution whose progress was determined not solely, and indeed perhaps not even primarily, by economic factors. Outside Ireland, the potato had made its greatest conquests in the English northwest. Cheapness and ease of growth commended its use to native as well as immigrant Lancastrians; but perhaps of equal importance was the variety which it gave to the working man's table. In Ireland the rising consumption of the potato was the mark of deteriorating living standards: in northern England the same phenomenon admits of a different explanation. Even if our statistical knowledge were increased, therefore, it is doubtful whether the case of an overall rise or decline in the standard of living could find any convincing basis in the changing consumption pattern of bread and potatoes. At best it suggests differences of experience between the agricultural and industrial communities.

Not so with meat. Here a decline in *per capita* consumption may well be taken as *prima facie* evidence of an overall deterioration in living standards. At this point the historian is more fortunate in his statistical sources. Both Professor Ashton and Dr. Hobsbawm have made important use of the Returns of the Collector of Beasts Tolls at Smithfield Market, the one to demonstrate a rise in meat consumption during the eighteenth century, the other to suggest its decline after 1800. The Smithfield returns present a continuous, though not necessarily always comprehensive, survey of the numbers of sheep and cattle brought to London for slaughter in the eighteenth and early nineteenth century, and in relation to population their trend is upward in the second half of the eighteenth, and downward in the first four decades of the nineteenth century. But, suggestive as they are of wider general tendencies, the Smithfield statistics must be approached with some caution. They do not take into account all classes of meat—the ubiquitous pig, for example, is omitted—nor do they allow for the weight, as distinct from the number, of beasts taken for consumption. The investigations of G. E. Fussell thirty years ago disproved the once commonly held view that the weight of animals at market more than doubled during the course of the eighteenth century. His findings were that the Smithfield cow or sheep of 1800 was little heavier, though rather meatier, than its 1700 forbear: but it would be dangerous, without similar close investigations, to carry over this conclusion into the nineteenth century. Even more questionable is the extent to which London's experience may be said to reflect that of the country as a whole. In its extremes of wealth and poverty London was no doubt a microcosm of the nation at large, but its economic progress ran a somewhat different course from that of either the industrial North or of the agricultural South. The evidence on meat, therefore, while it suggests a nineteenth-century decline and to that extent holds no comfort for the optimist, is of itself insufficient to establish any firm thesis of general deterioration.

When attention is turned from bread and meat to more quickly perishable foodstuffs like milk and green vegetables, historian and statistician part company. Contemporaries were virtually silent about the levels of consumption of these nutritively significant items of diet. It seems likely, however, that in the case of perishable commodities the years of rapid urbanization were years of declining consumption. Although cattle were grazing within a mile of Manchester Town Hall as late as 1850, and large-scale market gardening was developing on the fringe of the industrial areas, the carriage of fresh dairy produce and vegetables before the coming of the railway must have presented problems which could hardly fail to be reflected in shortages and high prices.

The conclusions to be drawn, therefore, from the evidence on food consumption are by no means clearly defined: but their general tenor is to suggest rising living standards towards the end of the eighteenth century and less certain progress or even decline thereafter. Food, however, though it remained the most important item of working-class expenditure and took up the greater part of every working-class budget, did not exhaust the worker's wants. We know less than we would wish about the movement of house rents, but perhaps sufficient to suggest that, in relation to the labourer's wage, rent rose rather than declined between 1800 and 1850. Fuel, on the other hand, was increasing in availability and tending to fall in price with the greater exploitation of inland coalfields and improvements in transportation.

It was outside the field of necessities, in the narrow sense, that increasing consumption was most evident. Between 1785 and 1840 the production of cotton goods for the home market increased ten times more rapidly than did population. An equally well-attested, if somewhat more limited, increase is to be seen in the output of soap and candles; and it is possible to infer similar increases in the production of a wide range of household articles from pots and pans to furniture and furnishings. It would be unwise to interpret this general expansion in output as synonymous with an equivalent increase in working-class consumption. The upper and middle classes, no doubt, took a disproportionate share of the products as they did of the profits of industrialization: but it is clear that improving standards of comfort were slowly percolating down to the mass of the population. By the 1840s working-class houses in Sheffield were said to be "furnished in a very comfortable manner, the floors . . . carpeted, and the tables . . . usually of mahogany." Similar conditions were to be found in the mining districts of Northumberland and Durham. If these improvements were purchased in part at the expense of so-called necessities, and specifically of food, this was a matter of the consumer's choice. A society slowly growing more prosperous may well prefer to sacrifice near-necessities in the pursuit of new luxuries.

There remains for consideration one further possible approach to the measurement of changing living standards. As long ago as 1816 John Rickman, the census-taker, expressed the opinion that "human comfort is to be estimated by human health and that by the length of human life." Longevity is in general a useful yardstick of changing living standards, and for this reason among others the debate on living standards has tended to keep company with that on the causes and nature of population growth.

Between 1780 and 1850 the population of England and Wales rose from some $7\frac{1}{2}$ to 18 millions, a rate of growth wholly unprecedented in this country. Contemporaries were made increasingly aware of this development and sought its explanation in terms either of a rising birth-rate or of a declining death-rate. The followers of Malthus, perhaps even more than Malthus himself, put particular stress on a high birth-rate, and by implication discounted the significance of increased longevity. The contrary viewpoint, laying emphasis on a falling death-rate, was neither so firmly nor perhaps so coherently held, but indications of it are to be found in Rickman, among others. In the present century the issue has been no less vigorously debated. Griffith, in 1926, came down heavily on the side of a declining death-rate as the primary factor in population growth, but his thesis, though widely accepted, has never received the general endorsement of demographers.

T. H. Marshall, for example, though giving full weight to the decline in the death-rate from 1780 onwards, insists that as much attention be given "to the forces which kept the birth-rate up as to those which pulled the death-rate down"; and J. T. Krause goes even further in concluding that "the national [statistical] materials suggest strongly that a rising birth-rate was the major cause of the growth of the English population in this period."

When there is such disagreement about causes of first instance, it is not surprising that equal divergence of opinion is to be found about the underlying causes of population growth and their implication for the movement of living standards. Neither an increasing population nor a rising birth-rate is in itself evidence of improving living standards: indeed the experience of some Asiatic societies suggests that the reverse may often be the case. A declining death-rate, on the other hand, unless—an important proviso—it is merely the statistical reflection of a rising birth-rate, implies an increased expectation of life and may therefore be regarded as *prima facie* evidence of an improving standard of life.

It is generally agreed that the crude death-rate fell sharply—perhaps by a quarter—between 1780 and the end of the French Wars, and rose significantly, though slightly, over the next two decades; since then its course has been consistently downward. In so far as it is possible to regard the overall reduction of the death-rate as synonymous with increased longevity, this increase in expectation of life has been traced to a variety of causes: to a growth in medical knowledge and facilities, to the recession of specific virulent diseases, to improvements in personal hygiene and public health, to better and more plentiful supplies of food, and to a marked reduction in maternal and infant mortality. Griffith, for example, while touching on all these factors, perhaps lays most stress on improvements in medical knowledge and practice, and on environmental factors—the latter to explain not only the decline in the death-rate before 1815 but also the temporary reversal of the trend in the post-war period. Marshall emphasizes the rapid decline in infant mortality before 1810 and its perceptible, if less marked, rise thereafter. More recently two medical investigators, T. McKeown and R. G. Brown, have, for the eighteenth century at least, questioned the importance of improvements in medicine and treatment, and by implication given added weight to the significance of advances in nutritional standards.

These statistics and explanations are broadly consistent with those changes in living standards—upwards in the late eighteenth century and arrested to the point of decline thereafter—which have already been suggested by the evidence of food consumption. Yet, notwithstanding this coincidence, the ambiguity of the death-rate still makes it highly suspect as an instrument for the measurement of changing living standards. This is the more the case when it is borne in mind that the growth in population of these years was not solely a British nor even a European phenomenon. The fundamental cause of population increase would accordingly appear to lie outside the narrow confines of the new British industrial economy. This does not mean that industrialization played no part in determining the pattern of Britain's population growth; but it suggests that industrialization was at least as much a consequence as a cause of the increase in population. Where cause and effect are seemingly so inseparably intertwined, head is apt to chase tail in disconcerting fashion. The demographer would be the first to admit that he has problems of his own to solve in this period before he can effectively come to the aid of the economic historian.

Where so much remains legitimately controversial, the historian can at best draw only tentative conclusions. The evidence, however, would appear to permit two immediate generalizations. There is reason to believe that after an early upsurge in living standards in the first stages of rapid industrialization, the pace of advance slackened, and decline may even have set in, by the beginning of the nineteenth century. It is also evident, notwithstanding Porter's assertion to the contrary, that the progress of the working class lagged increasingly behind that of the nation at large. Had working-class incomes kept pace with the growth of the national income, the average worker could have expected to find himself some 50 per cent better off in real terms in 1840 than thirty years earlier. Even the most sanguine of optimists would hardly claim that such was in fact the case.

To explain how this situation arose is in a measure to validate the facts themselves. Thorold Rogers, writing in the 1880s, attributed the poverty of the working classes in the earlier part of the century to a variety of causes: to the unrestricted employment, before the first effective factory act in 1833, of juvenile labour; to restrictions on, and the weakness of, trade unions; and to the attitude of employers and of the law. But, significantly, he added that, although "the sufferings of the working classes . . . might have been aggravated by the practices of employers, and were certainly intensified by the harsh partiality of the law . . . they were due in the main to deeper causes." Chief among these, Rogers cited the protracted wars against France, the economic derangements which accompanied them, and the behaviour of successive governments, which were slow to remedy social evils, yet intervened unwisely to maintain the price of bread and to impede the development of trade unionism.

Modern historians have tended to endorse Rogers' findings, though with varying degrees of emphasis. They have also added two other factors, made evident by more recent economic experience: the effect of the claims of long-term investment on current consumption, and the movement of the terms of trade. A brief examination of the interaction of these varied factors is relevant to our discussion of living standards.

In the early stages of rapid industrial growth, a society is obliged to make heavy investments not only in buildings, machinery, stocks and equipment, but also in communications and public utilities. Such investment must inevitably be made at the expense of current consumption, unless, as in the case of the United States, foreign investors are willing to prime the pump of economic development. Thus Soviet Russia declared a virtual moratorium on increased living standards while laying the foundations of her industrial greatness in the 1920s. Britain after 1780 was erecting textile-mills and iron-works, constructing a great network of canals and laying the nucleus of a greater railway system, and building reservoirs, gas-works and hospitals to meet the present and future needs of a rapidly growing urban population. Like Russia a century later, though less consciously, she was sacrificing present comfort to the pursuit of future wealth and prosperity. By 1850 this early investment was yielding abundant fruit, and future expansion, in terms of railways, steamships, steel-mills, and electrical plants, was no longer to be incompatible with rising living standards.

The needs of capital accumulation, therefore, supply a partial explanation of the relative depression of working-class living standards in this period of rising national wealth. It would be unwise to press this argument too hard, however. In Japan, for example, whose industrial growth after 1918 closely paralleled that of Britain in the early nineteenth century, it proved possible to reconcile industrial growth with a perceptible advance in living standards. We must, therefore, look further afield if we are to explain not only the slow but still more the inconstant rise of living standards in nineteenth-century England. It is here, in particular, that significance is to be attached to the effects of the French Wars and to the frequently adverse movement of the terms of trade.

The wars against revolutionary and Napoleonic France imposed a severe strain upon the resources of the nation, and offset, in part at least, the gains of industrial and commercial expansion. Large-scale borrowing by the state during the war, and the imposition of severely regressive taxation at its end, not only induced serious wartime inflation but tended further to redistribute the national income in favour of the men of property. War thereby, both directly and indirectly, acted on balance to the economic detriment of the nation at large and to that of the working class in particular.

The movement of the terms of trade also proved disadvantageous to the working class consumer. During the first half of the nineteenth century the terms on which Britain dealt in foreign markets steadily worsened, more particularly between 1800 and 1815, and between 1830 and 1840. In order to pay for a given volume of imported goods, Britain had to export almost twice as much in 1840 as she had done in 1800. Specifically, the price of cotton exports fell much more rapidly after 1815 than did that of imported foodstuffs. In part—though only in part—cotton manufacturers and their employees were able to find compensation in a reduction of the price of their imported raw material: for the rest they had no alternative but to accept lower profit margins and reduced piece-rates. A significant share of the benefits of Britains's new industrial efficiency, therefore, went neither to her workers nor to her industrialists, but to the foreign consumer.

Behind these pervasive but temporary factors lay the insistent force of population pressure. In so far as population increase may be ascribed a determinant rôle in the economic growth of this period, it is easy to understand how the upward thrust of population, though it facilitated and encouraged industrial advance, also retarded the improvement in living standards which industrialization brought in its train. Since the value of labour, as of any other commodity, gains with scarcity, an overabundant supply of labour is plainly inimical to the advance of working-class living standards.

How plentiful then was the supply of labour in early nineteenth-century England? The question admits of no categorical answer. The rapid increase in population, the influx of Irish immigrants, particularly into industrial Lancashire and western Scotland, the readiness with which women and young children could be employed in mills and workshops, are all pointers to an abundant labour supply. But the supply of workers must be measured against the demands of employers. That the number of those seeking employment in a year of intense depression like 1842 was far in excess of demand is tragically evident; but we need to deepen our knowledge of employment conditions in boom years like 1835 before we can pass final judgement on the general state of the labour market. The relative immobility of labour, in terms both of geographical and of occupational movement, tended to create not one but a number of virtually independent "markets" for labour, in some of which workmen were in short, and in others in abundant supply. If a generalization is to be ventured it must be that, except at the level of the skilled worker or in years of exceptional demand, employers had little difficulty in finding hands; and to this extent the worker, lacking effective trade union organization, was generally placed in a weak position in his dealings with his employer.

To dwell thus upon these three major forces is not to deny the significance of more traditional explanations of working-class discontent; but it may serve to place these in a new perspective. That the scales were heavily weighted against the working classes is indisputable. There is no shortage of evidence, in the blue books and elsewhere, of capitalist excesses, some of them committed in the name of so-called sound economics, some of them less worthily motivated. In face of these, the worker could find little help from a state which made him the weaker partner in every contract and frustrated his efforts at collective self-help. But these evils, although they were the most apparent and the most easily remediable, were neither the only, nor probably the most important, causes of the failure of the working classes to derive early benefits from the rapid growth of industrial enterprise and productivity.

We may now sketch in rather fuller detail the general movement of working-class living standards between 1780 and 1850. The limited evidence suggests that down to about 1795 working-class families were gaining at least a share in the benefits of quickening economic activity. Prices for manufactured goods in foreign markets were buoyant and industry was reaping the full reward of its increased productivity. Workers in the newly stimulated industries enjoyed rapidly rising living standards; this was above all the golden age of the Lancashire handloom weaver. From the mid-1790s a new and less happy trend is apparent. War, inflation, and worsening terms of trade spelt distress for all but limited sections of the working class. "Wages limped slowly behind the cost of living, the standard of living of the workers was lowered." Recovery after 1815 was slow and interrupted. There were good years like 1825, when employment was high and earnings moved upwards, and even better ones like 1836, when a strong demand for labour went hand in hand with falling food prices. At such times working-class living standards, particularly in the industrial North, reached heights much above those of the best years of the eighteenth century. But there were also years, like 1817 and 1842, when work was scarce and food dear, and the position of the labourer, not least in the towns, was little if at all better than that of his predecessor in the leanest years of the earlier age. It is evident that by 1840 the material progress of half a century had not yet sufficed to insulate the working class against the worst effects of economic depression. The ebb and flow of working-class fortunes, as of those of the economy in general, had in some respects tended to become more marked with the growth of industrialism and of the nation's export trade. To this extent the labourer suffered more sharply under the pressure of industrial distress, though he gained equally substantially when business activity moved upward. In the exact calculation of gain and loss which a comparison with an earlier age involves, it is necessary to take account not only of both prosperous and depressed years but also perhaps of the new insecurity which the changing character of the business cycle brought with it. But the calculation, however nicely weighted, depends on the accuracy of the information at the historian's disposal, and the vagaries of the evidence must leave the ultimate question still an open one.

To say this may appear tantamount to suggesting that a generation of historians has laboured to bring forth a mouse. But the appearance is deceptive. Although the central issue may remain unresolved — and is perhaps likely to remain so — the area of controversy has been substantially and significantly reduced.

Optimist and pessimist now agree in seeing the years before 1795 and from the early 1840s as periods of advance — the latter to be sustained until almost the end of the nineteenth century; each views the quarter century of war as a time of deterioration; and each also draws distinctions between the experiences of different types of worker. It is common ground that the skilled enjoyed relative prosperity; and among these are to be numbered not only the craftsmen called into existence by the new order, but also the older artisan, now pressed into fuller and wider service. In this group are to be found machine-makers, iron-moulders, builders, printers and not least hewers of coal and ore. There is similar agreement that decline in living standards was the lot of the domestic worker in those industries where the machine had taken early command, in cotton weaving and hosiery knitting, for example. But in 1840 the majority of English workers, including the vast and varied army of farm-labourers and the smaller company of textile operatives, fell outside these two groups, and their experience in terms of gain or loss can be neither so easily nor so indisputably defined.

All this would suggest that the area of disagreement has contracted. Certainly it has become more clearly defined: and this is also true in a further sense. It is perhaps no more than an accident that Professor Ashton speaks of the Standard of Life of the Workers in *England* and Dr. Hobsbawm of the *British* Standard of Life. Neither makes great play with the implicit distinction; but from the point of view of the general controversy its importance can scarcely be exaggerated, a fact which Proter recognized a century ago, when he restricted his claim of improving living standards, in the first instance, to England. In 1841 the inhabitants of England outnumbered those of Ireland by only two to one. Today, taking the same areas, the disproportion is almost ten to one. Ireland, politically integrated in the United Kingdom since 1801, loomed large in the British scene. Although in 1841 the tragedy of the Great Famine still lay in the future, the living standards of Ireland's eight millions were already close to the margin of subsistence. The 'Forties may not have been hungry in England; they were certainly so in Ireland. It would be too much to suggest that the pessimistic case rests on the inclusion, and the optimistic on the exclusion, of Ireland in the calculation of the nation's welfare; but the distinction between English and British is here clearly of more than marginal significance. The argument for declining living standards is patently strongest when the experience of Ireland is added to that of Great Britain, and correspondingly weakest when attention is confined to England and, more specifically, to its new industrial North and Midlands. If nothing else emerges from recent debate, therefore, it is evident that future controversialists will need to define their arguments in precise terms of date, area and the section of the population with which they are concerned.

Even more significant than this evidence of a narrowing area of dispute is the change in the nature of the debate which has accompanied it. Where argument was once primarily in terms of the new industrial classes, it has now shifted to the wider field of the British working class as a whole, among whom as late as 1840 the new industrial wage-earners were still only a minority. At the same time the extreme position adopted by some advocates of the pessimistic case — that the decline in working-class living standards in this period was only part of a permanent process of deterioration — now appears to be virtually abandoned. This move to fresh positions is in a sense a pessimist's retreat, but it has wider implications. In the past the debate over living standards has tended to become inseparable from a more general controversy about the merits and demerits of *laissez-faire* capitalism, in which optimists and pessimists might be broadly characterized as respectively the friends and foes of economic liberalism. This division would now seem too facile. To contend that living standards rose is not to extol the merits of liberal capitalism; nor does the view that they declined necessarily imply its denigration. The slowness of advance, or actual deterioration, in working-class living standards is now seen to be explicable, at least in part, in terms other than those of the excesses of capitalist individualism; and the retardation of living standards in the early stages of industrialization has revealed itself as the experience of socialist as well as of capitalist societies. At the same time it has been clearly demonstrated that rapid economic growth and social advance are as compatible with socialist as with capitalist institutions. From one standpoint, therefore, the significance of the debate may be said to have narrowed; but from another it has undoubtedly widened. Industrialization is now a world-wide phenomenon; and the controversy about the standard of life in nineteenth-century Britain will remain not only a favourite jousting-ground for economic historians but an issue relevant to the problems of the modern world.

WALT WHITMAN ROSTOW

THE TRADE CYCLE, LIVING STANDARDS, AND MOVEMENTS OF DISCONTENT

Educated at Yale, where he received the Ph.D., and at Oxford, where he was a Rhodes Scholar, Walt Whitman Rostow (1916–   ) is a recognized authority in the fields of economic history and contemporary affairs. He taught at Columbia University, 1940–41, lectured at both Oxford and Cambridge, and served as Professor of Economic History at the Massachusetts Institute of Technology, 1950–60. Rostow has held various government appointments, including that of Assistant Chief of the German-Austrian Economic Division, U.S. Department of State, 1945–46; Assistant to the Executive Secretary of the Economic Commission for Europe, 1947–49; United States Representative to the Inter-American Committee of the Alliance for Progress; Counselor to the U.S. Department of State. He has recently been appointed Special Assistant to President Johnson.

Rostow is the author of numerous books including, *The American Diplomatic Revolution* (1947), *Essays on the British Economy of the Nineteenth Century* (1948), *The Process of Economic Growth* (1952), *The Growth and Fluctuation of the British Economy, 1790–1850* (1953), *The Dynamics of Soviet Society* (1953), *The Prospects for Communist China* (1954), *An American Policy in Asia* (1955), *Proposal: Key to an Effective Foreign Policy* (1957), *The United States in the World Arena* (1960), and *The Stages of Economic Growth* (1960). He is also editor of *The Economics of Take-off into Sustained Growth* (1963). The following selection is taken from his *Essays on the British Economy of the Nineteenth Century*.

Historians of every shade of bias admit the importance of the influence of economic situations on political and social events. The weight attached to economic factors or, more precisely, the mechanism of their action is, however, by no means settled. The most familiar relation that has hitherto been emphasized in the years 1790–1850 links the mechanical inventions of the late eighteenth century to the growth of the factory system and to the consequent rise of a large urban proletariat and a powerful middle class. From these relations, which are essentially sociological, efforts have been made to explain the political forces that produced the Reform Bill of 1832, the Chartist Movement, the repeal of the Corn Laws. In the realm of cultural history, the rise to dominance of a philosophy of individualism and a cult of romanticism have been linked to the same forces, with ramifications in economic doctrine, religion, architecture, and poetry. Such attempts at interconnexion represent a long-run analysis of economic influences. For many purposes, especially where economic influences operate at several removes, that sort of generalization is adequate.

Experience of the inter-war years, however, impressed observers with the tremendous impact of economic forces, acting over shorter periods. Changes in social structure, in political atmosphere and policy, and in intellectual attitudes can be more or less directly traced to the depression after 1929.

From W. W. Rostow, "The Trade Cycle, Living Standards, and Movements of Discontent," from his *British Economy of the Nineteenth Century* (Oxford, 1948), pp. 108–22. Reprinted by permission of the Claredon Press, Oxford.

While it is true that these trends (and the causes of depression as well) have a long history reaching back, at least, to 1873, their timing, their intensity, and their unique character are closely connected with recent short-run developments. Many historians have taken account of this type of influence, but rarely have they done so systematically.

From 1790 to 1850 there were at least three major economic forces that contributed, at intervals, to British social and political unrest: cyclical unemployment, fluctuations in domestic harvests, and technological unemployment. The latter, by itself, was not likely to produce major disturbances; nor can it be sharply distinguished from cyclical unemployment. The underemployment of hand-loom weavers was, admittedly, an important element in the Luddite and Chartist movements; and the resentment of the hand-loom weavers against the introduction of machinery often gave a peculiar character to the activity of wider groups. The most serious unrest, however, was a product of cyclical depression and high food prices.

Good harvests with resulting low grain prices were calculated to call forth complaint from the landholders and from tenants burdened with fixed rent payments. The demand for grain was sufficiently inelastic to bring a decline in gross income when good harvests caused a sharp fall in price; and, until 1832 at least, the agrarian interest was disproportionately represented in Parliament. The simplest short-period, economic-political relation is that between the wheat price and the Corn Laws.

The Corn Laws were altered principally in the following years: 1791, 1804, 1815, 1822, 1828, 1842. Repeal came, of course, in 1846. A glance at the annual average wheat price reveals the principal setting for these amendments.

The wheat price fell from 56 shillings per quarter in May 1790 to 42s. in October 1791. The movement continued to a low point of 47.0s. in May 1792. The harvest of 1791 was "one of great abundance" and, under the prevailing corn law, the fall in price was sufficient to cause the ports to be closed to foreign grain: "but the low price was productive, as usual, of complaint on the part of the landed interest, and was the occasion of a fresh corn bill." The inadequate harvests of the following years, however, kept the wheat price at or above 50s., and the Act of 1791 was not called into operation.

The catastrophic fall in the wheat price, from 154s. per quarter in March 1801 to 50s. in February 1804, produced similar, though even more violent complaint. The Corn Laws were again modified. The area under cultivation had, of course, been greatly expanded between 1793 and 1804. A succession of abundant harvests brought forth an unparalleled supply of wheat. The import limit was raised to 63s. The cutting off of Baltic supplies resulting from the resumption of war, together with bad harvests, kept the wheat price above the new minimum until 1815. Like the Act of 1791, that of 1804 was never operative.

From August 1812, when the wheat price was 152s., to January 1816 a steady decline took place. The break-up of the continental system and finally, the return to peace, as well as good harvests, caused this fall. Despite considerable opposition it was judged that only an 80s. import limit could protect the capital newly invested in agriculture.

Until the close of 1818 the wheat price remained above 80s., aided largely by inadequate harvests on the Continent and considerable exports from Britain to France. But good harvests then brought on a decline to 39s. at the close of 1822. The period of severe agricultural distress has coloured the whole view of British agriculture in the three decades after the Napoleonic wars. In 1822, however, the Government was trapped between the farmers' petitions and the opposition to further protection from labour, commercial, and industrial interests. At Peterloo, three years before, "No Corn Laws" had appeared on the banners. Unlike the position in 1815 the decline in agricultural prices (1818–22) was accompanied by a decline in import prices and non-agricultural domestic prices. The Corn Law of 1822 modified only slightly the terms of the Act of 1815. "The farmers had asked for bread and gotten a stone"; but there were others, too, asking for bread between 1818 and 1822.

From the second quarter of 1823 to the last quarter of 1828 the price of wheat hovered between 50s. and 70s. per quarter. Although the farmers were far from content, their relative position was, with respect to profits, probably no worse than that of the manufacturer or exporter; after the crisis of 1825, in fact, it was probably better. And those who sought a reduction in agricultural protection were victorious in the Corn Law of 1828. It is probable that the growing prestige of free-trade ideas and the parliamentary influence of industrial and mercantile groups played some part in moderating the 1815 bill. There was however, an immediate economic basis reflected crudely in the movement of relative prices in the twenties:

	Domestic price index	Import price index	Wheat price (s. per quarter)
1823	97	99	52
1827	106	82	56

It is clear that, from 1823 to 1827, the wheat price did not share the net fall experienced in most other markets. After 1825, a peak year in general prosperity, this disparity was especially felt; and it was in the post-crisis atmosphere that antagonism to the Corn Law of 1815 developed.

Until the last quarter of 1832 the wheat price remained well above 50s. and, although the farmers never ceased to complain, their position was not desperate. The three following years (1833–6), however, brought abundant harvests, low prices, and extensive parliamentary investigations. Although the pressure for further protection increased, no action was taken by a Parliament in which anti-agrarian interests had been materially strengthened by the Reform Bill of 1832.

At the close of 1836 the wheat price again rose suddenly as the harvest of that year appeared inadequate. Chronically bad yields kept the price abnormally high until 1842. In this period the anti-Corn Law forces crystallized outside of Parliament, deriving additional strength from the generally depressed state of industry and the high level of unemployment, especially after 1839. This protracted pressure on real wages helped bring about the Whig tariff reforms of 1841: but "Corn duties they left where they were, crying over their shoulders as they were being pushed out of office that a reasonable fixed duty . . . was the right thing." Peel was elected on the issue of the sliding scale, and in 1842 his modifications of the Corn Law of 1828 consisted in lowering the maximum duty and in making the sliding scale less steep. He himself believed this arrangement to be a considerable reduction in protection, and it was put forward as such. There is no doubt that the high food prices and depression in the previous few years had, by 1842, helped to discredit the whole argument for agricultural protection and for tariffs generally.

The role of the Irish famine in the suspension and, ultimately, in the repeal of the Corn Laws is a familiar short-period sequence, as is also the tangled and dramatic political story of 1846. It is probable, in fact, that strictly economic considerations played a somewhat lesser part in the final repeal than in some of the earlier modifications. In 1845 and the first three quarters of 1846 the domestic wheat price ranged between 45s. and 59s. A few years before it had been over 70s. The Irish famine might have been dealt with by extraordinary measures short of actual repeal. The rise in the wheat price (to a peak of 93s. in June) in 1847, however, would almost certainly have ended agricultural protection then, if its end had not been accomplished earlier.

This account is not meant, of course, to deny the long-period factors making for a reduction in agricultural protection: the growth of population, the accelerated industrialization of Britain, the widening political power of the urban middle classes and their free-trade doctrines. But it is clear that the timing of the events leading up to repeal were closely connected with the British harvests and other short-run factors influencing the absolute and relative level of the prices of agricultural products.

1. *The Speenhamland System, 1795.*[1] The years 1794 and 1795 saw some industrial recovery in Great Britain, from the depression of 1793. A more powerful force, however, affecting labour's position, was a rise in foodstuff prices, due primarily to bad harvests. The wheat price was 43.2s. per quarter in January 1792, 108s. in August 1795. Although money wages rose, there seems little doubt that they rose "in a very inadequate proportion to the increased price of the necessaries of life." There was widespread evidence of physical distress, and the wage-subsidy scheme for out-of-door relief was instituted, much in the tradition of the Elizabethan poor laws.

2. *The Combination Acts, 1799 and 1800.* From the last quarter of 1796 until about the middle of 1799 the price of wheat and the cost of living remained moderately low. Despite the brief but severe depres-

---

[1]A system devised by the justices of Berkshire (at a meeting which met at Speenhamland) to supplement wages from public funds for those who were suffering from the economic effects of the depression. The amount of subsidy was tied to the price of bread measured against wages earned. The system spread to several other counties. [Editor's note.]

sion of 1797, these were, internally, years of relative peace. The wheat price (which, at the end of 1798, was down to 48s.) then rose to a peak of 154s. in March 1801. The government acted by offering bounties on grain imports, by sending agents to the Baltic ports, and by encouraging the process of inclosure. In 1799–1801, in general, the working classes were fairly well employed. Even the crisis in the Hamburg trade, in 1799, did not induce a prolonged deflation. Under these circumstances the workers had considerable market leverage in contracting money-wage bargains. In the attempt to maintain their real wage, at a time of rapidly rising costs of living, the men resorted to various types of combination. Even agricultural workers banded together in certain areas, notably in Norfolk.

Although the combination movement was very much the outgrowth of a particular short-period situation, and although the typical expression of discontent was the local bread riot or strike, the unrest was, at times, successfully linked with republican ideas. The corresponding societies, particularly, attempted to shape and unify the general dissatisfaction around the current liberal platform. With the memory of the French Revolution in mind, the Government acted to repress the corresponding societies and the combinations. The Acts of 1799 and 1800, reinforcing existing legislation, made illegal all collective working-class activity except the guild functions of the friendly societies.

3. *The Repeal of the Combination Acts, 1824 and 1825.* From 1820 through the early months of 1825 a fairly continuous increase in output and employment occurred. In the latter stages of the boom prices rose, relieving manufacturers briefly from the chronic downward pressure that had existed since 1814. But the period 1820–4 saw a coincidence of increased output and a sagging price level. Foodstuff prices, too, were fairly low. It is not surprising, then, that in the four years after Peterloo British labour was relatively peaceful.

The fact of increased prosperity, too, made it possible for the industrialists and the Government to afford a greater tolerance. Exceptional measures of repression were allowed gradually to lapse; the activities of spies were relaxed; and the law was set less freely in motion against working-class attempts at combination. It was in this atmosphere, early in 1824, that Place and Hume[2] manoeuvred the repeal of the Combination Acts.

The repeal immediately brought into the open the trade unions which had been operating under cover in the previous two decades; and it encouraged the formation of many others. A wave of strikes broke out and, in the following year, an aroused Parliament seriously limited the easy-going terms of the Act of 1824.

There can be little doubt that the strikes of 1824–5 can, in some measure, be attributed to the repeal of the Combination Acts. Two other factors, however, were operating. In the first place, in the latter half of 1824, the boom was suddenly accelerated, pushing the major British industries close to full employment. Enormous exports to South America and to the United States, as well as widespread internal enterprise, created a typical, late prosperity situation. Strikes for higher wages would normally be expected.

This tendency was accentuated by a second factor, a sudden rise in living costs.

In 1825, with a confidence born of some five years of increasing employment, the unions instituted numerous strikes for higher wages—in the cotton, wool, coal, iron, building, and other trades. At about the middle of 1825, however, the business cycle turned downward; and, although the strikes continued for some time, by the end of the year "combination . . . was knocked on the head. Bradford weavers and combers went back to work at the old wages . . . so did Renfrewshire colliers." In the bitter industrial conflicts that continued into 1826, labour was no longer on the offensive, but attempting to preserve wage rates in the face of a declining industrial demand.

The repeal of the Combination Acts is properly regarded as an expression of the general trend toward *laissez-faire*, paralleled, in the twenties, by the Huskisson[3] tariff reforms. Hume, in Parliament, presented the measure in such a light. Both Hume and Place regarded the unions as illiberal institutions brought into being by the repressive action of the Government; and they looked forward to their disap-

[2] Francis Place (1771–1854) was a reformer who led the struggle for the repeal of laws which prohibited trade unions, for election reform, and for other causes; he was also instrumental in formulating the program of the Chartists. Joseph Hume (1777–1855) was a physician who, as a member of Parliament, supported a broad range of reform programs. [Editor's note.]

[3] William Huskisson (1770–1830) was an important parliamentary leader between 1796 and 1830 and also held key governmental positions dealing with finances and trade. [Editor's note.]

pearance with the repeal of the Combination Acts. Nevertheless, the tolerant action of Parliament in 1824 was directly connected with the previous years of prosperity; the violence of the strikes of 1824–5 was largely the outgrowth of the situation in the labour market on either side of the cyclical turning-point, accentuated by the rising costs of living. It is possible, too, that the intemperance of the reaction of the Government in withdrawing, in 1825, a large part of the freedom granted in the previous year, may be linked to the change in the industrial outlook which occurred in that year. With commodity prices falling, and disillusion setting in with respect to the newly floated Latin-American mining issues, the doctrine of *laissez-faire,* as applied to labour organization, seemed somewhat more empty than in 1824.

4. *The Factory Act of 1847.* Factory acts in the first half of the nineteenth century were passed in 1802, 1819, 1833, 1842, and 1847. Each arose in a unique political setting; but each saw a similar combination of humanitarian and anti-industrial groups arrayed against the manufacturers. Within the ranks of the manufacturers there were, of course, notable exceptions: men like Peel and Whitbread and Owen,[4] to whom the conditions of factory labour were ethically outrageous and/or who believed that shorter hours and better conditions meant greater efficiency and profits. In parliamentary debate, humanitarian arguments led to rebuttal based on pleas for the freedom of the individual, or originating in attacks on state paternalism. To these the manufacturers would often add the claim that shorter hours meant a serious reduction or even the destruction of the existing margin of profit, and the loss of foreign markets.

There is, however, probably some significance in the fact that these acts were all passed at, or close to, a low point in cyclical fluctuations. The years 1819 and 1842 are such troughs in general business conditions, while 1833 and 1847 were also generally depressed years (the troughs were in 1832 and 1848). To a limited extent the children and women working in factories and mines were competing with the men available for the jobs. At a time of severe cyclical un-

employment it would be natural, then, that the men should complain, and attempt to oust their competitors or to limit their working time. A major driving force behind the movement which led to the Act of 1833, for example, was "the hope of absorbing men who are 'hanging on the trade idle.'"

In the case of the Ten-hour Bill of 1847 the role of the depression is even more clear. From 1845 onward unemployment was steadily increasing. In 1844 a Ten-hour Bill was defeated; in 1847 it was quietly passed. *The Times,* in a leading article on the following day, said it was not to be imagined that there had been any considerable degree of conversion on the subject. The argument stood very much where it had done in 1844, and had, in fact, been almost exhausted in that memorable struggle. The absence of fierce opposition was attributed in a large measure to the fact that the chief argument of the opponents —namely, that the country could not spare the last two hours of industry—could not be brought forward in 1847 without inviting its own refutation, for so great was the depression of trade that the mill owners found it impossible to keep their mills working for so long as ten hours.

From the side of the workers, too, a distinctly non-humanitarian factor can be detected in the ten-hour agitation. There seems to be little question that the labour unions viewed the measure as a means of restricting the labour supply and maintaining wage rates at a time of serious depression. At an early stage of the ten-hour agitation (December 1841) in a period of severe unemployment, Fielden[5] was reported to have said: "It is the duty of individuals to curtail the quantity of production when there is an over-abundant supply of the article they produce rather than increase it and reduce wages. He considered that a reduction of the hours of labour from twelve to ten would have this tendency, and was therefore desirable, as they had already got mills and machinery to produce more than they could find a vent for at a remunerating price."

To some extent, then, the Ten-hour Bill was passed because unemployment existed and because it was believed by some to be a recovery measure. In markets other than that for labour the restriction of supply, in an effort to maintain prices, was a typical depression phenomenon in these years.

[4] Sir Robert Peel (1788–1850) was Prime Minister, 1834–1835 and 1841–1846. Samuel Whitbread (1758–1815) was a London brewery owner who after being elected to Parliament became a strong opponent of all forms of oppression and exploitation. Robert Owen (1771–1858) was a business man with socialist leanings who agitated for a broad range of reforms and sought to ameliorate social conditions by establishing communities run on socialistic principles; one of the most famous of these establishments was at New Harmony, Indiana. [Editor's note.]

[5] John Fielden (1784–1849) was a member of Parliament who strongly supported reform causes after 1820. [Editor's note.]

The long-run economic and social influences reflected in the debates are perhaps more familiar. In Parliament, the factory question, from this time down to 1847, was really a part of the wider struggle between the agricultural landlords and the manufacturers over the repeal of the Corn Laws. The Tories were taunted with the condition of the labourers in the fields, and they retorted by tales of the conditions of the operatives in factories. The manufacturers rejoined by asking, if they were so anxious to benefit the workman, why did they not, by repealing the Corn Laws, cheapen his bread. The landlords and the mill owners each reproached the other with exercising the virtues of humanity at other people's expense. This is not to deny, of course, that sincere humanitarians worked within the Ten-hour Movement; nor does it underrate the importance of the strange political battle which led, finally, to the passage of the 1847 Bill. But it is clearly a case where the short-run position of the economic system—the degree of unemployment—played a part in determining the moment of its ultimate acceptance.

Testifying before the Committee on Manufactures (1832) William Mathews, Staffordshire iron manufacturer, was asked: "9991. Do you conceive that the depression of trade in late years has had any effect in producing . . . discontent?—Very great. 9992. Do you think the working classes of Staffordshire ever show political discontent so long as they are doing well in their particular trade?—Not at all; you cannot get them to talk of politics so long as they are well employed. 9993. Do you think that any man could create discontent among them so long as they were doing well?—It is utterly impossible." The converse of the dictum—"you cannot get them to talk of politics as long as they are well employed"—is not to be generalized without reservation; but within this period it serves to explain the political unrest of such years as 1811–12, 1816, 1819, 1826, 1837, 1839–42, and 1847–8. In each of these cases a fairly direct connexion can be traced between unemployment and mass dissatisfaction. In the case of the Reform Bill, for example, to which Mathews's questioners were referring, there can be little doubt that the intense depression of the latter months of 1831 and the early months of 1832 contributed significantly to the pressures that led to its passage.

The activities of the Chartists, covering more than a decade, offer an interesting, if somewhat crude confirmation of this thesis. General business conditions reached a peak in 1836; 1837 was a year of severe depression; some recovery followed through 1838, to a second peak early in 1839. From the later months of 1839 to the end of 1842 Britain suffered almost unbroken depression, exacerbated in its effects on the working classes by bad harvests. A recovery set in during 1843 which culminated in a peak in 1845. Business activity then declined to a low point in 1848. The phases of the most important Chartist activity occurred within severe depression; its temporary, but almost complete disappearance in 1843–5 coincides with the prosperity of those years.

The three focal points of Chartist activity came in 1839, 1842, and 1848. Beginning in 1837 the Movement gradually grew to the point where a petition boasting some million and a quarter signatures was presented to Parliament in 1839. The failure of this petition, and the Government's prosecution of the leaders, caused a temporary stagnation; but in 1842 a petition containing almost three and a third million names was placed in the hands of the Government. In that year, too, the Chartists helped lead a series of bitter strikes, marked by extensive sabotage.

The wheat price fell, with the advent of a promising harvest, in the summer of 1842, and in the following year recovery was well under way. For the Chartists a long period of discouragement and inactivity followed, until the return of depression in 1846. Still another petition went to Parliament in that year, and throughout 1847 the strength of the movement increased. Early in 1848 there were large meetings in the principal cities, climaxed by the presentation of the signatures of what purported to be almost six million British men and women. Threats of direct action, however, failed to materialize, and, in the following years, prosperity and inadequate leadership brought the movement to an end.

The demand for universal suffrage at this period in British history patently had roots deeper than cyclical unemployment. The chronically depressed position of the hand-loom weavers, many of whom were Chartists, was also more than a cyclical problem. Yet, apparently, depression was required before the political doctrines of the Chartist leaders could command wide or effective support.

These examples by no means exhaust the possibility of tracing important links between short-run economic fluctuations and political and social events in the years 1790–1850. There are innumerable other cases which might usefully be examined from this perspective, and those traced here deserve more detailed analysis. Even these brief summaries, however, reveal the manner in which cyclical fluctuations and cost-of-living movements served to detonate and to give expression to the familiar underlying trends. They should also emphasize the distinctive economic, social, and political atmosphere of each year, or even different parts of the same year. The use of long-run conceptions like "the growth of the Free-trade Movement," or the "development of working-class organizations," or "the Industrial Revolution" tends to blur this type of distinction. A necessary, but by no means sufficient requirement for a thorough interrelation of economic and other factors is a knowledge of fluctuations in general business activity and in costs of living.

EDWARD P. THOMPSON

THE INDUSTRIAL REVOLUTION AND CLASS CONSCIOUSNESS IN THE ENGLISH WORKING CLASS

The English historian, Edward P. Thompson, was born in Oxford, England in 1924 and educated at Corpus Christi College, Cambridge. Since 1947 he has taught in the Extra-mural Department of Leeds University. He is the author of *William Morris, Romantic to Revolutionary* (1961) and *The Making of the English Working Class* (1963), from which our selection has been taken. He was editor of *The New Reasoner*, 1957–59, and has been a contributor to this periodical and to the *Left Revue*.

The student will notice that as in the case of the pupils of Georges Lefebvre, [see problem on the nature of the French Revolution, pp. 554–84 above] Edward Thompson has attempted to view the revolutionary movements from below, that is to say, from the grass-roots movements of the English workers themselves. His emphasis is upon the ideas and aspirations of individuals rather than a statistical analysis of groups.

"The present mischief these two men [Owen and Hodgskin][1] have in some respects done is incalculable," noted Francis Place. The "mischief" is written across the years 1831–5. . . . To step over the threshold, from 1832 to 1833, is to step into a world in which the working-class presence can be felt in every county in England, and in most fields of life.

[1] Robert Owen (1771–1858) and Thomas Hodgskin (1787–1869) were both strong advocates of socialistic reforms. [Editor's note.]

The new class consciousness of working people may be viewed from two aspects. On the one hand, there was a consciousness of the identity of interests between working men of the most diverse occupations and levels of attainment, which was embodied in many institutional forms, and which was expressed on an unprecedented scale in the general unionism of 1830–4. This consciousness and these institutions were only to be found in fragmentary form in the England of 1780.

Condensed from *The Making of the English Working Class*, by E. P. Thompson, pp. 807–832 © Copyright 1963 by E. P. Thompson. Reprinted by permission of Pantheon Books, a Division of Random House, Inc., and Victor Gollancz Ltd.

On the other hand, there was a consciousness of the identity of the interests of the working class, or "productive classes," *as against* those of other classes; and within this there was maturing the claim for an alternative *system*. But the final definition of this class consciousness was, in large part, the consequence of the response to working-class strength of the middle class. The line was drawn, with extreme care, in the franchise qualifications of 1832. It had been the peculiar feature of English development that, where we would expect to find a growing middle-class reform movement, with a working-class tail, only later succeeded by an independent agitation of the working class, in fact this process was reversed. The example of the French Revolution had initiated three simultaneous processes: a panic-struck counter-revolutionary response on the part of the landed and commercial aristocracy; a withdrawal on the part of the industrial bourgeoisie and an accommodation (on favourable terms) with the *status quo*; and a rapid radicalisation of the popular reform movement until the Jacobin cadres who were tough enough to survive through the Wars were in the main little masters, artisans, stockingers and croppers, and other working men. The twenty-five years after 1795 may be seen as the years of the "long counter-revolution"; and in consequence the Radical movement remained largely working-class in character, with an advanced democratic "populism" as its theory. But the triumph of such a movement was scarcely to be welcomed by the mill-owners, iron-masters, and manufacturers. Hence the peculiarly repressive and anti-egalitarian ideology of the English middle classes. . . . Hence also the fact that the mildest measure of reform, to meet the evident irrationalities of Old Corruption, was actually *delayed*, by the resistance of the old order on the one hand, and the timidity of the manufacturers on the other.

The Reform Bill crisis of 1832 — or, to be more accurate, the successive crises from early in 1831 until the "days of May" in 1832 — illustrates these theses at almost every point. The agitation arose from "the people" and rapidly displayed the most astonishing consensus of opinion as to the imperative necessity for "reform." Viewed from one aspect, England was without any doubt passing through a crisis in these twelve months in which revolution was possible. The rapidity with which the agitation extended indicates the degree to which

experience in every type of constitutional and quasi-legal agitation was present among the people:

The systematic way in which the people proceeded, their steady perseverance, their activity and skill astounded the enemies of reform. Meetings of almost every description of persons were held in cities, towns, and parishes; by journeymen tradesmen in their clubs, and by common workmen who had no trade clubs or associations of any kind. . . .

"The great majority" of those who attended the swelling demonstrations, the King's private Secretary complained in March 1831 to Grey,[2] "are of the very lowest class." The enormous demonstrations, rising to above 100,000 in Birmingham and London in the autumn of 1831 and May 1832, were overwhelmingly composed of artisans and working men.

"We did not cause the excitement about reform," Grey wrote a little peevishly to the King, in March 1831: "We found it in full vigour when we came into office." And, viewed from another aspect, we can see why throughout these crisis months a revolution was in fact improbable. The reason is to be found in the very strength of the working-class Radical movement; the skill with which the middle-class leaders, Brougham, *The Times*, the *Leeds Mercury* both used this threat of working-class force, and negotiated a line of retreat acceptable to all but the most die-hard defenders of the *ancien régime;* and the awareness on the part of the Whigs and the least intransigent Tories that, while Brougham and Baines[3] were only blackmailing them, nevertheless if a compromise was not come to, the middle-class reformers might no longer be able to hold in check the agitation at their backs.

The industrial bourgeoisie desired, with heart and soul, that a revolution should not take place, since they knew that on the very day of its commencement there would be a dramatic process of radicalisation. . . . "Threats of a 'revolution' are employed by the middle classes and petty masters," wrote the *Poor Man's Guardian*. But —

[2] Charles Grey, Second Earl (1764–1845) was the Prime Minister who put through the Reform Bill of 1832. [Editor's note.]

[3] Henry Brougham, First Baron Brougham and Vaux (1778–1868) was a Scotsman by birth but settled in London. As a member of Parliament and an official in Whig cabinets, he was an active promoter of reform. He was especially popular among the people but considerably less so among his fellow party members. Edward Baines (1774–1848) was a member of Parliament who supported liberal causes; he was the director of the liberal *Leeds Mercury* and used it to promote the reform movement. [Editor's note.]

a violent revolution is not only beyond the means of those who threaten it, but is to them their greatest object of alarm; for they know that such a revolution can only be effected by the poor and despised millions, who, if excited to the step, might use it for their own advantage, as well as for that of themselves, who would thus . . . have their dear rights of property endangered: be assured that a violent revolution is their greatest dread. . . .

The middle-class reformers fought skillfully on both fronts. On the one hand *The Times* came forward as the actual organiser of mass agitation: "We trust there is not a county, town, or village in the United Kingdom which will not meet and petition for a reform. . . ." It even urged upon the people "the solemn duty of forming themselves into political societies throughout the whole realm." It supported . . . measures of enforcement which led directly on towards revolution: the run on the Banks, refusal to pay taxes, and the arming of members of Political Unions. On the other hand, the riots at Nottingham, Derby and Bristol in October 1831 underlined the dual function of the Political Unions on the Birmingham model:

These Unions were to be for the promotion of the cause of reform, for the protection of life and property against the detailed but irregular outrages of the mob, as well as for the maintenance of *other* great interests against the systematic violences of an oligarchy. . . .

These middle-class incendiaries carried in their knapsacks a special constable's baton. There were occasions when the Tories themselves hoped to outwit them, by encouraging the independent working-class reform movement to display itself in a form so alarming that Brougham and Baines would run to Old Corruption for protection. . . .

Throughout the country middle-class and working-class reformers manoeuvred for control of the movement. In the earliest stages, until the summer of 1831, the middle-class Radicals held the advantage. Seven years before Wooler had closed the *Black Dwarf*[4] with a sadly disillusioned final Address. There was (in 1824) no "public devotedly attached to the cause of parliamentary reform." . . . Many of the working-class leaders of the late 1820s shared his disillusion, and accepted the anti-political stance of their master, Owen. It was not until the

[4] Thomas Jonathan Wooler (1786?–1853) was a journalist and politician who constantly attacked conservative ministries and promoted reforming causes. The *Black Dwarf* was a Sunday paper published between 1817 and 1824; it was noted chiefly for its attacks on the government, which won it a wide audience among the lower classes. [Editor's note.]

summer of 1830, with the rural labourers' "revolt" and the July Revolution in France, that the tide of popular interest began to turn back to political agitation. And thenceforward the insanely stubborn last-ditch resistance of the die-hards (the Duke of Wellington, the Lords, the Bishops) to *any* measure of reform dictated a strategy (which was exploited to the full by the middle-class Radicals) by which popular agitation was brought to bear behind Grey and Russell,[5] and in support of a Bill from which the majority had nothing to gain.

Thus the configuration of forces of 1816–20 (and, indeed, of 1791–4), in which the popular demand for Reform was identified with Major Cartwright's[6] platform of manhood suffrage, was broken up. "If any persons suppose that this Reform will lead to ulterior measures," Grey declared in the House in November 1831:

they are mistaken; for there is no one more decided against annual parliaments, universal suffrage, and the ballot, than I am. My object is not to favour, but to put an end to such hopes and projects.

This was clearly enough seen by the older Radicals, the majority of whose articulate spokesmen poured scorn on the Whig Bill until the final "days of May." . . . George Edmonds, the witty and courageous Radical schoolmaster, . . . declared:

I am not a house-holder.—I can, on a push, be a musketholder. The nothing-but-the-Bill does not recognise George Edmonds as a citizen!—George Edmonds scorns the nothing-but-the-Bill, except as cut the first at the national robber.

This was the position also of the élite of London's Radical artisans, enrolled in the National Union of Working Classes and Others, whose weekly debates in the Rotunda in 1831 and 1832 were reported in Hetherington's[7] *Poor Man's Guardian*—undoubtedly the finest working-class weekly which had (until that time) been published in Britain. The

[5] Lord John Russell (1792–1878) was a prime force in framing and pushing through the Reform Bill of 1832. Later he became Prime Minister (1846–1852, 1865). [Editor's note.]

[6] John Cartwright (1740–1824) became an active advocate of political reform after a career in the navy and army. One of his most controversial proposals urged universal manhood suffrage. [Editor's note.]

[7] Henry Hetherington (1792–1849) was a publisher of "unstamped newspapers," an offense for which he was twice imprisoned; his publications supported a wide range of liberal causes. [Editor's note.]

debates were attended by Hetherington himself . . . , now pressing his proposal for a . . . month's general strike, in the course of which the productive classes would assume control of the nation's government and resources. The debates increasingly turned upon the definition of class. William Carpenter,[8] who shared with Hetherington the honour of initiating the struggle for the "unstamped" press, offered a dissentient opinion. The Whig Bill ought to be supported, as a "wedge." He complained that the *Poor Man's Guardian* used the words "middle men" and "middle class" as "convertible terms," whereas the middle classes "are not only *not* a class of persons having interests different from your own. They are the *same* class; they are, generally speaking, *working* or *labouring* men." Throughout the entire crisis the controversy continued. . . .

It is problematical how far the militant Owenities of the Rotunda represented any massive body of working-class opinion. They commenced by representing only the intelligentsia of the artisans. But they gathered influence most rapidly; by October 1831 they were able to organise a massive demonstration, perhaps 70,000 strong, many wearing the white scarves emblematic of manhood suffrage; perhaps 100,000 joined their demonstrations against the National Fast in March 1832. Place regarded the Rotundists . . . as constituting the greatest of threats to the middle-class strategy, and much of his manuscript history of the Reform Bill crisis . . . is devoted to the unscrupulous manoeuvres by which he sought to limit their influence, and displace it by that of his rival National Political Union. The Duke of Wellington himself saw the contest as one between the Establishment and the Rotunda, which he compared to two armies "*en présence.*" It confused his military mind very much to reflect that he could place no river between the armies, with adequate sentinels and posts on the bridges. The enemy was installed at sensitive points within his own camp.

The procession of October 1831, however, was mainly composed (it seems) of "shopkeepers and superior artisans." And while the numbers called out were impressive, they compare poorly with the even greater demonstrations at Birmingham, drawn from a smaller population. It would seem that, while the London artisans had at last succeeded in building a cohesive and highly articulate leadership, there remained a wide gulf between them and the mass of London labourers, and workers in the dishonourable trades. . . . Edward Gibbon Wakefield[9] . . . saw the Rotundists as "Desperadoes" and idealists, whose danger lay in the fact that they might unleash the destructive energies of the criminal classes, . . . "costermongers, drovers, slaughterers of cattle, knackers, dealers in dead bodies and dogs' meat, cads, brickmakers, chimney-sweepers, nightmen, scavengers, &c." His attitude to the Owenite Socialists of the Rotunda was ambiguous. On the one hand, they were mostly "sober men, who maintain themselves by industry" —men plainly marked off by superior talents from the dangerous classes. On the other hand, many were "loose single men living here and there in lodgings, who might set fire to London without anxiety for helpless beings at home. . . .

Many, he said (with some truth), "are provided with arms":

If an insurrection of the London populace should take place, they will be found at the most dangerous posts, leading the thieves and rabble, pointing out the most effectual measures, and dying, if the lot fall on them, with cries of defiance.

"These will be the fighting men of our revolution, if we must have one."

The picture is overdrawn; but it is not wholly without truth. The danger, from the point of view of authority (whether Whig or Tory), lay in a possible conjunction between the artisan Socialists and the "criminal classes." But the unskilled masses in London inhabited another world from that of the artisans—a world of extreme hardship, illiteracy, very widespread demoralisation, and disease, which was dramatised by the cholera outbreak of the winter of 1831–2. Here we have all the classic problems, the hand-to-mouth insecurity, of a metropolitan city swollen with immigrants in a period of rapid population-growth.

The unskilled had no spokesmen and no organisations (apart from friendly societies). They were as likely to have followed the lead of a gentleman as of an artisan. And yet the severity of the political

---

[8] William Carpenter (1798–1874) was a journalist who advocated political reforms in his pamphlets. [Editor's note.]

[9] Edward Gibbon Wakefield (1796–1862) was a political figure and writer whose main interests were in colonizing ventures in New Zealand and Australia; he was especially concerned with inducing people to migrate to these territories. [Editor's note.]

crisis which commenced in October 1831 was sufficient to crack the crust of fatalism, deference, and need, within which their lives were enclosed. The riots of that month . . . all were indicative of a deep disturbance at the foundations of society, which observers anxiously expected to be followed by the uprising of London's East End.

The Birmingham Political Union was an acceptable model, . . . because the local industrial context favoured a reform movement of the masses which still remained firmly under middle-class control. The history of Birmingham Radicalism is significantly different from that of the north Midlands and the north. There was no basis in its small-scale industries for Luddism,[10] and the "father" of the Political Unions, Thomas Attwood,[11] first gained public-prominence when he led, in 1812, a united agitation of the masters and artisans against the Orders in Council. There were undoubtedly groups of "physical force" Radicals in the Black Country in 1817–20, . . . Thomas Attwood was able in 1830 to "harmonize and unite" the diverse "materials of discontent" because the Industrial Revolution in Birmingham had "multiplied the number of producing units rather than added to the scale of existing enterprises." There had been little displacement of skilled labour by machinery; the numberless small workshops meant that the social gradients shelved more gently, and the artisan might still rise to the status of a small master; in times of economic recession masters and journeymen were afflicted alike. Hence, class antagonism was more muted than in Manchester, Newcastle, and Leeds. Throughout the Reform Bill crisis, Attwood controlled the Birmingham Union with "such a show of good-nature" . . . "that the Brummagem operatives seemed really to believe that they would be *virtually*, though not actually, presented in the 're-formed' parliament." . . .

To this body, more than to any other, is confessedly due the triumph (such as it was) of the Reform Bill. Its well-ordered proceedings, extended organization, and immense assemblages of people, at critical periods of its progress, rendered the measure irresistible.

[10] A movement by organized gangs to destroy machinery in the factories because it caused unemployment; the movement first appeared in 1811 in and around Nottingham. [Editor's note.]

[11] Thomas Attwood (1783–1856) was a local official in Birmingham whose concern over economic distress led him to found the Birmingham Political Union in 1829 for the purpose of bringing pressure for reform on the government. After the Reform Bill of 1832 passed, Attwood was elected to Parliament. [Editor's note.]

In such centres as Leeds, Manchester, and Nottingham the position of the middle-class reformers was very much more uneasy. At Manchester (as in London) rival political Unions co-existed, and from October 1831 onwards the manhood suffrage Union made the running. At Bolton in the same month the rejection of the Bill by the House of Lords resulted in a split in the Political Union, the largest (manhood suffrage) section organising a demonstration, 6,000 strong, behind the banners: "Down with the Bishops!" "No Peers!" In the Midlands and the north such incidents were repeated dozens of times. . . .

Indeed in the winter of 1831–2 the ridicule poured upon the Bill and upon its attendant proceedings in the *Poor Man's Guardian* takes on a somewhat academic air. No doubt the Rotundists were right to designate the Bill as a trap (and as a betrayal of the Radical movement). But the well-nigh neolithic obstinacy with which Old Corruption resisted *any* reform led on to a situation in which the nation stepped, swiftly and without premeditation, on to the threshold of revolution. Belatedly, the *Poor Man's Guardian* adjusted its tactics, publishing as a special supplement extracts from Colonel Macerone's *Defensive Instructions for the People* (a manual in street-fighting). Throughout the "eleven days of England's apprehension and turmoil" which preceded the final passage of the Bill through the Lords in May, Francis Place held his breath. On the evening of the day when it passed, he returned home and noted:

We were within a moment of general rebellion, and had it been possible for the Duke of Wellington to have formed an administration the Thing and the people would have been at issue.

There would have been "Barricadoes of the principal towns—stopping _circulation of paper money"; if a revolution had commenced, it "would have been the act of the whole people to a greater extent than any which had ever before been accomplished."

In the autumn of 1831 and in the "days of May" Britain was within an ace of a revolution which, once commenced, might well (if we consider the simultaneous advance in cooperative and trade union theory) have prefigured, in its rapid radicalisation, the revolutions of 1848 and the Paris Commune. . . .

. . . The fact that revolution did not occur was due,

in part, to the deep constitutionalism of that part of the Radical tradition of which Cobbett[12] (urging the acceptance of half a loaf) was the spokesman; and in part to the skill of the middle-class Radicals in offering exactly that compromise which might, not weaken, but strengthen both the State and property-rights against the working-class threat.

The Whig leaders saw their rôle as being that of finding the means . . . "to associate the middle with the higher orders of society in the love and support of the institutions and government of the country." The extreme care with which this line was drawn is evinced by a survey undertaken by Baines in 1831, to discover "the numbers and respectability of the £10 householders in Leeds." The results were communicated to Lord John Russell in a letter which should be taken as one of the classic documents of the Reform Bill crisis. Baines' pioneering psephological canvassers—

stated *unanimously*, that the £10 qualification did not admit to the exercise of the elective franchise a single person who might not safely and wisely be enfranchised: that they were surprised to find how comparatively few would be allowed to vote.

In answer to Russell's enquiry as to the proportion which £10 householders bore to the rest of the population, the canvassers reported:

. . . in the parts occupied chiefly by the working classes, not one householder in fifty would have a vote. In the streets principally occupied by shops, almost every householder had a vote. . . .

Even this estimate would appear to have been excessive. Returns made to the Government in May 1832 showed that in Leeds (population, 124,000) 355 "workmen" would be admitted to the franchise, of whom 143 "are clerks, warehousemen, overlookers, &c." The remaining 212 were in a privileged status, earning between 30s. and 40s. a week.

Such surveys no doubt reassured the Cabinet, which had meditated raising the £10 franchise qualification to £15. "The great body of the people," Place wrote, "were self-assured that either the

Reform Bills would be passed by Parliament, or that they should, by their own physical force, obtain much more than they contained, if they were rejected. . . ." It is the threat of this "much more" which hung over both Tories and Whigs in 1832, and which enabled that accommodation to be made, between landed and industrial wealth, between privilege and money, which has been an enduring configuration of English society. Upon the banners of Baines and Cobden,[13] were not *égalité* and *liberté* (still less *fraternité*) but "Free Trade" and "Retrenchment." The rhetoric of Brougham was that of property, security, interest. "If there is a mob," Brougham said in his speech on the second reading of the Reform Bill,

there is the people also. I speak now of the middle classes —of those hundreds of thousands of respectable persons —the most numerous and by far the most wealthy order in the community, for if all your Lordships' castles, manors, rights of warren and rights of chase, with all your broad acres, were brought to the hammer, and sold at fifty years' purchase, the price would fly up and kick the beam when counterpoised by the vast and solid riches of those middle classes, who are also the genuine depositaries of sober, rational, intelligent, and honest English feeling. . . . Rouse not, I beseech you, a peace-loving, but a resolute people. . . . As your friend, as the friend of my order, as the friend of my country, as the faithful servant of my sovereign, I counsel you to assist with your uttermost efforts in preserving the peace, and upholding and perpetuating the Constitution. . . .

Divested of its rhetoric, the demands of the middle-class Radicals were voiced by Baines, when the Bill had been passed:

The fruits of Reform are to be gathered. Vast commercial and agricultural monopolies are to be abolished. The Church is to be reformed. . . . Close corporations are to be thrown open. Retrenchment and economy are to be enforced. The shackles of the Slave are to be broken.

The demands of working-class Radicalism were less clearly formulated. A minimum political programme may be cited from the *Poor Man's Guardian*, the organ of the National Union of Working Classes:

Extirpation of the Fiend Aristocracy; Establishment of a Republic, viz. Democracy by Representatives elected by Universal Suffrage; Extinction of hereditary offices, titles and distinctions; Abolition of the . . . law of primogeniture; . . . Cheap and rapid administration of justice; Abolition of the Game Laws; Repeal of the diabolical

[12] William Cobbett (1763–1835) was the leading advocate of radical reform measures during the first third of the nineteenth century; his appeal was especially powerful among the working classes of England. He was an especially gifted writer and poured great energy into publicizing the causes he supported. In many respects his career is the best reflection of the rising tide of working-class consciousness and of the spirit of reform of any man of his generation. [Editor's note.]

[13] Richard Cobden (1804–1865) was a businessman, economist, and political figure who played a leading role in the agitation to repeal the corn laws. He was the directing force behind the Anti-Corn Law League. [Editor's note.]

imposts on Newspapers . . .; emancipation of our fellow-citizens the Jews; Introduction of Poor Laws into Ireland; Abolition of the Punishment of Death for offences against property; Appropriation of the Revenues of the "Fathers in God," the Bishops, towards maintenance of the Poor; Abolition of Tithes; Payment of every Priest or Minister by his Sect; The "National Debt" not the debt of the Nation; Discharge of the Machinery of Despotism, the Soldiers; Establishment of a National Guard.

This is the old programme of Jacobinism, with little development from the 1790s. . . . But around this "much more" other demands accrued, according to the grievances foremost in different districts and industries. . . . Doherty[14] . . . argued that "universal suffrage means nothing more than a power given to every man to protect his own labour from being devoured by others." The Owenites, the factory reformers, and "physical force" revolutionaries . . . were pressing still further demands. But, in the event, the terms of the contest were successfully confined within the limits desired by Brougham and Baines. It was (as Shelley had foreseen in 1822) a contest between "blood and gold"; and in its outcome, blood compromised with gold to keep out the claims of égalité. For the years between the French Revolution and the Reform Bill had seen the formation of a middle-class "class consciousness," more conservative, more wary of the large idealist causes (except, perhaps, those of other nations), more narrowly self-interested than in any other industrialised nation. Henceforward, in Victorian England, the middle-class Radical and the idealist intellectual were forced to take sides between the "two nations." It is a matter of honour that there were many individuals who preferred to be known as Chartists or Republicans rather than as special constables. But such men . . . were always disaffected individuals or intellectual "voices." They represent in no sense the ideology of the middle class.

What Edward Baines had done, in his correspondence with Russell, was to offer a definition of class of almost arithmetical exactitude. In 1832 the line was drawn in social consciousness by the franchise qualifications, with the crudity of an indelible pencil. Moreover, these years found also a theorist of stature to define the working-class predicament. . . . James "Bronterre" O'Brien (1805–64), the son of an Irish wine merchant, and a distin-

guished graduate of Trinity College, Dublin, arrived in London in 1829 "to study Law and Radical Reform":

My friends sent me to study law; I took to radical reform on my own account . . . While I have made no progress at all in law, I have made immense progress in radical reform. So much so, that were a professorship of radical reform to be instituted tomorrow in King's College (no very probable event by the way), I think I would stand candidate . . . I feel as though every drop of blood in my veins was radical blood. . . .

After editing the Midlands Representative during the Reform Bill crisis, he moved to London and assumed the editorship of the Poor Man's Guardian.

"We foresaw," he wrote of the Reform Bill, "that its effect would be to detach from the working classes a large portion of the middle ranks, who were then more inclined to act with the people than with the aristocracy that excluded them," And in his Introduction to Buonarotti's history of the Conspiracy of Equals, he drew a parallel: "The Girondists would extend the franchise to the small middlemen (just as our English Whigs did by the Reform Bill) in order the more effectively to keep down the working classes." "Of all governments, a government of the middle classes is the most grinding and remorseless."

It was a theme to which he often returned. His anger was refreshed by each new action of the Whig administration—the Irish Coercion Bill, the rejection of the 10 Hour Bill, the attack on the trades unions, the Poor Law Amendment Act. "Previously to the passing of the Reform Bill," he wrote in 1836:

the middle orders were supposed to have some community of feeling with the labourers. That delusion has passed away. It barely survived the Irish Coercion Bill, it vanished completely with the enactment of the Starvation Law. No working man will ever again expect justice, morals or mercy at the hands of a profit-mongering legislature.

A refugee from a middle-class culture himself, he took especial pleasure in writing of his own class in terms which imitated its own drawing-room small-talk about the servant classes: "The pursuits and habits [of the middle classes] are essentially debasing. Their life is necessarily a life of low cunning and speculation . . ."

And he sought, with considerable genius, to twist together the tradition of ultra-Radicalism with that of Owenism, into a revolutionary Socialism, whose

[14]John Doherty was a leader in Manchester who worked to establish both local and national organizations of workingmen in the 1830's. [Editor's note.]

goals were political revolution, the expropriation of the properties classes, and a network of Owenite communities:

We must have what Southey calls "a revolution of revolutions"; such an one as Robespierre and St. Just projected in France in the beginning of 1794; that is to say, a complete subversion of the institutions by which wealth is distributed . . . Property—property—this is the thing we must be at. Without a change in the institution of property, no improvement can take place.

Such a revolution (he hoped) would come, without violence, in the immediate aftermath of the attainment of manhood suffrage: "From the *laws of the few* have the existing inequalities sprung; by the laws of the many shall they be destroyed."

Historians today would certainly not accept O'Brien's overcrude assimiliation of the post-Reform Whig administration to the interests of the "middle class." . . . Nor is it proper to select this one theorist (middle-class in his own origins) as expressive of the new consciousness of the working class. But at the same time, O'Brien was very far from being an eccentric at the edges of the movement. As editor of the *Poor Man's Guardian* and other journals he commanded a large, and growing, working-class audience; he was later to earn the title of the "Schoolmaster" of Chartism. His writings are a central thread through the abundant agitations of the early 1830s, providing a nexus for the old democratic claims, the social agitations (against the New Poor Law and for Factory Reform), the Owenite communitarian experiments, and the syndicalist struggles of the trade unions. O'Brien was . . . an authentic voice of his times.

For most working men, of course, disillusion in the Reform Bill came in less theoretical forms. The proof of the pudding was in the eating. We may see the eating in microcosm in a few of the incidents at one of the contests in the ensuing General Election—at Leeds. Here Baines . . . brought forward in the Whig interest Marshall, one of the largest employers in Leeds, and Macaulay[15] (or "Mr. Mackholy" as one of the tail of Whig shopkeepers noted in his diary). Macaulay was one of the most complacent of the ideologists of the Reform Bill settlement, translating into new terms the Tory doctrine of "virtual representation":

The higher and middling orders are the natural representatives of the human race. Their interest may be opposed, in some things, to that of their poorer contemporaries, but it is identical with that of the innumerable generations which are to follow.

"The inequality with which wealth is distributed forces itself on everybody's notice," he lamented, while "the reasons which irrefragably proved this inequality to be necessary to the well-being of all classes are not equally obvious." . . .

The Tory candidate, on the other hand, was Sadler,[16] leading parliamentary spokesman of the 10 Hour Movement. Oastler[17] had launched, with the Short-Time Committees, his passionate campaign against child labour two years before. The amazing "Pilgrimage to York" had taken place in the previous April; and the 10 Hour agitation (like the Owenite agitation) continued without pause during the Reform Bill crisis months. In such a contest, therefore, Oastler could be counted upon to side with Sadler against Baines, who had conducted a mealy-mouthed defence of the mill-owners in the *Leeds Mercury*. Cobbett could be counted upon to do the same. . . .

A Tory-Radical alliance was therefore inevitable behind Sadler. It was also inevitable that the greater part of the Nonformist "shopocrat" vote would go to "Mr. Marshall Our Townsman and Mr. Mackholy the Scotchman." . . .

The working-class Radicals in Leeds, maintained their independent press and organisation. The men of Leeds (they declared) . . . had now been betrayed by the men who, in the days of May, had addressed their great assemblies and promised Reform or barricades:

Messrs. Marshall and Macaulay may . . . be very friendly to Reforms of all sorts and sizes, . . . but let the operatives of Leeds remember that if they support them, they do what they can to put legislative power into the hands of their enemies.

Moreover, the Radicals declared that the old forms of electoral bribery and influence employed by the aristocratic interest were now finding insidious new

[16] Michael Thomas Sadler (1780–1835) was a Leeds businessman and a Tory who became an advocate of factory reform. [Editor's note.]

[17] Richard Oastler (1789–1861) was also a strong advocate of factory reform; he was especially concerned with child labor. [Editor's note.]

[15] Thomas Babington Macaulay (1800–1859), the famous historian. [Editor's note.]

forms in the service of the manufacturing interest. Although the workers did not have votes, great efforts were made to offset the effects of 10 Hour demonstrations in favour of Sadler by compelling factory-hands to declare for Marshall and Macaulay at the hustings:

We could name more than a dozen mills, all the hands of which have received positive orders to be in the Yard on Monday, and to hold up their hands for the Orange Candidates . . . on pain of instant privation of employment. . . .

In the event, the scene on the hustings turned into riot, where Oastler and the 10 Hour men "rang matins on the thick skulls of the flying oranges." When Sadler was defeated at the poll, Marshall and Macaulay were burned in effigy in the same city centre where Paine had been burnt by the loyalists in 1792.

This Leeds election of 1832 was of more than local significance. It had focussed the attention of factory reformers throughout the country, drawing addresses in Sadler's favour from thousands of signatories in northern towns. There is no mistaking the new tone after 1832. In every manufacturing district a hundred experiences confirmed the new consciousness of class which the Bill had, by its own provisions, so carefully defined. It was the "reformed" House of Commons which sanctioned the transportation of the Dorchester labourers in 1834 ("a blow directed at the whole body of united operatives"), and who launched, with "the document" and the lockout, the struggle to break the trade unions, whose intensity and whose significance (in both political and economic terms) is still too little understood. . . .

"The very men," declared one Leeds trade unionist, "who had pampered Political Unions, when they could be made subservient to their own purposes, were now endeavouring to crush the Trades Unions":

It was but the other day that the operatives were led in great numbers to the West Riding meeting at Wakefield, for the purpose of carrying the Reform Bill. At that time, the very individuals who were now attempting to put down trades' unions, were arraying them to carry by the force of numbers, a political reform which he was sure would not otherwise have been obtained from the aristocracy of this country. . . .

The line from 1832 to Chartism is not a haphazard pendulum alternation of "political" and "economic" agitations but a direct progression, in which simultaneous and related movements converge towards a single point. This point was the vote. There is a sense in which the Chartist movement commenced, not in 1836 with the promulgation of the "Six Points,"[18] but at the moment when the Reform Bill received Royal Assent. Many of the provincial Political Unions never disbanded, but commenced at once to agitate against the "shopocrat" franchise. . . .

The characteristic ideology of Birmingham Radicalism, which united employers and journeymen in opposition to the aristocracy, the Banks, the National Debt, and the "paper-money system," was beginning to fall apart. . . . Once again, a monster demonstration gathered on Newhall Hill (May 1833), at which an attendance of 180,000 was claimed, and at which there was expressed—

. . . a sentiment of common hatred to the parties whom, having been mainly instrumental in forcing into power, they now assembled to express their disgust of the . . . treachery which they had manifested.

. . . The process of radicalisation which was to make Birmingham a Chartist metropolis had begun.

But the content of this renewed agitation was such that the vote itself implied "much more," and that is why it had to be denied. (The Birmingham of 1833 was not the Birmingham of 1831: it was now the home of an Equitable Labour Exchange, it was the headquarters of the socialist Builders' Union, it housed the editorial office of the Pioneer.) The vote, for the workers of this and the next decade, was a symbol whose importance it is difficult for us to appreciate, our eyes dimmed by more than a century of the smog of "two-party parliamentary politics." It implied, first, égalité: equality of citizenship, personal dignity, worth. "Instead of bricks, mortar, and dirt, man ought to be represented," wrote one pamphleteer, lamenting the lot of "the miserable, so-called 'free-born' Englishmen, excluded from the most valuable right that man can enjoy in political society," . . .

"Like the wild Irish of old, the British millions have been too long insolently placed without the pale of social governments":

[18] The "Six Points" represented the basic program advocated by the Chartist movement. They were universal suffrage, payment of members of Parliament, equal electoral districts, no property qualifications, voting by ballots, and annual parliaments. [Editor's note.]

I now speak the thoughts of my unrepresented fellow millions, the Wild English, the free-born slaves of the nineteenth century.

But in the context of the Owenite and Chartist years, the claim for the vote implied also further claims: a new way of reaching out by the working people for *social control* over their conditions of life and labour. At first, and inevitably, the exclusion of the working class provoked a contrary rejection, by the working class, of all forms of political action. . . . But in the post-1832 swing to general unionism, this anti-political bias was not quietist but embattled, militant, and even revolutionary. To examine the richness of the political thought of these years would take us further into the history of general unionism — and, indeed, into the early years of Chartism — than we intend to go. They are years in which Benbow canvassed his notion of the "Grand National Holiday" in the industrial districts; in which the printing-worker, John Francis Bray, carried forward Hodgskin's ideas, in lectures to Leeds artisans, later published as *Labour's Wrongs and Labour's Remedies*; in which the Builders' Union and the Grand National Consolidated Trades Union rose and fell; and in which Doherty and Fielden founded the "Society for National Regeneration" with its remedy of the General Strike for the Eight-Hour Day. The Owenite communitarians were fertile with notions and experiments prefiguring advances in the care of children, the relations between the sexes, education, housing, and social policy. Nor were these ideas canvassed among a limited intelligentsia only; building workers, potters, weavers, and artisans were willing, for a while, to risk their livelihood to put experiments to the test. . . . In the silk mills of the Colden Valley, isolated on the Pennines between Yorkshire and Lancashire, the Owenite journals were read.

Two themes only may be mentioned of those which arose again and again in these years. The first is that of internationalism. This was, to be sure, part of the old Jacobin heritage; and one which the Radicals had never forgotten. . . . Cobbett could always find time to add a stop-press to his journals:

I have just room to tell you, that the people of BELGIUM, the *common people,* have *beaten the Dutch armies,* who were marched against them to compel them to *pay enormous taxes.* This is excellent news.

The French Revolution of 1830 had a profound impact upon the people, electrifying not only the London Radicals but working-class reformers in distant industrial villages. The struggle for Polish independence was followed anxiously in the working-class press; while Julian Hibbert, in the Rotunda, carried a vote of sympathy with the Lyons weavers, in their ill-fated insurrection, likening them to the weavers of Spitalfields. In the Owenite movement this political tradition was extended to embrace social and class solidarities. In 1833 a "Manifesto of the Productive Classes of Great Britain and Ireland" was addressed to "the Governments and People of the Continents of Europe and of North and South America," commencing: "Men of the Great Family of Mankind . . ." By the end of the same year, the question of some common alliance between the trade unionists of England, France, and Germany had already come under discussion.

The other theme was that of industrial syndicalism. When Marx was still in his teens, the battle for the minds of English trade unionists, between a capitalist and a socialist political economy, had been (at least temporarily) won. The winners were Hodgskin, Thompson, James Morrison and O'Brien; the losers were James Mill and Place.[19] "What is capital?" asked a writer in the *Pioneer*. "'It is reserved labour!' cried M'Culloch.[20] . . . From whom and what was it reserved? From the clothing and food of the wretched." Hence the workers who had been "insolently placed without the pale of social government" developed, stage by stage, a theory of syndicalism, or of "Inverted Masonry." "The Trades Unions will not only strike for less work, and more wages," wrote "A Member of the Builder's Union,"

but they will ultimately ABOLISH WAGES, become their own masters, and work for each other; labour and capital will no longer be separate but they will be indissolubly joined together in the hands of the workmen and workwomen.

The unions themselves could solve the problem of political power; a "Parliament" of the industrious

[19] We have already become acquainted with Hodgskin, O'Brien, and Place as leading advocates of reform. George Thompson (1804–1878) was an advocate of the abolition of slavery; he carried his cause to the United States in 1834 and was denounced by Andrew Jackson. After his return to England he fought for parliamentary reform and the repeal of the corn laws. James Morrison (1790–1857) was a rich merchant who as a member of Parliament supported the Reform Bill of 1832 and tried to promote labor reform. James Mill (1773–1836) was the famous advocate of utilitarianism and a promoter of reform. [Editor's note.]

[20] John Ramsey M'Culloch (1789–1864) was an economist who wrote on wages and the forces that determined them. [Editor's note.]

classes could be formed, delegated directly from workshops and mills: "the Lodges send Delegates from local to district, and from district to National Assemblies. Here are Universal Suffrage, Annual Election, and No Property Qualification, instanter." . . .

This vision was lost, almost as soon as it had been found, in the terrible defeats of 1834 and 1835. And, when they had recovered their wind, the workers returned to the vote, as the more practical key to political power. Something was lost: but Chartism never entirely forgot this preoccupation with social control, to the attainment of which the vote was seen as a means. These years reveal a passing beyond the characteristic outlook of the artisan, with his desire for an independent livelihood "by the sweat of his brow," to a newer outlook, more reconciled to the new means of production, but seeking to exert the collective power of the class to humanise the environment:—by this community or that co-operative society, by this check on the blind operation of the market-economy, this legal enactment, that measure of relief for the poor. And implicit, if not always explicit, in their outlook was the dangerous tenet: production must be, not for profit, but for *use*.

This collective self-consciousness was indeed the great spiritual gain of the Industrial Revolution, against which the disruption of an older and in many ways more humanly-comprehensible way of life must be set. It was perhaps a unique formation, this British working class of 1832. The slow, piecemeal accretions of capital accumulation had meant that the preliminaries to the Industrial Revolution stretched backwards for hundreds of years. From Tudor times onwards this artisan culture had grown more complex with each phase of technical and social change. Delaney, Dekker and Nashe: Winstanley and Lilburne: Bunyan and Defoe[21]—all had

at times addressed themselves to it. Enriched by the experiences of the 17th century, carrying through the 18th century the intellectual and libertarian traditions which we have described, forming their own traditions of mutuality in the friendly society and trades club, these men did not pass, in one generation, from the peasantry to the new industrial town. They suffered the experience of the Industrial Revolution as articulate, free-born Englishmen. Those who were sent to gaol might know the Bible better than those on the Bench, and those who were transported to Van Diemen's Land might ask their relatives to send Cobbett's *Register* after them.

This was, perhaps, the most distinguished popular culture England has known. It contained the massive diversity of skills, of the workers in metal, wood, textiles and ceramics, without whose inherited "mysteries" and superb ingenuity with primitive tools the inventions of the Industrial Revolution could scarcely have got further than the drawing-board. From this culture of the craftsman and the self-taught there came scores of inventers, organisers, journalists and political theorists of impressive quality. It is easy enough to say that this culture was backward-looking or conservative. True enough, one direction of the great agitations of the artisans and outworkers, continued over fifty years, was to *resist* being turned into a proletariat. When they knew that this cause was lost, yet they reached out again, in the Thirties and Forties, and sought to achieve new and only imagined forms of social control. During all this time they were, as a class, repressed and segregated in their own communities. But what the counter-revolution sought to repress grew only more determined in the quasi-legal institutions of the underground. Whenever the pressure of the rulers relaxed, men came from the petty workshops or the weavers' hamlets and asserted new claims. They were told that they had no rights, but they knew that they were born free. The Yoemanry rode down their meeting, and the right of public meeting was gained. The pamphleteers were gaoled, and from the gaols they edited pamphlets. The trade unionists were imprisoned, and they were attended to prison by processions with bands and union banners.

Segregated in this way, their institutions acquired a peculiar toughness and resilience. Class also acquired a peculiar resonance in English life: everything, from their schools to their shops, their chapels to their amusements, was turned into a battle-ground

[21] Thomas Delaney [Deloney] (1543?–1607?) was a ballad writer and pamphleteer who wrote in a popular vein. Thomas Dekker (c. 1572–c. 1632) was a dramatist and pamphleteer whose writings gave an excellent picture of life in Tudor London. Thomas Nashe (1567–1601) was a poet and playwright whose works showed a keen critical spirit and an ability to portray society realistically. Gerrard Winstanley (1609–1660?) was an advocate of a communistic society; his writings formed the basis for a group of agrarian communists known as the Diggers who flourished briefly about 1650. John Lilburne (1614–1657) was an advocate of radical democracy during the era of the English Civil War and the age of Cromwell; he was the leader of the Levellers. John Bunyan (1628–1688) was the great religious poet who wrote *Pilgrim's Progress*. Daniel Defoe (c. 1660–1732) was an essayist and novelist whose numerous writings provided a brilliant and critical picture of life in his day; best known of his works are *Moll Flanders* and *Robinson Crusoe*. [Editor's note.]

of class. The marks of this remain, but by the outsider they are not always understood. If we have in our social life little of the tradition of *égalité*, yet the class-consciousness of the working man has little in it of deference. "Orphans we are, and bastards of society," wrote James Morrison in 1834. The tone is not one of resignation but of pride.

Again and again in these years working men expressed it thus: "they wish to make us tools," or "implements," or "machines." A witness before the parliamentary committee enquiring into the hand-loom weavers (1835) was asked to state the view of his fellows on the Reform Bill:

Q. Are the working classes better satisfied with the institutions of the country since the change has taken place?

A. I do not think they are. They viewed the Reform Bill as a measure calculated to join the middle and upper classes to Government, and leave them in the hands of Government as a sort of machine to work according to the pleasure of Government.

Such men met Utilitarianism in their daily lives, and they sought to throw it back, not blindly, but with intelligence and moral passion. They fought, not the machine, but the exploitive and oppressive relationships intrinsic to industrial capitalism. In these same years, the great Romantic criticism of Utilitarianism was running its parallel but altogether separate course. After William Blake, no mind was at home in both cultures, nor had the genius to interpret the two traditions to each other. It was a muddled Mr. Owen who offered to disclose the "new moral world," while Wordsworth and Coleridge had withdrawn behind their own ramparts of disenchantment. Hence these years appear at times to display, not a revolutionary challenge, but a resistance movement, in which both the Romantics and the Radical craftsmen opposed the annunciation of Acquisitive Man. In the failure of the two traditions to come to a point of junction, something was lost. How much we cannot be sure, for we are among the losers.

Yet the working people should not be seen only as the lost myriads of eternity. They had also nourished, for fifty years, and with incomparable fortitude, the Liberty Tree. We may thank them for these years of heroic culture.

1234567890